Tick...Tick...

Hear that clock ticking? It's the countdown to the SAT Mathematics Level 1 and Level 2 subject tests, and they'll be here before you know it. Whether you have one year or one day to go, now's the time to start maximizing your score.

The Test Is Just a Few Months Away!

You're ahead of the game. But you still need to make the most of your time. Start on page 199, where we'll help you devise year-round strategies to make the most of your time so you'll be well-prepared for the big day.

Actually, I Only Have a Few Weeks!

That's plenty of time for a full review. Turn to Part II, where you'll find a comprehensive guide to the multiple-choice section, as well as a review of all the vocabulary you'll need to know.

Let's Be Honest. The Test Is Tomorrow and I'm Freaking Out!

No problem. Read through the last-minute study guide (page 1). Then grab a pencil and take a practice test (page 208). Don't worry about the scores—just focus on getting to know the test. Before you go to bed, go through the test day tips (page 5) and keep it close. It'll walk you through the day ahead.

Relax. Everything you need to know, you've already learned. We're just here to keep it fresh in your mind for test day.

My Max Score

SAT MATH 1 & 2
SUBJECT TEST

Maximize Your Score in Less Time

Chris Monahan

Published by Sourcebooks, Inc.
P.O. Box 4410, Naperville, Illinois 60567-4410
(630) 961-3900
Fax: (630) 961-2168
www.sourcebooks.com

Library of Congress Cataloging-in-Publication Data

Monahan, Chris.
  My max score SAT math 1 & 2 subject test : maximize your score in less time / Chris Monahan.
    p. cm.
  1. Mathematics—Problems, exercises, etc. 2. Mathematics—Examinations—Study guides. 3. SAT (Educational test)—Study guides. I. Title.
  QA43.M76 2012
  510.76—dc23

                              2011022517

Printed and bound in the United States of America.
VP 10 9 8 7 6 5 4 3 2 1

Also Available in the *My Max Score* Series

AP Exam Prep

AP Calculus AB/BC
AP English Language and Composition
AP English Literature and Composition
AP U.S. Government & Politics
AP U.S. History

SAT Subject Test Prep

SAT Literature Subject Test
SAT U.S. History Subject Test

Coming Soon

AP Biology
AP European History
AP World History
Armed Services Vocational Aptitude Battery

Contents

Introduction

The SAT Mathematics Level 1 and Level 2 subject tests each consist of 50 multiple-choice questions for which the student has one hour to complete as many questions as possible. The College Board, in its document "Getting Ready for the SAT Subject Tests," suggests that you consider which level to take based on your level of preparation. Students are not expected to have studied every topic on either test.

- Mathematics Level 1: Three years of college-preparatory math, including two years of algebra and one year of geometry

- Mathematics Level 2: More than three years of college-preparatory math, including two years of algebra, one year of geometry, and elementary functions (precalculus) and/or trigonometry

If you have had preparation in trigonometry and elementary functions and have attained grades of B or better in these courses, select Level 2. If you are sufficiently prepared to take Level 2 but take Level 1 in hopes of receiving a higher score, you may not do as well as you expect.

The breakdown of the questions on the test can also be found in this same document. Both Level 1 and Level 2 have a strong emphasis on algebra. Approximately 40 percent of the Level 1 test and 50 percent of the Level 2 test involve algebra. Approximately 40 percent of the

Level 1 test and 30 percent of the Level 2 test involve questions about geometry and the numerical relationships found in plane geometry. An estimated 10 percent of each test involves coordinate geometry, 10 percent goes towards probability and statistics, and 10 percent covers numerical relationships and operations. Approximately 5 percent of the Level 1 test and 10 percent of the Level 2 test involves trigonometry, and approximately 5 percent of each level is geared towards three-dimensional reasoning. For those of you who are adding, the percentages for each level well exceed 100 percent, which indicates that the actual structure of each exam will vary each time the test is administered. It also indicates that some questions can cover more than one topic. For example, a question that gives the measures of the angles of a triangle as algebraic expressions and asks for the measure of the largest angle involves geometric measurement and algebra.

The material in this text will help you prepare to score your best on your chosen level test. Hopefully, you have given yourself plenty of time to prepare for this test. Take the time to read chapters 2–4 before jumping into the diagnostic test and working through all of the material in the mini-review in chapters 6–14. There is one sample test for each level following the mini-review section with the solutions to each problem at the end of the text.

Visit mymaxscore.com for an additional practice test for each level of the SAT Mathematics Level 1 & 2 Subject Tests, as well as practice tests for other subjects.

THE ESSENTIALS: A LAST-MINUTE STUDY GUIDE

How to Cram for the Test

I f this is a worst case-scenario for you and you feel like you need to cram for the test in a short period of time, it would be worth your while to first read Chapter 2: "Test-Taking Strategies." Take the time to look at the formulas you really do need to know when you walk into the test. This will help you as you work through some of the material in this book to prepare yourself for the test.

You should next work through Chapter 3: "15 Problems You Must Be Able to Solve." These will give you a sense of the topics that are on the test as well as an idea of the level of depth and the connections among topics that are common on the test. This test is unlike the tests you've taken in school in that it is cumulative over many years, is all multiple-choice, and attempts to integrate topics when it can. The test is unlike the general SAT exam in that the Math section of the general exam tests your quantitative aptitude. This test questions you on specific topics as wells as your quantitative ability.

Give yourself an hour and work through the diagnostic test in Chapter 4. If you did not complete the test in the given hour, make note of which questions you were able to complete, and then finish the test. The solutions immediately follow the test. Don't look at the answers until you have decided you've answered all the questions that you can. Make note of the questions you answered incorrectly to determine if there is a topic that you should review. If so, go to the appropriate chapter and work through the examples in the chapter—don't just read the examples, work them through on your own. Do the exercises at the end of the chapter to see if you have a better understanding of the material.

Finally, take the time to do the practice tests for the level of the SAT Mathematics Subject test that you will be taking. Try to do this in as quiet an environment as you can find, so as to simulate the testing conditions. Solutions are provided at the end of each test.

Test-Taking Strategies

Each of the Level 1 and Level 2 tests consist of 50 questions, and you have 60 minutes with which to do them. This gives you an average of 1.2 minutes, or 72 seconds, per question. Some questions will take much less time, some will take a minute or so, and some will require more time. As simple as this sounds, it is something that you need to be comfortable with when you walk in to take the test. The questions on the test are grouped into what the exam writers consider to be the easier questions first, followed by the medium-level difficulty, and finishing with the more challenging questions. You should expect to spend more time on questions as the test progresses.

There Is No Partial Credit

Most students have been trained in class to show work so that (a) your teacher can see how you are approaching the material being tested and (b) partial credit might be awarded should your answer not be completely correct.

This is a multiple-choice test, and the answer to each question is either correct, incorrect, or blank. Work that you can do mentally or with your calculator will save time. Every few seconds you save on the "easy" questions gives you more time for the more challenging problems.

Writing down each step as you go uses time. *But*, if you need to write things down to get the correct solution, do so. As the problems get more challenging, you will want to write some of your steps so that you can see your thinking should your answer not match one of the choices. The end goal is for you to score as high as you can. Write as much as you feel you need in order to achieve this goal.

Calculators

Being fluent with your calculator is a great advantage! Knowing how to change from radian to degree mode and real to complex mode will save time. If you are using a graphing calculator, being able to quickly establish windows for graphs, to find intercepts, and to find extreme values will enable you to solve more complicated problems without having to do a lot of algebra. Many calculators have a cache feature in which previous steps can be retrieved and edited, should you need to make a correction or alteration in an entry. Take the time to learn how to do this before the exam. (It will also be beneficial to you in class and on class exams.) QWERTY and interactive calculators are not allowed on the exam, but a calculator with a Computer Algebra System (CAS) is allowed.

Do not try to use a calculator on the exam if you are not comfortable using it. However, it would be to your advantage to practice so that you are able to take advantage of its features.

No matter which calculator you choose to bring to the test with you, be sure that you have a fresh set of batteries with you in case the batteries in the calculator lose their energy.

Example: Solve: $x^3 - 5x^2 + 6x \geq 0$

(A) $x \leq 0$ or $2 \leq x \leq 3$ (B) $x \leq -6$ or $0 \leq x \leq 1$
(C) $0 \leq x \leq 2$ or $x \geq 3$ (D) $-3 \leq x \leq -2$ or $x \geq 0$
(E) $-6 \leq x \leq 0$ or $x \geq 1$
Sketch this graph on your calculator and determine when the graph is on or above the x axis.

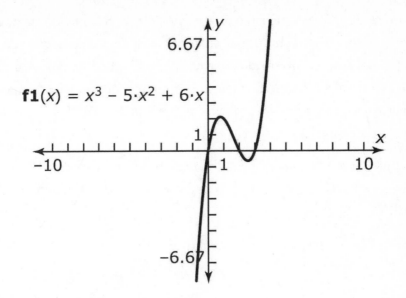

$$f1(x) = x^3 - 5 \cdot x^2 + 6 \cdot x$$

Choice (C) is the correct choice.

Know What You Know

Spending time working on a problem that you can solve is worthwhile, so long as it does not take an inordinate amount of time. Taking a minute and a half or more on a question early in the exam is not a wise decision. Taking this time on question number forty-something might be acceptable if you know what the other questions are and have determined that the time spent on this one problem gives you the best chance of correctly answering a question from this section.

Knowing your own knowledge base can help you score well. If you run into a question that always has given you trouble or a topic of which you have only a surface knowledge (and the question seems to go below the surface), skip it. There is no penalty for a blank answer. Come back to those questions you have passed over after you have answered the questions covering the material that you know well.

Beware—the Educational Testing Service (ETS), the company that writes and scores the exam, has spent a lot of money writing and testing the questions on the exam. The choices presented to you for each question have been developed based on answers provided on field tests. The incorrect alternatives are based on common errors given by previous test takers, common misconceptions students have displayed about certain topics, and correct intermediate answers found while working through a problem. Take the time to underline or circle the piece of information you are asked to find in the problem so that you don't fall for the trap of a correct intermediate answer.

Example: In $\triangle ABC$, $m\angle A = 7x + 1$, $m\angle B = 11x - 27$, $m\angle C = 8x + 24$, $AB = 4y + 8$, $AC = 9y + 4$, and $BC = 5y + 24$. What is the perimeter of $\triangle ABC$?

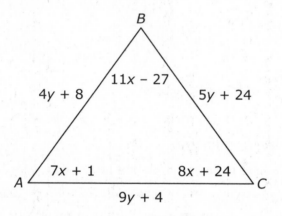

    (A)   49 (B)   50 (C)   80 (D)   126 (E)   180

    A student who mistakenly adds the sides of the triangle and sets the sum to 180 will determine that $y = 8$ and will find, not surprisingly, that the sum of the sides is 180. Do you see how the question about perimeter might lead someone to do this?

    Setting the sum of the angles to 180 will yield the result that $x = 7$. This in turn will reveal that the measure of $\angle A$ is 50, choice (B). In turn, $m\angle B = 80$, choice (C), and $m\angle C = 50$. You now know that $\triangle ABC$ is isosceles and that $AB = BC$. Solve this equation to determine that $y = 5$ and that $AB = BC = 49$, choice (A). After determining that $AC = 28$, the only choice left for the perimeter is the correct choice (D), 126.

Smart Guessing

Should you guess if you do not know the answer to a question? As a rule, the answer is no. A blind guess has a one-fifth chance of being correct and a four-fifths chance of losing a quarter of a point on your raw score. It is better to skip the question and move on to the rest of the test.

However, if you can eliminate an answer or two as being impractical, then the chances of picking a correct answer increase, and you may want to consider taking a guess.

Example: In $\triangle ABC$, $m\angle C = 50°$, $AC = 77$, and $BC = 77$. What is the perimeter of $\triangle ABC$?

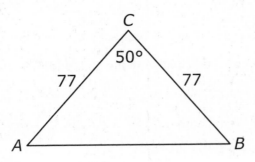

(A)   154   (B)   219   (C)   231   (D)   253   (E)   263

Even if you do not remember that you can use the Law of Cosines to find the third side of this triangle, choice (A) makes no sense, as it is the sum of two sides of the triangle. Choice (C) is not correct, since the third side of the triangle would also need to be 77. This is not the case because the triangle is isosceles, not equilateral.

This leaves you with three answers. You may reason that $m\angle A= m\angle B = 65$, so AB must be smaller than 77, so choices (D) and (E) are not correct. Therefore, choice (B) is correct.

You May Not Run Out of Choices

The test is entirely multiple-choice. There are some questions with which you may be better served by working through the choices rather than by working through the algebra of the problem.

Example: Solve: $x^3 - 64 = 0$

    (A)   4   (B)   4, $2 + 2i\sqrt{3}$, $2 - 2i\sqrt{3}$

    (C)   4, $-2 + 2i\sqrt{3}$, $-2 - 2i\sqrt{3}$ (D)   4, $2\sqrt{3} + 2i$, $2\sqrt{3} - 2i$

    (E)   4, $-2\sqrt{3} + 2i$, $-2\sqrt{3} - 2i$

Any calculator that has a complex number mode can be used to solve this problem.

Since 4 is a choice for all the problems, you need not check it. Enter $(2 + 2i\sqrt{3})^3$ into your calculator. If the answer is 64, you can check the value of $x^3 - 64$ with $2 - 2i\sqrt{3}$. $(2 + 2i\sqrt{3})^3 = -64$. Be careful: $-64 - 64 \neq 0$, so choice (B) is not correct. Try $(-2 + 2i\sqrt{3})^3$ from choice (C) next. $(-2 + 2i\sqrt{3})^3 = 64$. Since none of the other choices have this number as an option, choice (C) is the correct choice.

Know This!

The only formulas you are given on the exam are some formulas about volume and surface area of solids. There are some formulas and relationships beyond the Pythagorean Theorem and sum of the measures of the angles of a triangle that you should know. Some of these are:

ALGEBRA

Multiplication and Factoring Formulas

$(a - b)(a + b) = a^2 - b^2$

$(a - b)^2 = a^2 - 2ab + b^2$

$(a + b)^2 = a^2 + 2ab + b^2$

$(a - b)(a^2 + ab + b^2) = a^3 - b^3$

$(a + b)(a^2 - ab + b^2) = a^3 + b^3$

The notation $n\left(\dfrac{n}{r}\right) = {}_nC_r = \dfrac{n!}{r!(n-r)!}$ represents the number of combinations of n taken r at a time. The Binomial Theorem states:

$$(a+b)^n = a^n + \left(\frac{n}{1}\right)a^{n-1}b + \left(\frac{n}{2}\right)a^{n-2}b^2 + \left(\frac{n}{3}\right)a^{n-3}b^3 + \ldots + \left(\frac{n}{n-2}\right)a^2b^{n-2} +$$

$$\left(\frac{n}{n-1}\right)ab^{n-1} + \left(\frac{n}{n}\right)b^n$$

Notice how the values of r start at 0 and increase by 1 until r reaches n; the value of r is also the exponent of b; and the sum of the exponents is always n.

TRIGONOMETRY

$\sin^2(\theta) + \cos^2(\theta) = 1$

$1 + \tan^2(\theta) = \sec^2(\theta)$

$1 + \cot^2(\theta) = \csc^2(\theta)$

$\sin(A+B) = \sin(A)\cos(B) + \cos(A)\sin(B)$

$\sin(A - B) = \sin(A)\cos(B) - \cos(A)\sin(B)$

$\cos(A - B) = \cos(A)\cos(B) + \sin(A)\sin(B)$

$\cos(A + B) = \cos(A)\cos(B) - \sin(A)\sin(B)$

$\sin(2A) = 2\sin(A)\cos(A)$

$\cos(2A) = \cos^2(A) - \sin^2(A)$

$\cos(2A) = 2\cos^2(A) - 1$

$\cos(2A) = 1 - 2\sin^2(A)$

$\sin(-A) = -\sin(A)$

$\cos(-A) = \cos(A)$

Law of Sines: $\dfrac{a}{\sin(A)} = \dfrac{b}{\sin(B)} = \dfrac{c}{\sin(C)}$

Law of Cosines: $z^2 = x^2 + y^2 - 2xy\cos(Z)$

Area of a Triangle: $K = \dfrac{1}{2}bc\,\sin(A)$

The Last Bit of Advice

Get a good night's sleep and have a good breakfast before taking the test.

15 Problems You Must Be Able to Solve

There are some basic problems you should know how to solve to help move you along through the test. On many questions, you will need to stop, think about what you are being asked to solve, and then determine how to find the solution. You should be able to recognize some problems immediately. Here is a list of 15 problems with solutions and some suggestions for related issues you will want to be sure you know.

1. Law of Exponents

Simplify: $\left(\dfrac{45x^{-3}y^8z}{20x^5y^{-6}z^7}\right)^{-\frac{3}{2}}$

(A) $\dfrac{27y^{21}}{8x^{12}z^9}$ (B) $\dfrac{8x^{12}z^9}{27y^{21}}$ (C) $\dfrac{27y^{21}}{12x^{12}z^9}$

(D) $\dfrac{27x^{12}z^9}{12y^{21}}$ (E) $\dfrac{135x^{12}y^{21}z^9}{60}$

The rules for exponents are a fundamental tool in the study of mathematics and one in which errors occur more because of carelessness than lack of understanding. Recall that the basic properties are:

I	$\left(b^m\right)\left(b^n\right)=b^{m+n}$	When the bases are the same, products are found by keeping the base and adding the exponents
II	$\dfrac{b^m}{b^n} = b^{m-n}$	When the bases are the same, quotients are found by keeping the base and subtracting the exponents
III	$\left(b^m\right)^n = b^{mn}$	When a term raised to a power is also raised to a power, multiply the exponents
IV	$(ab)^n = a^n b^n$	When a product is raised to a power, each of the factors is raised to the power and the results are multiplied
V	$b^0 =1$	Any nonzero number raised to the zero power is equal to 1
VI	$b^{-n} = \dfrac{1}{b^n}$	A negative exponent means a reciprocal
VII	$b^{\frac{1}{n}} = \sqrt[n]{b}$	Fractional exponents translate to radical expressions

Simplify: $\left(\dfrac{45x^{-3}y^8z}{20x^5y^{-6}z^7}\right)^{-\frac{3}{2}}$

Start with the terms inside the parentheses. $\dfrac{45}{20}$ reduces to $\dfrac{9}{4}$. $\dfrac{x^{-3}}{x^5}$ becomes $\dfrac{1}{x^8}$, since $5 - (-3) = 8$. The term with the larger exponent was in the denominator originally, so the result is written in the denominator. $\dfrac{y^8}{y^{-6}}$ becomes y^{14}. $\dfrac{z}{z^7}$ becomes $\dfrac{1}{z^6}$.

The expression inside the parentheses is now $\left(\dfrac{9y^{14}}{4x^8z^6}\right)^{-\frac{3}{2}}$. Apply rule VI to get $\left(\dfrac{4x^8 z^6}{9y^{14}}\right)^{\frac{3}{2}}$. Apply rule IV to get $\dfrac{(4^{\frac{3}{2}})(x^8)^{\frac{3}{2}}(z^6)^{\frac{3}{2}}}{(9^{\frac{3}{2}})(y^{14})^{\frac{3}{2}}}$, which

becomes $\dfrac{8x^{12}z^9}{27y^{21}}$, choice B.

Being comfortable with the rules of exponents is essential for suc-
ceeding on the SAT Math Level 1 and Level 2 exams. For more practice
with the rules of exponents, see the chapter Exponents and Logarithms.

2. Working with Functions

Given $f(x) = 2\sqrt{3x + 4} + x$ and $g(x) = 4x - 11$. Solve $f(x) = g(x)$.

   I. 0
  II. 5/3
 III. 7

(A) I only   (B) II only   (C) III only
(D) II and III   (E) I, II, and III

The function notation in this problem is used to mask a much easier
problem—solve the equation $2\sqrt{3x + 4} + x = 4x - 11$. Solving equations with square roots can be tedious. Subtracting x and then squaring
both sides of the equation gives $(2\sqrt{3x + 4}^2) = (3x - 11)^2$. This in turn
becomes $4(3x+4) = 9x^2 - 66x + 121$, or $9x^2 - 78x + 105 = 0$. Factor,
use the quadratic formula, or graph the parabola to determine that $x =$
5/3 or 7. As tempting as choice (D) is, stop and check that 5/3 does not
work—it is, in fact, an extraneous root—it's extra and erroneous. Only
$x = 7$ solves this problem. Choice (C) is correct.

The trouble with the solution described in the previous paragraph is
that it takes a long time to perform. Hopefully, you are proficient with a
graphing calculator and can graph these two functions to find the point
of intersection. Window settings may be an issue, so be sure you are
comfortable with how to change the window settings.

As good as these classroom approaches are, the fastest way to answer this question is probably to just substitute the three numbers into the equations to determine the correct solution.

Functions are a big piece of the study of mathematics, and you should expect to see some questions about them on the test. Function notation such as $f(x) = 2\sqrt{3x + 4} + x$ and $g(x) = 4x - 11$ is just another way for writing $y = 2\sqrt{3x + 4} + x$ and $y = 4x - 11$, with the benefit of being able to distinguish between the equations with a single letter, f or g. You must also be able to identify that x is the input variable and that $f(x)$ is the output variable. Function notation is a nice way to indicate substitutions. For example, $f(4)$ directs you to replace the x with a 4 in the function $f(x)$, so that $f(4) = 2\sqrt{3(4) + 4} + 4 = 2\sqrt{16} + 4 = 2(4) + 4 = 12$. Translated, that means that when the input value is a 4, the output value is 12.

The equation $f(x) = 17$ indicates that the output value is 17. Solve the equation $2\sqrt{3x + 4} + x = 17$ to determine that $x = 7$.

A function such as $g(x) = 4x - 11$ allows for any number to serve as the input. That is, the domain is the set of real numbers. With $f(x)$, you need to be sure that the number under the radical is not negative, because the square root of a negative number is an imaginary number, and the discussion with functions is usually limited to real numbers. What is the domain for $f(x)$? Set $3x + 4 \geq 0$ and solve to get $x \geq -4/3$. Thus, the domain is the set of real numbers greater than or equal to $-4/3$.

The domain and range of $g(x)$ consist of the set of all real numbers. The line $y = 4x - 11$, with its positive slope, allows for any output value which can be considered. The range for $f(x)$ is more complicated. The range for the square root function is $y > -4/3$ as this is the value of $f(-4/3)$.

Functions are the basic building blocks of advanced mathematics. For more information and practice with functions, see the chapter Algebra and Functions.

3. Pythagorean Theorem

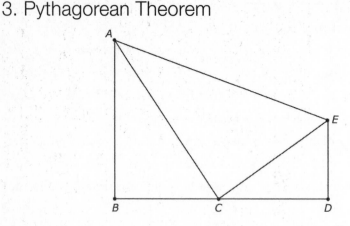

In the figure, $\overline{AB} \perp \overline{BD}$, $\overline{ED} \perp \overline{BD}$, $\overline{AC} \perp \overline{CE}$, $\overline{BC} \cong \overline{DE}$, $AB = CD + 7$, $AC = 20$, and $CE = 15$. The perimeter of $ABDE$ is

    (A) 9   (B) 12   (C) 49   (D) 74   (E) 109

The figure consists of three right triangles. Knowing some basic Pythagorean triples will certainly assist in answering the question quickly. The 3-4-5 triangle is the best known, and most often used of all the Pythagorean triples. With $CE = 15$ (that is, $5 \cdot 3$) and $AC = 20$ ($5 \cdot 4$), it is easy to see that AE must be 25 ($5 \cdot 5$). CE is also the hypotenuse of right $\triangle CDE$. Could it be that CD and ED are $3 \cdot 3$ and $4 \cdot 3$? Thus, ED would equal 12, CD would equal 9, AB would equal 16 (or 9 + 7), and BC would also equal 12. Since you know AE equals 25, the perimeter can be written as 25 + 16 + 12 + 12 + 9, or 74.

You now know the lengths of the sides of the triangles. The question asked you to find the perimeter of the quadrilateral. Don't lose sight of that. In fact, you may want to underline that piece of information in the problem. Remember what it is that you are solving. You can see that choices (A) and (B) are there to distract you once you find the lengths of the sides of the component triangles.

The perimeter of the quadrilateral is the sum of AB, BC, CD, ED, and AE. The test writer is checking to be sure that you did not forget about AE. The correct answer is (D). Forget about EA, and choice (C) is waiting for you. Be careful not to make the mistake of including AC and CE to get choice (E).

This method of solution for determining the sides of the triangle does not take as long to do as it took you to read the paragraphs. Keep in mind that not all right triangles are 3-4-5. It is worthwhile to take a moment to look at the possibility given the numbers 15 and 20.

This problem can be solved algebraically. Letting $BC = DE = b$, $CD = a$, and $AB = a + 7$, you can write the system of equations

$$(a + 7)^2 + b^2 = 20^2$$
$$a^2 + b^2 = 15^2$$

Do you see that subtracting the two equations will cause the b^2 terms to be eliminated? $20^2 - 15^2$ is a simple calculator problem. [Although, if you treat this as the difference of squares, $(20 - 15)(20 + 15) = (5)(35) = 175$.] Finally, $(a + 7)^2 - a^2 = 14a + 49$. Knowing the formula

$$(x + y)^2 = x^2 + 2xy + y^2$$

can save you a great deal of time from multiplying.

You are now left with solving the equation $14a + 49 = 175$ (that is, $400 - 225$). A couple of computations on the calculator and you know that $a = 9$. A leg of 9 and a hypotenuse of 15 should lead to the conclusion that the other leg is 12, also the missing leg of the third triangle. Remember—answer the question asked—find the perimeter of the quadrilateral.

Which Pythagorean triples should you know besides the 3-4-5? 9-12-15, 5-12-13, 8-15-17, and 7-24-25 are fairly common. 9-40-41, 11-60-61, and 12-35-37 are worth knowing. The two special right triangles from trigonometry, the 45°-45°-90° and 30°-60°-90° triangles, with their sides 1-1-$\sqrt{2}$ and 1-$\sqrt{3}$-2, should always be on your mind.

Some other things that you may want to consider:

- Observe that $ABDE$ is a trapezoid, so the area of the quadrilateral could have been sought. Recall that the area of a trapezoid is $A = \frac{1}{2}h(b_1 + b_2)$. The bases are the parallel sides of the figure and the height is perpendicular to these.

- $\angle ACB$ and $\angle DCE$ are complimentary as are $\angle CED$ and $\angle BAC$, because the triangles are similar.

- $\angle BAC \cong \angle DCE \cong AEC$ and $\angle BCA \cong \angle DEC \cong EAC$

The Pythagorean Theorem is a relationship used to build many problems in plane and coordinate geometry. For more practice with the Pythagorean Theorem, see the chapter Geometry and Measurement.

4. Parallel Lines

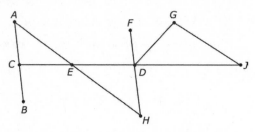

Figure not drawn to scale.

In the diagram, C, E, D, and J are collinear, $\overline{ACB} \parallel \overline{HDF}$, $\overline{AEH} \parallel \overline{JG}$, and $\overline{DG}$ bisects $\angle FDJ$. If $m\angle AEC = 34°$ and $m\angle G = 97°$, then $m\angle H + m\angle ACE =$

(A) 48°   (B) 98°   (C) 131°   (D) 146°   (E) 180°

Parallel lines yield a number of different relationships. You know that when parallel lines are cut by a transversal

- alternate interior angles are congruent

- corresponding angles are congruent

- alternate exterior angles are congruent

- same-side interior angles are supplementary

You know then that $m\angle J = 34°$ because it is a corresponding angle with $\angle AEC$.

Since the sum of the angles of a triangle is 180°, you can determine that $m\angle GDJ= 49$.

Because of the angle bisector, $m\angle FDJ = 98$. $m\angle EDH = 98$ (vertical angles are congruent) and $m\angle ACE = 98$ because it is a corresponding angle with $\angle FDJ$ as well as an alternate interior angle for $\angle EDH$.

$\angle DEH$ is vertical to $\angle AEC$, so its measure is 34. This makes $m\angle H = 48$. Finally, $m\angle H + m\angle ACE = 48 + 98 = 146$.

You can see how some of the intermediate answers were chosen for alternate choices (A) – (C) and that a student might choose (E) should he mistakenly assume that $\angle H$ and $\angle ACE$ are supplementary.

Being comfortable with the relationships of the angles of parallel lines, the angles in a triangle, and the language used with angles (e.g., congruent, supplementary, complementary) is an important skill in taking the SAT Math Level 1 and Level 2, because many problems can be constructed from these principles. For more information about this topic, see the chapter Geometry and Measurement.

5. Quadrilaterals

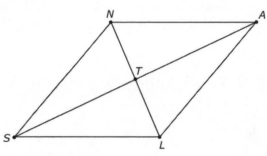

The diagonals of rhombus *SLAN* intersect at point *T*. If $SA = 150$ and $NL = 50\sqrt{3}$, the perimeter of *SLAN* is approximately

(A) 87 (B) 302 (C) 346 (D) 348 (E) 6495

By definition, all sides of a rhombus have the same length. You can determine the perimeter of the rhombus by finding the length of one side and multiplying by four.

The diagonals of a rhombus are perpendicular bisectors of each other. (You should also note that the diagonals of a rhombus bisect the opposite angles of the quadrilateral.) $ST = 75$ and $TL = 25\sqrt{3}$. You can use the Pythagorean Theorem to determine the length of SL. You should also recognize that $(25\sqrt{3})\sqrt{3} = 75$. Since the longer leg of the triangle is $\sqrt{3}$ times longer than the shorter leg, this must be a 30-60-90 triangle and the hypotenuse of the triangle, $SL = 50\sqrt{3}$, or 86.6 as a decimal. (Do you see why the test makers included choice (A) as a misleading option?)

The perimeter of $SLAN = 4(50\sqrt{3}) = 200\sqrt{3}$, or 346. The correct answer is (C).

Choice (D) is waiting for those who round the length of SL to be 87 before they compute the perimeter. **Never round off a decimal until the end of a problem, unless the directions within the problem direct you to do so.** Choice (B) is a consequence of using your calculator incorrectly and determining that the square of $25\sqrt{3}$ is 75 rather than 1875. That is, the square of $25\sqrt{3}$ should be written into your calculator as $(25\sqrt{3})^2$ rather than $25\sqrt{3}^2$. Finally, choice (E) is the area of the rhombus rather than the perimeter.

Properties of the rhombus, the parallelograms, and many other polygons can be found in the chapter Geometry and Measurement.

6. Volume of Three-Dimensional Solids

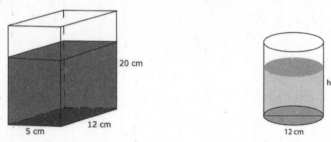

A rectangular container which measures 5 cm × 12 cm × 20 cm is 3/4 full of water. If the water is poured into a cylindrical container with a diameter of 12 cm, the height to which the water rises in the cylinder is approximately how many centimeters?

(A) 1.99   (B) 7.96   (C) 19.64   (D) 23.87   (E) 78.54

If the volume of water in the rectangular container is 3/4 the capacity of the container, the height of the water must be 15 cm, 3/4 of 20 cm. The volume of water in the rectangular container is $(5)(12)(15) = 900$ cm^3 (which could also be computed by multiplying $(5)(12)(20)(3/4)$).

The volume of a cylinder is given by the formula $V = \pi r^2 h$. The radius of the cylinder is 6 cm, and the height is the item to be found. Solve the equation $36\pi h = 900$ by dividing both sides of the equation by 36π. $h = \dfrac{900}{36} = 7.96$. Choice (B) is the correct answer.

Choice (A) is present should one use the diameter, 12 cm, rather than the radius, 6 cm, in the volume formula. Choice (D) is present should one use 12 rather than 36 in the formula (either miscalculating 6^2 or just using the diameter will cause this). Choices (C) and (E) are present should one not enter the data into the calculator correctly. Choice (E) comes from entering $\dfrac{900}{36\pi}$, and choice (C) comes from $\dfrac{900}{144\pi}$.

Solids in which the top base is parallel and congruent to the bottom base, and the lateral sides are perpendicular to these bases, are called prisms. One usually thinks of the base of a prism as being a polygon, but it is reasonable to think of a cylinder as a circular prism. It is common to call the area of the base of the prism B. The volume of the prism is $V = Bh$, the area of the base times the height. The lateral surface area (LSA) is equal to the perimeter of the base times the height of the prism. Consequently, the LSA of a cylinder is $2\pi rh$.

Solids with one base and whose lateral sides converge to a single point are called pyramids. The volume of a pyramid is one-third the volume of a prism. The LSA is found by computing the areas of the triangles that form the faces of the pyramid. For more information and examples on the solids, see the chapter Three-Dimensional Geometry.

7. Quadratic Equations

One solution to $4.1x^2 - 5.3x + 9.7 = 0$ is

    (A) 2.315   (B) 0.6463   (C) 9.4905
    (D) $0.6463 + 1.3957i$ (E) $2.65 + 5.7225i$

There are four ways you are taught to solve quadratic equations—factoring, using the quadratic formula, completing the square, and graphing. Your first thought when you read the sample problem might have been, "4.1 and 9.7 do not have factors that I easily recognize, so factoring is not an option," or something to that effect. That's absolutely the correct thing to think. Completing the square is rarely a good option for a test such as the SAT Level 1 and 2, except for when you are dealing with conic sections. That will be examined later.

This brings you to either graphing or using the quadratic formula. If the solutions to the equation are real numbers, graphing is an easy way to solve the problem. However, two of the choices are complex numbers, and quadratic equations with complex solutions will not intersect the x-axis, making the graphing option unsuccessful.

The quadratic formula turns out to be the best approach for this problem. However, you must be careful when entering the information into the calculator to ensure that the order of operations is correctly used. When solving the quadratic equation $ax^2 + bx + c = 0$, the quadratic formula gives $x = \dfrac{-b \pm \sqrt{b^2 - 4ac}}{2a}$. If you are comfortable using your calculator, then entering this information may not present a problem.

If you feel the need to be more cautious, then you may want to consider breaking the problem into simpler steps. Start with calculating the value of $(b)^2 - 4ac$, the *discriminant* of the equation. b is written in parentheses to remind you that the calculator will compute -5.3^2 as -28.09, whereas the square of -5.3 is 28.09. Getting into the habit of using the parentheses will eliminate this potential mistake.

$(-5.3)^2 - 4(4.1)(9.7) = -130.99$. The answer to this problem will be a complex number, either (D) or (E). Which is it? The real terms of the complex numbers are different. The real term of the answer, based on the quadratic formula, is $\dfrac{-b}{2a}$, so for this problem the real number is $\dfrac{-(-5.3)}{2(4.1)} = 0.646$. Choice (D) is correct. Choices (A) – (C) and (E) are based on whether you know that the discriminant is $(b)^2 - 4ac$ rather than $(b)^2 + 4ac$, as well as potential errors in entering the numbers for computation in your calculator.

For more information about the quadratic equations, including items such as the sum and product of the roots of the equation and their relationship to the coefficients of the equation, see the chapter Algebra and Functions.

8. Absolute Value

Solve $|3x - 5| > 7$

    I. $x > 4$

    II. $x > -2/3$

    III. $x < -2/3$

    (A) I only   (B) III only   (C) I and II only

    (D) I and III only   (E) I, II, and III

Solving the inequality $3x - 5 > 7$ gives $3x > 12$, so that $x > 4$. Statement I is correct. Are there any other correct statements? You write $3x - 5 > 7$ and $3x - 5 < -7$. This is **WRONG!**

You know that when you are asked to solve $|x| = 4$, the answer is $x = \pm 4$, because both these points are 4 units from 0 on the number line. Consider what this looks like:

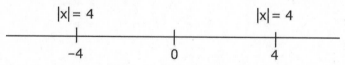

There are two points on the number line for which $|x| = 4$. What is true of all the points between -4 and 4? What is true of all the points to the left of -4 and to the right of 4?

All the points between -4 and 4 have the property that their distance to 0 is less than 4, while the remaining points on the line, those to the left of -4 and those to the right of 4, have the property that their distance to 0 is greater than 4.

What do you do about $|3x - 5| > 7$? Start with the equation $|3x - 5| = 7$. This becomes $3x - 5 = 7$, so $x = 4$, and $3x - 5 = -7$, so $x = -2/3$. These are the two points that satisfy the notion of equality. The points between them satisfy the condition that $|3x - 5| < 7$ while the remaining points, $x < -2/3$ and $x > 4$, satisfy the condition that $|3x - 5| > 7$. The correct answer is choice (D).

For more examples of solving equations and inequalities with absolute value, see the chapter Algebra and Functions.

9. Transformations

If $f(x)$ is defined by the graph below, determine the zeros of the function $g(x) = -\dfrac{1}{2}f(x - 3) - 1$.

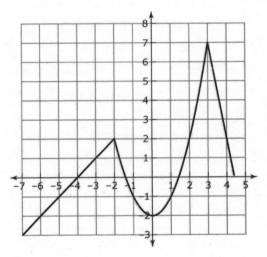

(A) {1}   (B) {1, 3}   (C) {1, 5}
(D) {3, 7}   (E) {1, 5, 7}

The graph of $g(x)$ is found by

- translating the graph of $f(x)$ to the right 3,

- reflecting this result over the x-axis

- dilating this new graph from the x-axis by a factor of 1/2

- translating this third graph down 1 unit.

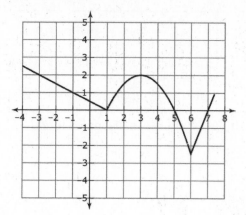

If $g(x) = 0$, then $\frac{1}{2}f(x-3) - 1 = 0$, or $f(x-3) = 2$. Start with those values of $f(x)$ that equal 2. $f(x) = 2$ when $x = -2$, $x = 2$, or $x = 4$. Therefore, for $g(x) = 0$, it must be the case that $x - 3 = -2$, $x - 3 = 2$, or $x - 3 = 4$. Therefore, $x = 1$, 5, or 7. Choice (E) is correct.

Those values of x associated with y-coordinates of -2 on the graph of $f(x)$, $x = -6$ or 0, have y-coordinates of 2 in the graph of $g(x)$. That is, the point $(-6,-2)$ maps to $(-3,2)$, while $(0,-2)$ maps to $(3,2)$. The negative coefficient before $f(x)$ does inform you that the vertical translation is up and not down.

Understanding transformations is helpful is working among families of functions. The table below summarizes the transformations. Assume that a, h, and k are positive values.

Equation	Action
$y = f(x - h)$	Translates the graph of $f(x)$ to the right h units
$y = f(x + h)$	Translates the graph of $f(x)$ to the left h units
$y = f(x) + k$	Translates the graph of $f(x)$ up k units
$y = f(x) - k$	Translates the graph of $f(x)$ down k units
$y = -f(x)$	Reflects the graph across the x-axis

$y = f(-x)$	Reflects the graph across the y-axis
$y = af(x)$	Stretches the graph from the x-axis by a factor of a
$y = f(ax)$	Stretches the graph from the y-axis by a factor of $1/a$

For more examples of transformations of functions, see the chapter Algebra and Functions.

10. Sequences

If the first three terms in a geometric sequence with positive common ratio r are $2r + 1$, $5r$, and $7r + 6$, find the tenth term of the sequence.

    (A) 2   (B) 7   (C) 195   (D) 2560   (E) 5120

A geometric sequence is one in which the ratio of consecutive terms is a constant. In this example, the terms in the sequence are written as expressions in r, the common ratio. You can write $\dfrac{5r}{2r+1} = r$ or $\dfrac{7r+6}{5r} = r$ as the equation for the ratio of consecutive terms. Solving the first equation for r, you get $r = 0$ or 2. Solving the second equation for r yields $r = -3/5$, or 2. Since the common ratio is positive, $r = 2$.

The first term is 5, the second 10, and the third 20. The equation for the rule that creates the geometric sequence is $a^n = 5(2)^{n-1}$. The tenth term of this sequence is $a_{10} = 5(2)^9 = 2560$. Choice (D) is the correct choice. Choice (E) is there in case you use an exponent of 10 instead of 9.

If the numbers a, b, and c form a geometric sequence, in that order, then b is the *geometric mean* between a and c, and $b^2 = ac$. Therefore, you could find r by solving the equation $(5r)^2 = (2r + 1)(7r + 6)$ to find that $r = -3/11$ or 2. Again, r is positive for this problem, so $r = 2$.

A sequence is simply a listing of numbers. There are a number of common sequences that you should know.

Fibonacci Sequence	1, 1, 2, 3, 5, 8, 13, 21, ...
Triangular Numbers	1, 3, 6, 10, 15, 21, 28, ...
Powers	1, 2^n, 3^n, 4^n, 5^n, 6^n, ...

More important are the geometric and arithmetic sequences. As was just discussed, a geometric sequence is one in which the ratio of consecutive terms is a constant. The rule for creating geometric sequences always contains an exponential function of the form $a_n = a_1(r)^{n-1}$, where a_1 is the first term and r is the common ratio. (Please do not assume from the preceding example that the value of r needs to be positive. It does not. The statement of that example specified that the ratio was positive.)

An arithmetic sequence in one in which the difference of successive terms is constant. That is, one adds a constant value from one term to the next to create an arithmetic sequence. The rule that creates an arithmetic sequence will always be linear in the form $a_n = dn + b$ or $a_n = a_1 + (n-1)d$, where a_1 is the first term and d is the common difference. Do you see how the two forms of the line, slope-intercept and point-slope, come into play?

Choices (B) and (C) were included in case you did the problem as an arithmetic sequence.

Another way to define a sequence with some type of algebraic rule involves what is called a *recursive definition*. For example, consider the definition

$$a_1 = 5$$
$$a_n = 2 \quad a_{n-1} + 3$$

The first term, a_1, is 5. What is the second term? Using the second line of the definition with $n = 2$, you get $a_2 = 2\,a_{2-1} + 3 = 2\,a_1 + 3 = 2(5) + 3 = 13$. What are the next three terms?

$$a_3 = 2\,a_{3-1} + 3 = 2\,a_2 + 3 = 2(13) + 3 = 29$$
$$a_4 = 2\,a_{4-1} + 3 = 2\,a_3 + 3 = 2(29) + 3 = 61$$
$$a_5 = 2\,a_{5-1} + 3 = 2\,a_4 + 3 = 2(61) + 3 = 125$$

This sequence is neither arithmetic nor geometric. The difficulty with most sequences defined recursively is that there is no easy way to find a term in the sequence without finding all the terms that precede it.

To get more information and examples about sequences and series, see the chapter Numbers and Operations.

11. Law of Sines

Given $\triangle KNM$ with $KN = 20$, $NM = 30$, and $m\angle M = 40°$. Find, to the nearest degree, the measure of $\angle N$.

 (A) 35   (B) 65   (C) 35 or 65
 (D) 75   (E) 75 or 105

The Law of Sines states that the ratio of the length of a side of a triangle to the sine of the opposite angle is always a constant. That is, in $\triangle KNM$, $\dfrac{k}{\sin(K)} = \dfrac{m}{\sin(M)} = \dfrac{n}{\sin(N)}$.

For this example, $m = 20$, $k = 30$, and $m\angle M = 40°$. Using the first and third ratios in the above proportion, you write $\dfrac{30}{\sin(K)} = \dfrac{20}{\sin(40)}$. Solving for $\sin(K)$, $\sin(K) = \dfrac{30\sin(40)}{20}$. To solve for the measure of angle K, you need to use the inverse sine function. That is, $K = \sin^{-1}\left(\dfrac{30\sin(40)}{20}\right)$.

This is where the problem gets interesting. Is your calculator in radian or degree mode? It should be in degree mode.

One of the basic inequalities for triangles is that in any triangle the larger angle is opposite the larger side.

Since $30 > 20$, $m\angle K > m\angle M$. Your calculator will display that $\sin^{-1}\left(\dfrac{30\sin(40)}{20}\right) = 74.6°$, rounded to 75° as directed. BUT, $m\angle K$ could also be 105° (because $\sin(A) = \sin(180 - A)$). You do not know for sure which it is. This is the *ambiguous case*. All you know for certain is that $m\angle K > m\angle M$. Because the sum of the angles must be 180°, if $m\angle K = 75$, then $m\angle N = 65$ and if $m\angle K = 105$, then $m\angle N = 35$. Therefore, the correct answer is choice (C).

The Law of Sines and the Law of Cosines allow you to "solve triangles," that is, find missing information about a triangle from three pieces of information. Using the familiar abbreviations from geometry for triangle information, the Law of Sines applies when the information given is AAS, ASA, or even SSA (although you must stay aware that the ambiguous case may be lurking within the problem). Use the Law of Cosines $(k^2 = m^2 + n^2 - 2mn \cos(K))$ when you are given SAS or SSS information.

Particular care must be taken when working with SSS information. For example, suppose in $\triangle KNM$, $k = 20$, $m = 30$, and $n = 24$. What is the measure of $\angle M$? Using the Law of Cosines,

$$30^2 = 20^2 + 24^2 - 2(20)(24)\cos(M)$$
$$900 = 400 + 576 - 960\cos(M)$$
$$900 = 976 - 960\cos(M)$$

The temptation to subtract 960 from 976 is too strong for people to resist. As you read this page, you can see that subtracting violates the order of operation or "combining like terms," as 976 does not have a $\cos(M)$ attached to it. Be careful here!

Continuing with the correct solution,

$$-76 = -960 \cos(M)$$

$$\cos(M) = \frac{76}{960}$$

$$M = \cos^{-1}\left(\frac{76}{960}\right)$$

$$M = 85.5°$$

For more information and examples, see the chapter Trigonometry.

12. Exponential Data

The price of a lift ticket to ski for a day in Vail, Colorado in 1963 was approximately $5. If the price has increased at a rate of 7% per year, which equation can be used to determine the price for a daily lift ticket to ski in Vail in 2003?

(A) $p = 5(.7)^{40}$ (B) $p = 5 + 5 \cdot .07 \cdot 40$ (C) $p = 5(1.7)^{40}$

(D) $p = 5(1.07)^{40}$ (E) $p = 5^{(.07)(40)}$

Exponential functions are a vital tool in understanding the magnitude of quantities that grow or decline at a rate proportional to the current value. That is, quantities whose rate of change are reported as percentages (energy usage, crime statistics, population growth, economic changes) behave under this model.

The basic formula for exponential growth is $A = A_0(1 + r)^t$. The variable A_0 represents the amount at the initial stage for the problem (e.g., the price of a lift ticket was \$5 in 1963). The variable r represents the rate of change (written as a decimal) in a time period. If the quantity is growing, r will be positive. If the quantity is dropping in size, r will be negative. The variables r and t must agree in time frame (the change in the price for a lift ticket is reported annually). The variable A is the amount at a given point in time. The equation that will correctly give the price of a lift ticket for a day's skiing in Vail in 2003 is (D). (Remember: 7% written as a decimal is 0.07, not 0.7.)

For more information on exponential functions, see the chapter Exponents and Logarithms.

13. Trig Equations/Identities

Solve: $\sec^2(\theta) + \tan(\theta) - 3 = 0$ for $0 \le \theta \le 2\pi$

(A) -1.107 (B) $\frac{\pi}{4}, \frac{5\pi}{4}$ (C) $\frac{\pi}{4}, \frac{3\pi}{4}, \frac{5\pi}{4}, \frac{7\pi}{4}$

(D) $2.034, 5.176$ (E) $\frac{\pi}{4}, \frac{5\pi}{4}, 2.034, 5.176$

This is an example of a trigonometric equation that is solved using one of the three Pythagorean Identities:

$$\sin^2(\theta) + \cos^2(\theta) = 1$$
$$1 + \tan^2(\theta) = \sec^2(\theta)$$
$$1 + \cot^2(\theta) = \csc^2(\theta)$$

Making the substitution for $\sec^2(\theta)$, the equation becomes

$$1 + \tan^2(\theta) + \tan(\theta) - 3 = 0$$
$$\tan^2(\theta) + \tan(\theta) - 2 = 0$$
$$(\tan(\theta) + 2)(\tan(\theta) - 1) = 0$$
$$\tan(\theta) = -2, 1$$

The domain for θ is $0 \le \theta \le 2\pi$, so the answers need to be in radians. $\tan(\theta) = 1$ yields the answers $\pi/4$ and $5\pi/4$. The reference angle for $\tan(\theta) = -2$ is $\tan^{-1}(2) = 1.107$. Subtracting this number from π and from 2π yields the answers 2.034 and 5.176. The correct answer is (E).

These three identities, along with the identities for the sum and difference of the sine and cosine functions, form the basis for a very large portion of the study of trigonometry.

$$\sin(A + B) = \sin(A)\cos(B) + \sin(B)\cos(A)$$
$$\sin(A - B) = \sin(A)\cos(B) - \sin(B)\cos(A)$$
$$\cos(A + B) = \cos(A)\cos(B) - \sin(A)\sin(B)$$
$$\cos(A - B) = \cos(A)\cos(B) + \sin(A)\sin(B)$$

From these, the identities for the sum and difference of the tangent function and the double angle formulas are derived. Recall, $\tan(\theta) = \dfrac{\sin(\theta)}{\cos(\theta)}$.

Using the difference formulas, you can prove that

$$\sin(180 - \theta) = \sin(\theta)$$
$$\sin(90 - \theta) = \cos(\theta)$$
$$\cos(-\theta) = \cos(\theta)$$
$$\sin(-\theta) = -\sin(\theta)$$

Each of these identities has an impact on being able to solve trigonometric problems more quickly. For more information and examples on the identities, see the chapter Trigonometry.

14. Trig Equations/Multi-Angles

Solve: $3\cos(2x) = 2\sin(x) - 1$ for $0° \le x \le 360°$

(A) 41.8°, 90°   (B) 221.8°, 270°   (C) 41.8°, 138.2°, 270°
(D) 41.8°, 138.2°, 90°   (E) 221.8°, 318.2°, 270°

The identities for the double angles are a big part of solving trigono-metric equations and will appear again as part of your study of integral calculus. There is only one identity for the sine of the double angle and one for the tangent of the double angle. There are three different iden-tities for the cosine of the double angle. All are derived from the sum identities and the Pythagorean Identities.

$$\sin(2\theta) = 2\sin(\theta)\cos(\theta)$$
$$\cos(2\theta) = \cos^2(\theta) - \sin^2(\theta)$$
$$\cos(2\theta) = 2\cos^2(\theta) - 1$$
$$\cos(2\theta) = 1 - 2\sin^2(\theta)$$
$$\tan(2\theta) = \frac{2\tan(\theta)}{1 - \tan^2(\theta)}$$

Learning to determine which of the variations to use for $\cos(2\theta)$ is usually the biggest issue for students. The rule of thumb is to see which other function is used in the problem and to use the equivalent expres-sion for $\cos(2\theta)$ that only uses that function.

In this problem, $\sin(x)$ is the other function in the problem. Using $\cos(2x) = 1 - 2\sin^2(x)$, the equation becomes

$$3(1 - 2\sin^2(x)) = 2\sin(x) - 1$$
$$3 - 6\sin^2(x) = 2\sin(x) - 1$$
$$0 = 6\sin^2(x) + 2\sin(x) - 4$$

Divide by 2:

$$0 = 3\sin^2(x) + \sin(x) - 2$$
$$0 = (3\sin(x) - 2)(\sin(x) + 1)$$
$$\sin(x) = \frac{2}{3}, -1$$

$\sin(x) = -1$ when $x = 270°$. $\sin(x) = 2/3$ has a reference angle $x = \sin^{-1}(2/3)$ $= 41.8°$. The sine function is positive in quadrant II as well, so x could also equal $180\,° - 41.8° = 138.2°$. The correct answer is (C). The other choices are there in case you make a mistake in the signs when you factor.

The half angle identities are derived from the double angles without too much fuss.

Let $A = 2\theta$.

$\cos(2\theta) = 2\cos^2(\theta) - 1$ becomes $\cos(A) = 2\cos^2\left(\frac{A}{2}\right) - 1$. Solving for $\cos\left(\frac{A}{2}\right)$, you get $\cos\left(\frac{A}{2}\right) = \pm\sqrt{\dfrac{1 + \cos(A)}{2}}$. The sign of the answer is dependent upon the range of values for $\frac{A}{2}$.

$\cos(2\theta) = 1 - 2\sin^2(\theta)$ becomes $\cos(A) = 1 - 2\sin^2\left(\frac{A}{2}\right)$. Solving for $\sin\left(\frac{A}{2}\right)$, you get $\sin\left(\frac{A}{2}\right) = \pm\sqrt{\dfrac{1 - \cos(A)}{2}}$.

Using the relationship that $\tan(\theta) = \dfrac{\sin(\theta)}{\cos(\theta)}$, $\tan\left(\frac{A}{2}\right) = \dfrac{\sin\left(\frac{A}{2}\right)}{\cos\left(\frac{A}{2}\right)}$

$= \pm\sqrt{\dfrac{1 + \cos(A)}{1\ \cos(A)}}$.

For example, given $\cos(A) = -8/17$ with $\sin(A) < 0$, find $\cos\left(\frac{A}{2}\right)$ and $\sin\left(\frac{A}{2}\right)$.

With $\cos(A) < 0$ and $\sin(A) < 0$, it must be the case that $\pi < A < \frac{3\pi}{2}$ (or $180 < A < 270$), so that $\frac{A}{2}$ must be in the interval $\frac{\pi}{2} < \frac{A}{2} < \frac{3\pi}{4}$ (or $90 < \frac{A}{2} < 135$). Therefore, you know that $\cos\left(\frac{A}{2}\right) < 0$ and $\sin\left(\frac{A}{2}\right) > 0$.

$\cos\left(\frac{A}{2}\right) = -\sqrt{\dfrac{1 + \cos(A)}{2}} = -\sqrt{\dfrac{1 + \frac{-8}{17}}{2}} = -\sqrt{\dfrac{\frac{9}{17}}{2}} = -\sqrt{\dfrac{9}{34}} = -\dfrac{3}{\sqrt{34}}$

$$\sin\left(\frac{A}{2}\right) = \sqrt{\frac{1-\cos(A)}{2}} = \sqrt{\frac{1-\frac{-8}{17}}{2}} = \sqrt{\frac{\frac{25}{17}}{2}} = \sqrt{\frac{25}{34}} = \frac{5}{\sqrt{34}}$$

For more information and examples of trigonometric identities with double angles and half angles, see the chapter Trigonometry.

15. Conic Sections

The coordinates of the foci of the conic with equation $36x^2 + 20y^2 - 288x + 120y + 36 = 0$ are

    (A) $(4,-7)$ and $(4,1)$ (B) $(0,-3)$ and $(8,-3)$

    (C) $(4,-9)$ and $(4,3)$ (D) $(4 - 2\sqrt{5},-3)$ and $(4 + 2\sqrt{5},-3)$

    (E) $(4,-3 - 2\sqrt{14})$ and $(4,-3 + 2\sqrt{14})$

You should be able to identify that this is an equation for an ellipse because it has the form $Ax^2 + By^2 +$ other terms. Complete the square to get the equation into standard form.

$$36x^2 + 20y^2 - 288x + 120y + 36 = 0$$
$$36x^2 - 288x + 20y^2 + 120y = -36$$
$$36(x^2 - 8x) + 20(y^2 + 6y) = -36$$

To complete the square, take half the linear coefficient, square it, and add it inside the parentheses. **Be sure to account for the coefficient in front of the parentheses when balancing the right-hand side of the equation.**

$$36(x^2 - 8x + 16) + 20(y^2 + 6y + 9) = -36 + 36(16) + 20(9)$$
$$36(x - 4)^2 + 20(y + 3)^2 = 720$$

Divide by 720: $\dfrac{(x-4)^2}{20} + \dfrac{(y+3)^2}{36} = 1$

Ellipses can have a horizontal major axis or a vertical major axis. The clue to you is the larger denominator in the equation. When the major axis is horizontal, the equation is $\dfrac{(x-h)^2}{a^2} + \dfrac{(y-k)^2}{b^2} = 1$, and when the

major axis is vertical, the equation is $\dfrac{(x-h)^2}{b^2} + \dfrac{(y-k)^2}{a^2} = 1$. Recall that

a^2 is always greater than b^2 in the equation for the ellipse. In these equations, the center of the ellipse is at the point (h,k).

For the equation in this problem, the center is $(4,-3)$, $a^2 = 36$, $b^2 = 20$, and the major axis is vertical because a^2 is the denominator for the term in y.

The foci for an ellipse are located on the major axis at a distance c units from the center. This distance is called the *focal* length. The value of c is found from the equation $b^2 + c^2 = a^2$. (This really is the Pythagorean Theorem—you need to think of the theorem as it is written. In a right triangle, the sum of the squares of the legs is equal to the square of the hypotenuse. The mathematics community has gotten a little lax in always referring to the hypotenuse as c "to help students remember the theorem.") See page 167 for diagrams of ellipses with horizontal and vertical axes.

Substituting the values from the equation, you get $20 + c^2 = 36$, $c^2 = 16$, and $c = 4$. The foci are then located 4 units above and below the center of the ellipse at $(4,-7)$ and $(4,1)$. Choice (A) is the correct answer.

Choice (B) has the foci on a horizontal segment, not appropriate for this problem. Choice (C) are the endpoints (vertices) of the major axis. Choice (D) are the endpoints of the minor axis, and choice (E) is there should you use the relationship $a^2 + b^2 = c^2$ to find the focal length.

You should also be comfortable with finding the vertex, focus, directrix, and focal chord (latus rectum) for a parabola, and the center, vertices, foci, and asymptotes for a hyperbola. For more information and examples about these figures, see the chapter Conics, Parametric Equations, and Polar Coordinates.

THE MAIN COURSE: COMPREHENSIVE STRATEGIES AND REVIEW

Diagnostic Test

The test that follows is designed to give you a sense of the types of questions you will see when you take the Mathematics subject test. Throughout this book, material preceded by double asterisks (**) appears only on the Level 2 test.

Do not concern yourself with trying to complete this test in an hour. Take your time and do the best that you can. Explanations to the answers for each of the questions follow the test. Do not look at these until you are done with the test. After reading the explanations, you may get a better sense of which topics you have to spend more time preparing than you will for other topics.

Diagnostic Test

1. Simplify $\sqrt{50} - 3\sqrt{8}$

    (A) $3\sqrt{58}$ (B) $8\sqrt{2}$ (C) $11\sqrt{2}$ (D) $17\sqrt{2}$ (E) $37\sqrt{2}$

2. $\left(\dfrac{36x^{-3}y^5}{27x^{-2}y^{-4}} \right)^{-2} =$

(A) $\dfrac{16y^{11}}{9x^3}$ (B) $\dfrac{3x^3}{4y^1}$ (C) $\dfrac{8y^{11}}{3x^3}$

(D) $\dfrac{16y^{118}}{9x^2}$ (E) $\dfrac{9x^2}{16y^{18}}$

3. $(4 + 5i)^2 =$

(A) $16 + 25i$ (B) -9 (C) 41
(D) $-9 + 20i$ (E) $-9 + 40i$

4. If $\dfrac{2x}{3} - \dfrac{5}{8} = \dfrac{x}{4} + \dfrac{7}{12}$, then $\dfrac{12}{5x} =$

(A) $\dfrac{29}{10}$ (B) $\dfrac{24}{29}$ (C) $\dfrac{29}{50}$ (D) $\dfrac{10}{29}$ (E) $\dfrac{95}{120}$

5. The circumference of the circle that is half as large as the circle with equation $(x - 4)^2 + (y + 7)^2 = 8$ is

(A) 2π (B) 4π (C) 8π (D) $2\pi\sqrt{2}$ (E) $4\pi\sqrt{2}$

6. $\dfrac{\left(216x^6y^9z^{9/4} \right)^{2/3}}{\left(16x^8y^{-4}z^3 \right)^{3/2}} =$

(A) $\dfrac{9}{16x^8z^3}$ (B) $\dfrac{9}{16x^3z^3}$ (C) $\dfrac{9}{16x^8y^{12}z^3}$

(D) $\dfrac{3}{4x^8z^3}$ (E) $\dfrac{9y^{12}}{16x^8z^3}$

7. A summary for a set of data is given by the following box-and-whisker plot. What is the value of the interquartile range?

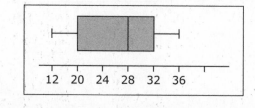

(A) 12   (B) 16   (C) 20   (D) 24   (E) 28

8. The difference between the measure of interior angle of a regular 20-sided polygon and the measure of an exterior angle of the same polygon is

   (A) 0   (B) 18   (C) 144   (D) 162   (E) 180

9. Given $\triangle ABC$ with midpoints D, E, and F as shown in the figure. What is the ratio of the area of $\triangle AFE$ to the area of quadrilateral $BCEF$?

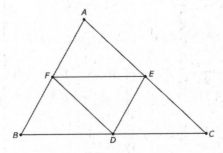

   (A) 1:3   (B) 1:4   (C) 1:5   (D) 2:3   (E) 2:5

10. Given $\triangle ABC$ with midpoints D, E, and F as shown in the figure. If $AB = 4$ cm, $AC = 8$ cm, and $BC = 9$ cm, what is the perimeter of $BCEF$?

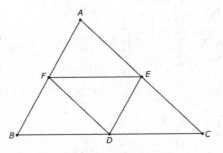

   (A) 10.5 cm   (B) 15 cm   (C) 19.5 cm
   (D) 21.5 cm   (E) 25.5 cm

11. In right $\triangle GHJ$, $\angle H$ is a right angle, $GH = 3$ cm, and $m\angle HGJ = 56°$. To the nearest tenth of a centimeter, what is the length of $\overline{JG}$?

(A) 1.7 cm   (B) 2.5 cm   (C) 3.6 cm   (D) 4.4 cm   (E) 5.4 cm

12. In the accompanying diagram of isosceles $\triangle ABC$, $AB = BC$, $m\angle B = 104°$, $\overline{CD}$ and $\overline{AD}$ bisect angles BCA and BAC, respectively. The measure of $\angle CDA$ is

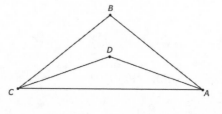

(A) 38°   (B) 76°   (C) 90°   (D) 142°   (E) 161°

13. The graph shows a set of data for the cost, in dollars, for using electricity (measured in kilowatt hours, kwh). Which of the following is an appropriate equation for the cost, C, in terms of the number of kilowatt hours used, k?

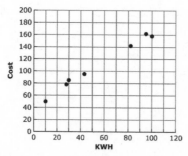

(A) $C = 1.2k + 40$ (B) $C = 3k + 20$ (C) $C = 5k + 30$
(D) $C = 1.5k - 15$ (E) $C = 1.4k + 75$

14. In figure 3, $\overline{LN} \perp \overline{KM}$, $m\angle LKN = 30°$, $m\angle LMN = 45°$, and $LN = 10$. Find the perimeter of $\triangle KLM$.

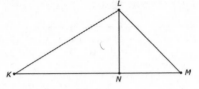

(A) $10 + 10\sqrt{3}$ (B) $30 + 10\sqrt{3}$ (C) $30 + 10\sqrt{2}$

(D) $30 + 10\sqrt{3} + 10\sqrt{2}$ (E) $40 + 10\sqrt{3} + 10\sqrt{2}$

15. $\dfrac{2}{3} \pm \dfrac{\sqrt{5}}{6}i$ are the roots to which of the following quadratic equations?

(A) $12x^2 - 16x + 7 = 0$ (B) $12x^2 - 7x + 16 = 0$
(C) $12x^2 + 16x + 7 = 0$ (D) $3x^2 - 4x + 7 = 0$
(E) $36x^2 - 4x + 21 = 0$

16. A bag contains 5 red, 3 white, and 6 blue marbles. Three marbles are picked without replacement. What is the probability of selecting one marble of each color?

(A) $\dfrac{1}{90}$ (B) $\dfrac{1}{15}$ (C) $\dfrac{7}{45}$ (D) $\dfrac{45}{182}$ (E) $\dfrac{15}{364}$

17. The Venn diagram shows the results of a survey of 100 college freshmen at a small university regarding the courses they are currently taking. How many of the respondents are currently taking calculus?

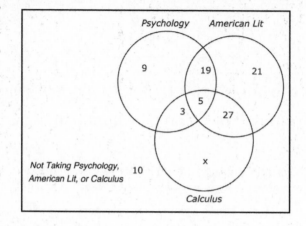

(A) 6   (B) 16   (C) 35   (D) 41   (E) 51

18. When the region bounded in the first quadrant by the equation of $3x + 4y = 12$ is rotated about the y-axis, the volume of the solid formed is

(A) 4π (B) 12π (C) 16π (D) 36π (E) 48π

19. Given the equation $4x^2 + 9x + 27 = 0$. The difference between the product of the roots and the sum of the roots is

(A) $\frac{81}{64}$ (B) $\frac{9}{4}$ (C) 9 (D) 18 (E) 36

20. The equation of the line that is perpendicular to $3x - 4y = 12$ and that passes through the point $(4,-2)$ is

(A) $3x - 4y = 20$ (B) $4x - 3y = 22$ (C) $4x + 3y = 10$
(D) $3x + 4y = 4$ (E) $-3x + 4y = -20$

21. Given $f(x) = 2x^3 + 3x + 2$. $f(3) + f(-3) =$

(A) $f(1) + f(-2)$ (B) $f(1) + f(-1)$ (C) $f(1) + f(0)$
(D) $f(1) + f(1)$ (E) $f(1) + f(3)$

22. Solve: $-8 < 7 - 3x \leq 11$

    (A) $5 < x \leq -6$ (B) $5 > x \geq -6$ (C) $5 > x \geq -4/3$

    (D) $5 < x \leq -4/3$ (E) $-4/3 < x \leq 5$

23. A company increases the number of employees by 25% to help with seasonal sales. By what percent must the company reduce its number of employees to return to the original number employed before the hiring increase?

    (A) 10%   (B) 20%   (C) 25%   (D) 80%   (E) 90%

24. If $3\begin{bmatrix} 2 & -1 \\ -3 & 5 \end{bmatrix} - 4\begin{bmatrix} -1 & 2 \\ 3 & 1 \end{bmatrix} = \begin{bmatrix} x & y \\ z & 11 \end{bmatrix}$, then $x + y - z =$

    (A) -22 (B) 0   (C) 10   (D) 20   (E) 42

25. Given $q(x) = \dfrac{x^2 - 3x - 4}{x^2 - 16}$. For which values of x does $q(x) = 0$?

    (A) $\{-4, 4\}$ (B) $\{-4, 1\}$ (C) $\{-1, 4\}$

    (D) $\{4\}$ (E) $\{-1\}$

26. In the accompanying diagram of $\triangle ABC$, $\overline{CE} \parallel \overline{AB}$, and $\angle CDE \cong \angle CBA$. Which of the following statements is true?

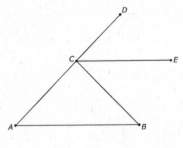

    I. $AC = BC$

    II. $\overline{CE}$ bisects $\angle DCB$

    III. $m\angle ACB = 90$

    (A) I only   (B) II only   (C) I and II only

    (D) I and III only   (E) I, II, and III

27. If $\cos(\theta) = \frac{7}{8}$, $0 \le \theta \le 90°$, what is the value of $\sin(180 - \theta)$?

   (A) $\frac{7}{8}$ (B) $-\frac{7}{8}$ (C) $\frac{-\sqrt{15}}{8}$ (D) $\frac{\sqrt{15}}{8}$ (E) $\frac{8}{7}$

28. Given: $2x + 3y - 4z = 123$
                   $4x - 2y + z = 79$
                   $5x + 4y - 3z = 37$

   What is the value of $x - 3y$?

   (A) 239   (B) 165   (C) 81   (D) $\frac{321}{15}$ (E) $-\frac{8969}{7}$

29. In a circle with area 75π, a central angle forms an arc with length 45. The measure of the central angle, in radians, is

   (A) $3\sqrt{3}$ (B) $3\sqrt{5}$ (C) $9\sqrt{3}$ (D) $3\pi\sqrt{3}$ (E) $3\pi\sqrt{5}$

30. In the accompanying figure, $\overline{DE} \perp \overline{AB}$ at E in $\triangle ABC$. Which is the longest segment?

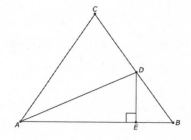

   (A) $\overline{AD}$ (B) $\overline{AC}$ (C) $\overline{BC}$ (D) $\overline{AB}$
   (E) Cannot be determined from the given information.

31. The range of the function $f(x) = -3x^2 + 9x + 7$ is

   (A) $x = 1.5$ (B) $y = 13.5$ (C) $[13.5, \infty)$
   (D) $(-\infty, 13.5]$ (E) All real numbers

32. An inverted cone (vertex at the bottom) with radius 8 inches and height 12 inches is filled to half its volume. To the nearest hundredth of an inch, what is the height of the water when the cone is half full?

   (A) 2.88   (B) 4.00   (C) 6.00   (D) 6.60   (E) 9.52

33. Solve: $4\sin(x) + 3\cos(x) = 0$ for $0 \le x \le 2\pi$

   (A) {0.644, 3.785}   (B) {2.498, 5.640}   (C) {0.927, 4.069}
   (D) {2.214, 5.356}   (E) {4.545}

34. If $25^{a^2+2ab} = 125^{a^2-ab}$ and if a and b do not equal 0, then $b =$

   (A) $-a$ (B) a (C) $\frac{a}{3}$ (D) $\frac{a}{7}$ (E) $7a$

35. In right $\triangle ACB$, $\overline{CD}$ is perpendicular to hypotenuse $\overline{AB}$. Which of the following equations is false?

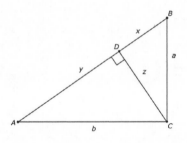

   I. $z^2 = ab$
   II. $z^2 = xy$
   III. $a^2 = y(x + y)$

   (A) I and II only   (B) I and III only   (C) II and III only
   (D) I, II and III   (E) All of the equations are true.

36. What is the 25th term in the sequence 8, 11, 14, 17, 20, ...?

   (A) 80   (B) 83   (C) 86   (D) 195   (E) 198

37. The graph of $y = f(x)$ is shown. Which is the graph of $y = \frac{-1}{2}f(x+2) - 1$?

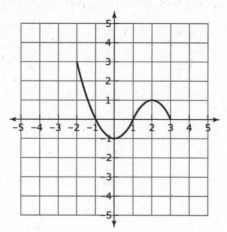

A.

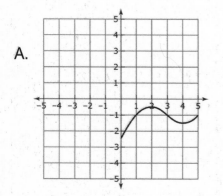

B.

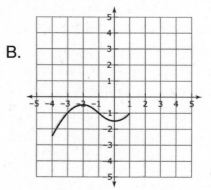

C.

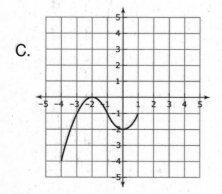

D.

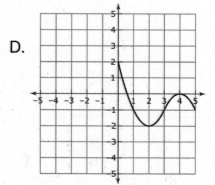

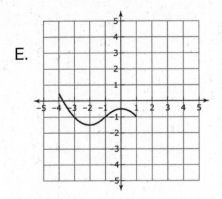

E.

38. Given $f(x) = \dfrac{x^2 - x - 6}{x^2 + 6x + 8}$ with a domain $-3 \le x \le 4$. The range of this function is

(A) $y < 1$ (B) $y \le 1/8$ (C) $y < 1$ and $y \ne 5/2$
(D) $y \le 1/8$ and $y \ne 5/2$ (E) All real numbers

39. If $f(x) = 3x - 5$ and $g(x) = 3x^2 + 1$, $g \circ f(-2) =$

(A) -360 (B) -143 (C) -38 (D) 34 (E) 364

40. If the solution to $f(x) = 0$ is $\{-3, -1.5, 2, 5\}$ and $g(x) = 4f(x + 3)$, the solution to $g(x) = 0$ is

(A) $\{-3, -1.5, 2, 5\}$ (B) $\{0, 1.5, 5, 8\}$ (C) $\{-12, -6, 8, 20\}$
(D) $\{0, 6, 20, 32\}$ (E) $\{-6, -4.5, -1, 2\}$

**41. $\dfrac{\sin(2x)}{2\sin(x)} - \dfrac{\cos(2x)}{2\cos(x)} =$

(A) $\frac{1}{2}\sec(x)$ (B) $\frac{1}{2}\sin(x)$ (C) $\frac{1}{2}\cos(x)$

(D) $\frac{1}{2}\csc(x)$ (E) $\frac{1}{2}\tan(x)$

**42. $\triangle ABC$ has $m\angle A = 39$, $AB = 20$, and $BC = 28$. To the nearest tenth of a degree, $m\angle B =$

(A) 26.7 (B) 26.7 or 153.3 (C) 114.3
(D) 56.3 (E) 56.3 or 123.7

**43. The foci of an ellipse are at $(2,-1)$ and $(-4,-1)$. If the coordinates of a vertex of the ellipse are $(4,-1)$, the equation of the ellipse is

(A) $\dfrac{(x+1)^2}{25}+\dfrac{(y+1)^2}{9}=1$ (B) $\dfrac{(x+1)^2}{25}+\dfrac{(y-1)^2}{16}=1$

(C) $\dfrac{(x+1)^2}{25}+\dfrac{(y+1)^2}{16}=1$ (D) $\dfrac{(x+1)^2}{9}+\dfrac{(y+1)^2}{25}=1$

(E) $\dfrac{(x+1)^2}{16}+\dfrac{(y+1)^2}{25}=1$

**44. The parametric equation for a curve is given by $x(t) = 3\sin(t) - 1$ and $y(t) = 7\cos(t) + 2$. The equation for this curve in rectangular coordinates is

(A) $\dfrac{x-1}{3}+\dfrac{y+2}{7}=1$ (B) $\dfrac{(x-1)^2}{3}+\dfrac{(y+2)^2}{7}=1$

(C) $\dfrac{(x+1)^2}{9}+\dfrac{(y-2)^2}{49}=1$ (D) $\dfrac{(x-1)^2}{3}-\dfrac{(y+2)^2}{7}=1$

(E) $\dfrac{(x+1)^2}{9}-\dfrac{(y-2)^2}{49}=1$

**45. Given: $a_1=12$

$$a_n = a_{n-1} + n$$
$$a_{10} =$$

(A) –7   (B) –6   (C) 12   (D) 16   (E) 17

**46. If vector $a= [-3, 2]$ and vector $b = [2, 5]$, then the head of the vector $4a + 6b$ lies

      (A) in Quadrant I   (B) in Quadrant II (C) in Quadrant III
      (D) in Quadrant IV (E) on the y-axis

**47. If $\log_b(c) = a$, then $\log_b(c^2b^3)=$

      (A) $a^2 + b^3$ (B) $3a^2$ (C) $2a + 3$ (D) $6a$ (E) $\dfrac{2a}{3}$

**48. $\cos\left(\sin^{-1}\left(\dfrac{x-1}{3}\right)\right)=$

      (A) $\dfrac{2(x-1)\sqrt{x-1}}{9}$ (B) $\dfrac{-2x^2 + 4x + 7}{9}$ (C) $\dfrac{-2x^2 + 4x + 25}{9}$

      (D) $\dfrac{2x^2 - 4x - 25}{9}$ (E) $\dfrac{-2x^2 + 4x - 15}{9}$

**49. The point with rectangular coordinates $(-5, 5\sqrt{3})$ corresponds to

      (A) $\left(10, \dfrac{\pi}{3}\right)$ (B) $\left(10, \dfrac{4\pi}{3}\right)$ (C) $\left(10, \dfrac{5\pi}{3}\right)$

      (D) $\left(10, \dfrac{-5\pi}{3}\right)$ (E) $\left(10, \dfrac{-4\pi}{3}\right)$

**50. The graph of the function $f(x) = \begin{cases} 3x - 2 & x < 1 \\ 2(x-2)^2 - 1 & x \geq 1 \end{cases}$ is

A.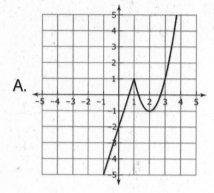

B.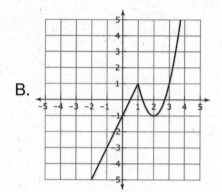

C.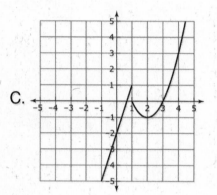

D.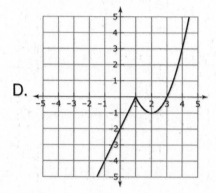

E.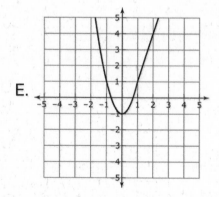

Diagnostic Test Solutions

1. The correct answer is (C). Remember to simplify the radical expressions by removing all those factors that are perfect squares. $\sqrt{50} = 5\sqrt{2}$ and $3\sqrt{8} = 3(2\sqrt{2}) = 6\sqrt{2}$. Take the time to write down each of these steps. Choices (B), (D), and (E) are designed to trip you up in case you should forget to simplify a part of a statement. Choice (A) should be eliminated immediately, as the numbers under the radicals are not the same, a requirement for adding and subtracting irrational numbers.

2. The correct answer is (E). Simplify the term inside the parentheses first to get $\left(\dfrac{4y^9}{3x}\right)^{-2}$. The negative exponent directs you to take a reciprocal, $\left(\dfrac{3x}{4y^9}\right)^2$. You can then square the term to get $\dfrac{9x^2}{16y^{18}}$. Be careful with the rules of exponents. $(a^m)^n = a^{mn}$, not a^{m+n}, which is the process behind the incorrect choices (A), (B), and (C).

3. The correct answer is (E). Squaring a binomial always gives three terms. Recall that $(a + b)^2 = a^2 + 2ab + b^2$. $(4 + 5i)^2 = 4^2 + 2(4)(5i) + 25i^2$. Since $i^2 = -1$, this becomes $-9 + 40i$. Choices (A), (B), and (C) should be eliminated, because the responses simply square the 4 and 5. Choice (A) and ignores the i. Choice (B) does square the i, so that the sum is $16 - 25$, and choice (C) uses i^2 as 1, not -1. Choice (D) does not correctly expand the binomial, because the middle term is $(4)(5i)$ rather than $2(4)(5i)$.

4. The correct answer is (B). A clue to this problem is the unusual quantity you are asked to find. Many people would begin this question by multiplying both sides of the equation by 24 to remove the fractions from the problem. However, if you gather the terms in x, $\dfrac{2x}{3} - \dfrac{x}{4}$, you get $\dfrac{5x}{12}$. You are looking for the reciprocal of this number. The reciprocal of $\dfrac{5}{8} - \dfrac{7}{12}$ is $\dfrac{24}{29}$. Choice (A) is the value of x that solves the problem and choice (D) is the reciprocal of this number.

5. The correct answer is (D). The radius of the circle given is $2\sqrt{2}$. This is also the diameter of the smaller circle. Use $C = \pi d$ to get the correct answer. Choice (A) is the area rather than the circumference of the small circle. Choice (C) is the area of the larger circle, and choice (B) is half this number. Choice (E) is the circumference of the original circle.

6. The correct answer is (A). The numerator simplifies to be $36x^4y^{-6}z^{3/2}$, and the denominator is $64x^12y^{-6}z^{9/2}$. The terms in y are exactly the same, so they will cancel out (divide to be 1). The larger of the exponents for both x and z are in the denominator of the fractions. When reduced, the fraction has the constant 9 in the numerator and the monomial $16x^8z^3$ in the denominator. As before in problem 2, be careful when simplifying $(a^m)^n$.

7. The correct answer is (A). The interquartile range (IQR) is the difference between the third quartile, Q_3, and the first quartile, Q_1. These numbers are the boundaries of the rectangle in the box-and-whisker plot. $Q_3 = 32$ and $Q_1 = 20$, so the IQR = 12. Choice (B) is the difference between the median and the minimum, choice (C) is Q_1, choice (D) is the range, and choice (E) is the median.

8. The correct answer is (C). The sum of the exterior angles for all convex polygons is $360°$. For a regular (all sides equal and all angles equal) 20-sided polygon, each exterior angle is $18°$ (choice (B)), and each interior angle is the supplement, $162°$ (choice (D)).

9. The correct answer is (A). The segment joining the midpoints of two sides of a triangle forms two triangles that are similar to each other. The ratio of the lengths of corresponding sides is 1:2, and the ratio of the areas is the square of this value, 1:4. That is, the area of $\triangle ABC$ is 4 times that of $\triangle AFE$. Quadrilateral $BCEF$ has area equal to the area of $\triangle ABC$ minus the area of $\triangle AFE$.

10. The correct answer is (C). The segment joining the midpoints of two sides of a triangle is half as long as the third side. Therefore, $FE = 4.5$, $FB = 4$, and $CE = 2$. The perimeter of a figure is the sum of the

lengths of the segments that form the outside of the figure. The perimeter of $BCEF$ = FB + BC + CE + EF = 2 + 9 + 4 + 4.5 = 19.5. Choice (A) is half the perimeter of $\triangle ABC$, and this would be the perimeter of any one of the four triangles contained within $\triangle ABC$. Choice (B) is the perimeter of $BDEF$ or $DCEF$. Choice (D) adds ED to the perimeter, and choice (E) adds ED and FD to the perimeter. Since ED and FD are not sides of the quadrilateral, they are not included in the computation of the perimeter.

11. The correct answer is (E). GH is the length of the segment adjacent to the $\angle G$, and JG is the length of the hypotenuse. Therefore, use $\cos(G) = \dfrac{GH}{JG}$. Multiply to get $JG \cdot \cos(G) = GH$ so that $JG = \dfrac{GH}{\cos(G)}$. Be sure to write the steps out in solving this problem. Choice (A) is the product of 3 and $\cos(56)$, not the quotient. Choices (B) and (C) use the sine function, while choice (D) uses the tangent function.

12. The correct answer is (D). The vertex angle of the triangle measures 104°, so each of the base angles measures 38° (choice (A)). The measures of $\angle DAC$ and $\angle DCA$ are each 19°. The measure of $\angle CDA$ is 180 – (19 + 19) = 142°.

13. The correct answer is (A). Use a straightedge piece of paper to draw your guess as to the line of best fit. The vertical intercept is approximately 40, with a slope that is almost 1. You can estimate the coordinates of two of the plotted points, one from each extreme. For example, (10,50) and (100,155) give a slope of $\dfrac{155-50}{100-10} = \dfrac{105}{90} = 1.17$. The other choices offered have too inappropriate a slope or a y-intercept to be considered a good line of fit.

14. The correct answer is (D). $\triangle KLN$ is a 30-60-90 triangle, so the longer leg, KN, is $\sqrt{3}$ times longer than the shorter leg, and the hypotenuse, KL, is twice the length of the shorter leg. $\triangle LNM$ is a 45-45-90 triangle. $LN = MN$, and LM is $\sqrt{2}$ times the length of the legs. $KM = KN + NM$. Choices (A) – (C) use some of the segments that form the perimeter,

but not all of them. Choice (E) includes LN, which is not part of the perimeter of $\triangle KLM$.

15. The correct answer is (A). The sum of the roots, $\left(\dfrac{2}{3}+\dfrac{\sqrt{5}}{6}i\right)+\left(\dfrac{2}{3}-\dfrac{\sqrt{5}}{6}i\right)=\dfrac{4}{3}$ and the product of the roots,

$\left(\dfrac{2}{3}+\dfrac{\sqrt{5}}{6}i\right)\left(\dfrac{2}{3}-\dfrac{\sqrt{5}}{6}i\right)=\left(\dfrac{2}{3}\right)^{2}-\left(\dfrac{\sqrt{5}}{6}i\right)^{2}=\dfrac{4}{9}+\dfrac{5}{36}=\dfrac{21}{36}=\dfrac{7}{12}=\dfrac{c}{a}$. Rewrit-

ing the sum of the roots as $\dfrac{16}{12}$, so that both denominators are 12, gives

$a = 12$, $b = -16$, and $c = 7$.

16. The correct answer is (D). Because the marbles are not being replaced, the probability of getting a red, a white, and a blue in that order

is $\left(\dfrac{5}{4}\right)\left(\dfrac{3}{13}\right)\left(\dfrac{6}{12}\right)=\left(\dfrac{15}{364}\right)$. You also have to consider the other orders in which the three marbles are selected. Drawing a quick tree diagram will help you to see that there are 3 choices for the first color chosen, 2 for the second, and 1 for the third. That is there are 6 different ways to arrange the colors, each with a probability of $\dfrac{15}{364}$. Therefore, the prob-

ability of getting one marble of each color is $6\left(\dfrac{15}{364}\right)=\dfrac{45}{182}$. You could

also use combinations to compute the probability of selecting one marble of each color. $\dfrac{\left(_5C_1\right)\left(_3C_1\right)\left(_6C_1\right)}{_{14}C_1}=\dfrac{45}{182}$.

17. The correct answer is (D). There are 100 students in the survey, but only 90 accounted for, so x must equal 6 (choice (A)). There are $6 + 3 + 5 + 27 = 41$ students taking calculus. Choice (B) would be the value of x if the 10 students not enrolled in any of the three courses were ignored, and choice (E) is the sum. Choice (C) ignores x and only adds the numbers displayed in the diagram.

18. The correct answer is (C). The region described in the problem is a triangle with vertices (0,0), (0,3), and (4,0). When this region is rotated about the y-axis, a cone is formed with radius 4 and height 3. The volume of the cone is $(1/3)\pi(4^2)(3) = 16\pi$. Choice (B) is the volume of the cone rotated about the x-axis, and the other choices involve using the wrong formula for the volume of the cone.

19. The correct answer is (C). The product of the roots for a quadratic equation $ax^2 + bx + c = 0$ is c/a, and the sum of the roots is $-b/a$. For this problem, the product is 27/4, and the sum is –9/4. The difference between these numbers is $36/4 = 9$.

20. The correct answer is (C). Because the slopes of perpendicular lines are negative reciprocals, the equation of the perpendicular line must be of the form $4x + 3y = C$. Substitute the coordinates (4,–2) into this equation to get choice (C). Choice (A) is parallel to the original line, choice (B) switches the coefficients but not the sign between the terms, and choice (D) switches the signs but not the coefficients. Choice (E) is the same as choice (A).

21. The correct answer is (B). This problem can be done by substituting values into your calculator. A quicker method would be to note that $f(3) = 2(3)^3 + 3(3) + 2$ and $f(-3) = 2(-3)^3 + 3(-3) + 2$. $2x^3$ and $3x$ are odd terms, meaning that whenever a value for x is substituted by its negative (like 3 and –3), the results will always be opposite each other, so the result to this sum is 4. $f(a) + f(-a)$ will always equal 4 for this function.

22. The correct answer is (C). Subtract 7 from all three terms to get $-15 < -3x \le 4$. Remember to reverse the orientation of the inequalities when you divide by –3 to get $5 > x \ge -4/3$. Choices (A) and (B) involve adding 7 and 11, while choice (D) fails to reverse the inequalities, and choice (E) puts the equality with 5 rather than with –4/3.

23. The correct answer is (B). After hiring the seasonal workers, the number of employees is 125% of normal. To bring this number back to 100%, solve the equation $125P = 100$, where P is the percent change, to

determine the correct answer. Remember that the percent change is not 25%, because the base you are working from (125%) is different from the number you originally used (100%).

24. The correct answer is (D). Scalar multiplication of matrices is performed by multiplying each element in the matrix by the coefficient. In

this case, $3\begin{bmatrix} 2 & -1 \\ -3 & 5 \end{bmatrix} = \begin{bmatrix} 6 & -3 \\ -9 & 15 \end{bmatrix}$ and $4\begin{bmatrix} -1 & 2 \\ 3 & 1 \end{bmatrix} = \begin{bmatrix} -4 & 8 \\ 12 & 4 \end{bmatrix}$.

Matrix subtraction is done with terms in corresponding positions, so

$\begin{bmatrix} 6 & -3 \\ -9 & 15 \end{bmatrix} - \begin{bmatrix} -4 & 8 \\ 12 & 4 \end{bmatrix} = \begin{bmatrix} 10 & -11 \\ -21 & 11 \end{bmatrix} = \begin{bmatrix} x & y \\ z & 11 \end{bmatrix}$.

$x + y - z = 10 + (-11) - (-21) = -1 + 21 = 20$.

25. The correct answer is (E). Even though the solution to $x^2 - 3x - 4 = 0$ is $x = 4$ or -1, you must first remember to look at the entire fraction and realize that it reduces to $\dfrac{(x-4)(x+1)}{(x-4)(x+4)} = \dfrac{x+1}{x+4}$. Setting the reduced fraction equal to zero will get the correct answer.

26. The correct answer is (C). Because of the parallel lines, $\angle CDE \cong \angle CAB$ (corresponding angles) and $\angle CBA \cong \angle BCE$ (alternate interior angles). Substitution gives $\angle CDE \cong \angle BCE$ (therefore, angle bisector) and $\angle CAB \cong \angle CBA$ (therefore, it is an isosceles triangle, and $AC = BC$). There is no reason for $\angle ACB$ to be 90°.

27. The correct answer is (D). If $\cos(\theta) = 7/8$ and θ is an acute angle, the Pythagorean Theorem (or the Pythagorean Identity $\cos^2(\theta) + \sin^2(\theta) = 1$) can be used to determine that $\sin(\theta) = \dfrac{\sqrt{15}}{8}$. $\sin(180 - \theta) = \sin(\theta)$ because the angles are a reflection across the y-axis from one another and $\sin(180 - \theta) = \dfrac{\sqrt{15}}{8}$.

28. The correct answer is (B). You can set up a matrix equation to solve the system fairly quickly to find that $x = \dfrac{429}{49}$, $y = \dfrac{-2531}{49}$, and $z = \dfrac{-3159}{49}$.

$x - 3y = 165$. The quicker approach to doing this problem is to see that $x - 3y$, the expression you are asked to find, can be determined by adding the first and second equations and then subtracting the third equation. It only takes a moment to look for a tricky relationship among the facts of the problem to see if the solution can be found quickly before going to a more traditional problem solving approach.

29. The correct answer is (A). Use the formula $s = r\theta$, where s is the arc length, r is the radius, and θ is the radian measure of the central angle. The radius of the circle is $\sqrt{75} = 5\sqrt{3}$. Therefore, $\theta = \dfrac{45}{5\sqrt{3}} = \dfrac{9}{\sqrt{3}} = 3\sqrt{3}$. Many students believe that radian angles always have a π in the answer, so choice (D) is there to tempt them. Choices (B) and (E) are in case a student writes $\sqrt{75}$ as $3\sqrt{5}$.

30. The correct answer is (E). While you can be sure that $\angle AED$ is a right angle, and angles $\angle ADE$ and $\angle EDB$ are acute, there is nothing else of which you are certain. You are being tempted to make assumptions about the problem. Do not fall into this trap.

31. The correct answer is (D). $f(x)$ is a parabola that opens down, has its axis of symmetry at $x = 1.5$, and its vertex at $(1.5, 13.5)$. The range, or set of outputs, will always be less than or equal to 13.5. The interval notation $(-\infty, 13.5]$ means the same as $y \le 13.5$.

32. The correct answer is (E). The volume of the original cone is $(1/3)\pi(8^2)(12) = 256\pi$. Half this amount is 128π.

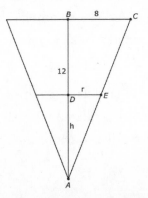

If AB is the height of the original cone and AD is the height of the water when the cone is filled to a level h, $\triangle DAE \sim \triangle BAC$ because of the right angles and the shared angle at vertex A. Therefore, $\dfrac{r}{h} = \dfrac{8}{12}$ and $r = \dfrac{2}{3}h$.

Solve $128\pi = \dfrac{1}{3}\pi r^2 h$ by substituting $\dfrac{2}{3}h$ for r to get $128\pi = \dfrac{1}{3}\pi\left(\dfrac{2h}{3}\right)^2 h$

or $\dfrac{1}{3}\pi\left(\dfrac{2h}{3}\right)^2 h$. This becomes $h^3 = 32 \cdot 27$, so $h = 6\sqrt[3]{4} = 9.52$.

33. The correct answer is (B). Solve $4\sin(x) + 3\cos(x) = 0$ by changing the equation to $4\sin(x) = -3\cos(x)$ and then $\dfrac{\sin(x)}{\cos(x)} = \dfrac{-3}{4}$ or $\tan(x) = -3/4$. The reference angle for $\tan^{-1}(3/4) = 0.644$. Choice (A) is tempting, but the signs of the tangent are wrong. Find the correct answers by computing $\pi - 0.644$ and $2\pi - 0.644$. Choices (C) and (D) are in case a student solved $\tan(x) = -4/3$.

34. The correct answer is (D). Rewrite the equation with the common base of 5. $25^{a^2 + 2ab} = 125^{a^2 - ab}$ becomes $5^{2(a^2 + ab)} = 5^{3(a^2 - ab)}$. Set the exponents equal to each other and solve. $2(a^2 + 2ab) = 3(a^2 - ab)$ becomes $2a^2 + 4ab = 3a^2 - 3ab$, or $0 = a^2 - 7ab$. $a(a - 7b) = 0$ becomes $a = 0$, or $a - 7b = 0$, $a = 7b$, or $a/7 = b$.

35. The correct answer is (B). When the altitude is dropped to the hypotenuse of a right triangle, three pairs of similar triangles are formed, and each pair contains a common side. In the diagram given, $z^2 = xy$, $a^2 = x(x + y)$, and $b^2 = y(x + y)$.

36. The correct answer is (A). The common difference for this arithmetic sequence is 3. The equation for the sequence is $a_n = 8 + 3(n - 1)$, so $a_{25} = 8 + 3(24) = 80$.

37. The correct answer is (B). The graph of $f(x)$ is translated left 2 units, reflected over the x-axis, dilated towards the x-axis by a factor of 1/2, then finally translated down 1. Move the points $(-2,3)$ and $(2,1)$ by these rules:

left 2		reflect		dilate		down	
(–2,3)	→	(–4,3)	→	(–4,–3)	→	(–4,–1.5)	→	(–4,–2.5)
(2,1)	→	(0,1)	→	(1,–1)	→	(0,–.5)	→	(0,–1.5)

38. The correct answer is (B). Sketch this graph with your graphing calculator with the window $x$min = –3 and $x$max = 4, the domain of the problem.

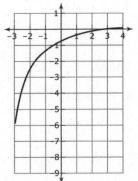

You can see that the range has a maximum value of 1/8 and that there is a vertical asymptote at $x = -3$.

39. The correct answer is (E). The open circle between g and f represents a composition, not a multiplication. Compositions are evaluated from right to left. $f(-2) = -11$ and $g(-11) = 3(-11)^2 + 1 = 3(121) + 1 = 364$.

40. The correct answer is (E). The dilation factor 4 has no impact on the answers to this problem because the output values are zero. Translate each of the solutions of $f(x) = 0$ to the left 3 units to get the solutions of $g(x) = 0$.

41. The correct answer is (A). Use the identity $\cos(2x) = 2\cos^2(x) - 1$ to rewrite the problem as $\dfrac{\sin(2x)}{2\sin(x)} - \dfrac{\cos(2x)}{2\cos(x)} = \dfrac{2\sin(x)\cos(x)}{2\sin(x)} - \dfrac{2\cos^2(x) - 1}{2\cos(x)}$

$= \cos(x) - \cos(x) + \dfrac{1}{2\cos(x)} = \dfrac{1}{2\cos(x)} = \dfrac{1}{2}\sec(x)$.

42. The correct answer is (C). Use the Law of Sines on this SSA problem to first find the measure of $\angle C$. You should know that because $BC > AB$,

$m\angle A > m\angle C$. It will save you time if you observe that because $BC > AB$, there is only one triangle that can be constructed. (The potential problems associated with the ambiguous case happen when the side opposite the known angle, BC, is greater than the altitude drawn from vertex B but less than AB.) $\dfrac{\sin(C)}{\sin(39)} = \dfrac{20}{28}$ becomes $\sin(C) = \dfrac{20\sin(39)}{28}$ so that $m\angle C = 26.7°$. Therefore, $m\angle B = 180 - (26.7 + 39) = 114.3°$.

43. The correct answer is (C). With the foci at $(2,-1)$ and $(-4,-1)$, the center of the ellipse is $(-1,-1)$, and the focal length (the distance from the center to a focus) is $c = 3$. The ellipse is horizontal, as the focal axis is horizontal. The equation for the horizontal ellipse is $\dfrac{(x - h^2)}{a^2} + \dfrac{(y - k^2)}{b^2} = 1$. The distance from the center to the end of the major axis is 5 units $((-1,-1)$ to $(4,-1))$. Finally, use the equation $a^2 = b^2 + c^2$ to determine that $b^2 = 16$. The equation for this ellipse is $\dfrac{(x + 1)^2}{25} + \dfrac{(y + 1)^2}{16} = 1$.

44. The correct answer is (C). Rewrite each of the equations to get $\sin(t) = \dfrac{x+1}{3}$ and $\cos(t) = \dfrac{y - 2}{7}$. Use the Pythagorean Identity $\sin^2(t) + \cos^2(t) = 1$ to get $\dfrac{(x + 1)^2}{9} + \dfrac{(y - 2)^2}{49} = 1$.

45. The correct answer is (B). There is no shortcut to doing this problem. You can use the Sequence mode on the TI-83/84 series calculator to create the recursion and then compute the 10th term or set up a spreadsheet on the TI-Nspire to achieve the same result. The first 10 terms of the sequence are 12, –10, 13, –9, 14, –8, 15, –7, 16, –6.

46. The correct answer is (E). $4a + 6b$ equals $4[-3, 2] + 6[2, 5] = [-12, 8] + [12, 30] = [0, 38]$. The vector terminates on the y-axis. Scalar multiplication is a dilation of the vector and can be computed by multiplying the vector components by the scalar factor.

47. The correct answer is (C). Use the properties of logarithms to expand $\log_b(c^2b^3)$ to $2\log_b(c) + 3\log_b(b) = 2a + 3(1) = 2a + 3$.

48. The correct answer is (B). If $\theta = \sin^{-1}\left(\dfrac{x-1}{3}\right)$, then $\sin(\theta) = \dfrac{x-1}{3}$.

The length of the leg adjacent to θ must have length $\sqrt{3^2 - (x-1)^2} =$

$\sqrt{9 - (x^2 - 2x + 1)}$. $\sqrt{9 - x^2 + 2x - 1} = \sqrt{8 + 2x - x^2}$, and $\cos(\theta) =$

$\dfrac{\sqrt{8 + 2x - x^2}}{3}$.

$$\cos(2\theta) = \cos^2(\theta) - \sin^2(\theta) = \left(\frac{\sqrt{8 + 2x - x^2}}{3}\right)^2 - \left(\frac{x-1}{3}\right)^2$$

$$= \frac{8 + 2x - x^2}{9} - \frac{x^2 - 2x + 1}{9}$$

$$= \frac{8 + 2x - x^2 - \left(x^2 - 2x + 1\right)}{9}$$

$$= \frac{8 + 2x - x^2 - x^2 + 2x - 1}{9}$$

$$= \frac{-2x^2 + 4x + 7}{9}.$$

You need to be careful with distributing the negative signs throughout the problem.

49. The correct answer is (E). The point $(-5, 5\sqrt{3})$ lies in the second quadrant of the rectangular plane and has a reference angle of $\pi/3$ because $\tan^{-1}\left(\dfrac{5\sqrt{3}}{5}\right) = \tan^{-1}(\sqrt{3}) = \dfrac{\pi}{3}$. The radius is 10 (all the choices have the same radius). Of all the angle choices, the only angle to terminate in quadrant II is $-4\pi/3$.

50. The correct answer is (A). For all values of $x < 1$, $f(x)$ is defined by the line $y = 3x - 2$. You can use the y-intercept of -2 and the point $(1,1)$ For $x \geq 1$, the parabola $2(x-2)^2 - 1$ defines the function. Use the values $x = 1, 2, 3$ to find the points $(1,1)$, $(2,-1)$, and $(3,1)$. When you examine the choices, option (A) is the only graph that has all these points.

How to Use the Mini-Review

Mathematics is not a spectator subject. One does not learn the subject merely by watching someone else do the material. Whether you are in the classroom or reading this text, you need to have pencil, paper, and a graphing calculator with you, and you need to put them to work. The chapters that follow contain a summary of much of what you have learned in high school. Within the text of each chapter are exercises the author has worked out for you. Don't read the solutions!

"What?" you say. "I bought this book so that I can see how problems are done."

That, dear reader, is exactly the point. Before you see how the problems are done, do the problems. Take the time to answer the problems based on what you have learned in school and from the reading in the chapter. You can look at the author's solution. This solution might be identical to yours or might have a different approach. Solutions are given with the end in mind that they should be as efficient as possible considering the time limit you have when taking the test. Any extra wordage given in a solution is meant to help clarify the process for you.

At the end of each chapter, you will find five review problems. Solutions to these problems follow after the review questions. Throughout these chapters, material preceded with a double asterisk (**) is intended to highlight Level 2 material, so that students who are taking the Level 1 test do not find themselves discouraged. Take the time to work out each of the problems in the review sections. Level 2 test takers should do all the problems.

Use your calculator efficiently. As wonderful a tool as the calculator is, it takes time to key in all the information needed to do a problem. Be mindful of this as you are preparing. Gauge when you can answer questions without the calculator, when the use of the calculator is a required, and when the use of the calculator gives you a greater sense of confidence in your solution. You should be using plenty of paper as you write your solutions. Consider using a separate notebook for just this purpose. You can section off part of the notebook for your notes—concepts and formulas that you want to go over regularly or that are new to you—and sections for problem solving. Keep notes on when you used a calculator and when you did not, so that when you get to the test, you will have a better sense of when to incorporate the graphing calculator in your solution.

Topic 1: Numbers and Operations

Order of Operations

Keep in mind the order of operations, especially when using a calculator. Too often, one will get an incorrect answer using a calculator because the expression was not entered correctly into the calculator. This is especially true with complex fractions and algebraic expressions with negative numbers.

The order of operations is

- parentheses or grouping

- exponents

- multiplication and division as they occur from left to right

- addition and subtraction as they occur from left to right.

Example: Simplify $\dfrac{\frac{2}{3} + \frac{7}{12}}{\frac{3}{4} - \frac{1}{2}}$

Entering this into a calculator as 2/3 + 7/12 / 3/4 – 1/2 will not yield the correct answer. The calculator will do 2/3, then [(7/12)/3]/4, and 1/2. It will then take these answers and combine them to get $\dfrac{31}{144}$.

The correct entry into the calculator (without using the fraction feature that is on many calculators) is (2/3 + 7/12) / (3/4 – 1/2). This will yield the correct answer, 5.

As is often the case, this problem can be solved more easily without a calculator than with one. Multiply the numerator and denominator by the common denominator of ALL the fractions (in this case, 12) to get

$$\frac{\left(\dfrac{2}{3}+\dfrac{7}{12}\right)}{\left(\dfrac{3}{4}-\dfrac{1}{2}\right)}\frac{12}{12}=\frac{8+7}{9-6}=\frac{15}{3}=5$$

Ratio and Proportion

Ratios have a number of applications, as they denote relative measurements as well as rates of change. If 1 euro = 1.60 U.S. dollars, then you can convert from one currency to another by setting up an equation called a proportion.

Convert 25 euros to U.S. dollars: $\dfrac{1}{1.6}=\dfrac{25}{d}$. Cross-multiply to get $d = 40$.

$$1 \cdot d = 1.6 \cdot 25$$
$$d = 40$$

Convert \$100 U.S. to euros: $\dfrac{1}{1.6}=\dfrac{e}{100}$. Cross-multiply to get $1.6e = 100$, or $e = 62.5$.

If a car travels 300 miles in 4.5 hours, how much time is needed to travel 500 miles? (Of course, the assumption is that the average speed is constant.) $\dfrac{300}{4.5}=\dfrac{500}{h}$. Solve to get $h = 7.5$.

In general, the proportion $\dfrac{a}{b}=\dfrac{c}{d}$ has a number of consequences.

Cross-multiply: $ad = bc$

Reciprocals: $\dfrac{b}{a}=\dfrac{d}{c}$

Exchange the means: $\dfrac{a}{c} = \dfrac{b}{d}$

Exchange the extremes: $\dfrac{d}{b} = \dfrac{c}{a}$

Do you see that when you cross-multiply, the products are still the same?

Add the denominator to the numerator: $\dfrac{a+b}{b} = \dfrac{c+d}{d}$ (Do you see this as adding 1 to both sides of the equation?)

Take the reciprocal of both sides of this equation to get: $\dfrac{a}{a+b} = \dfrac{c}{c+d}$. This is the same as adding the numerator to the denominator.

When would any of these be used?

Example: In $\triangle ABC$, D is a point on $\overline{AC}$ so that $\overline{DE} \parallel \overline{AB}$. If $\dfrac{AD}{DC} = \dfrac{2}{3}$, what is $\dfrac{DE}{AB}$?

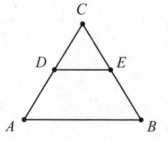

With $\overline{DE} \parallel \overline{AB}$, $\triangle DEC \sim \triangle ABC$ and $\dfrac{DE}{AB} = \dfrac{CD}{CA}$. Since $\dfrac{AD}{DC} = \dfrac{3}{2}$,

$\dfrac{DC}{AD} = \dfrac{3}{2}$, and when you add the numerator to the denominator,

you get $\dfrac{DC}{AD+DC} = \dfrac{3}{2+3}$, or $\dfrac{DE}{AB} = \dfrac{3}{5}$.

Rules for Exponents

The rules for exponents are a fundamental tool in the study of mathematics and one in which errors occur more because of carelessness than lack of understanding. Recall that the basic properties are

I	$\left(b^m\right)\left(b^n\right)=b^{m+n}$	When the bases are the same, products are found by keeping the base and adding the exponents
II	$\dfrac{b^m}{b^n}=b^{m-n}$	When the bases are the same, quotients are found by keeping the base and subtracting the exponents
III	$\left(b^m\right)^n = b^{mn}$	When a term raised to a power is also raised to a power, multiply the exponents
IV	$(ab)^n = a^n\, b^n$	When a product is raised to a power, each of the factors is raised to the power and the results are multiplied
V	$b^0 = 1$	Any nonzero number raised to the zero power is equal to 1
VI	$b^{-n} = \dfrac{1}{b^n}$	A negative exponent means a reciprocal
VII	$b^{1/n} = \sqrt[n]{b}$	Fractional exponents translate to radical expressions

Simplify: $\sqrt[3]{\left(\dfrac{50x^{-5}y^{17}}{150x^4y^2}\right)^2}$

Begin by simplifying the fraction and by rewriting the radical as a term with a fractional exponent.

$$\sqrt[3]{\left(\frac{50x^{-5}y^{17}}{150x^4y^2}\right)^2} = \sqrt[3]{\left(\frac{27y^{15}}{125x^9}\right)^2} \quad \text{Apply Rule IV to get } \left(\frac{27y^{15}}{125x^9}\right)^{2/3}.$$

This becomes $\dfrac{9y^{10}}{25x^6}$.

Irrational Numbers

Adding and subtracting irrational numbers is similar to addition and subtraction in algebra—combine like terms. Just as $2x + 5x = 7x$, $2\sqrt{3} + 5\sqrt{3} = 7\sqrt{3}$.

Problems such as $2\sqrt{12} + 5\sqrt{27}$ at first appear as though they cannot be added because the numbers under the square roots (the radicands) are different. However, because $12 = 4 \cdot 3$ and $27 = 9 \cdot 3$, the terms can be simplified first to $2\sqrt{12} = 2\sqrt{4 \cdot 3} = 2\sqrt{4}\sqrt{3} = 4\sqrt{3}$ and $5\sqrt{27} = 5\sqrt{9 \cdot 3} = 5\sqrt{9}\sqrt{3} = 15\sqrt{3}$. $2\sqrt{12} + 5\sqrt{27} = 4\sqrt{3} + 15\sqrt{3} = 19\sqrt{3}$.

You cannot add $\sqrt{3}$ and $\sqrt{5}$ because the radicands are different. You cannot add $\sqrt{3}$ and $\sqrt[5]{3}$ because their indices are different—one is a square root, and the other is a fifth root.

Multiplication of irrational numbers is straightforward, as long as the irrational expressions have the same index. For terms with different radicands, such as $(5\sqrt{2})(8\sqrt{6})$, multiply the coefficients and multiply the radicands to get $40\sqrt{12}$. This answer can be simplified to $40\sqrt{12} = 40\sqrt{4}\sqrt{3} = 80\sqrt{3}$.

**Example: Multiplication of expressions with different indices is possible if the radicands are common. Rewrite the problem using fractional exponents to get the result. For example, $(\sqrt[3]{32})(\sqrt{32}) = (32)^{1/3}(32)^{1/2}$. As with all multiplication problems using exponents, keep the base and add the exponents to get $32^{5/6}$. In this case, 32 can be rewritten as 2^5, so $32^{5/6} = (2^5)^{5/6} = 2^{25/6} = 2^4 \cdot 2^{1/6} = 16\sqrt[6]{2}$. Therefore, $(\sqrt[3]{32})(\sqrt{32}) = 16\sqrt[6]{2}$.

Multiplication of irrational binomials also works as it does in algebra.

$$(3 + 2\sqrt{15})(4 - 3\sqrt{6}) = 12 + 8\sqrt{15} - 9\sqrt{6} - 6\sqrt{90}$$

$$= 12 + 8\sqrt{15} - 9\sqrt{6} - 18\sqrt{10}(5 + 3\sqrt{6})^2 = 25 + 30\sqrt{6} + (3\sqrt{6})^2$$

$$= 25 + 30\sqrt{6} + 9(6)$$

$$= 79 + 30\sqrt{6}$$

Division with irrational numbers takes advantage of the factoring formula for the difference of squares, $(a + b)(a - b) = a^2 - b^2$. $a + b$ and $a - b$ are called conjugates.

If the divisor of the problem is a binomial with an irrational term, you will rationalize the denominator by getting an equivalent fraction. You can find this fraction by multiplying the numerator and denominator by the conjugate of the denominator.

$$\frac{36}{4 - 2\sqrt{3}} = \left(\frac{36}{4 - 2\sqrt{3}}\right)\left(\frac{4 + 2\sqrt{3}}{4 + 2\sqrt{3}}\right) = \frac{36(4 + 2\sqrt{3})}{16 - 12} = \frac{36(4 + 2\sqrt{3})}{4} =$$

$$9(4 + 2\sqrt{3}) = 36 + 18\sqrt{3}$$

Complex Numbers

By definition, $\sqrt{-1} = i$. The ramifications of this definition are that $i^2 = -1$, $i^3 = -i$, and $i^4 = 1$. This pattern of i, -1, $-i$, 1 will continue forever. The quick way to evaluate i^n is to divide n by 4.

If the remainder is	the answer is
0	1
1	i
2	-1
3	$-i$

Evaluate i^{479}. Since $\frac{479}{4} = 119$ with a remainder of 3 (your calculator will read 119.75), $i^{479} = -i$.

Equality of Complex Numbers—Two complex numbers $a + bi$ and $c + di$ are equal only if $a = c$ and $b = d$. That is, the real parts must be equal, and the imaginary parts must be equal.

Graphing Complex Numbers—The number line you have known forever consists of all the real numbers. To graph complex numbers, you need to work with the complex plane. It looks like a traditional coordinate plane, except that the values on the vertical axis are the pure imaginary numbers (complex numbers in which the real component is 0). As always, a real number will be plotted on the (horizontal) real number line. A complex number such as 3 + 4i has a real component of 3 and an imaginary component of 4, and looks like the directed line segment below.

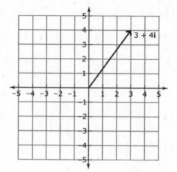

Absolute Value of a Complex Number—Absolute value represents the distance a number is from the origin. With a number such as 3 + 4i, you can see that the graph forms the traditional right triangle with legs 3 and 4, so the hypotenuse must be 5. That is, |3 + 4i| = 5. The distance formula, or Pythagorean Theorem, will always yield the absolute value of a complex number, $|a + bi| = \sqrt{a^2 + b^2}$. In the real number system, the equation |x| = 5 has two solutions, 5 and –5. In the complex number plane, the equation |a + bi| = 5 has an infinite number of solutions—all the points on a circle centered at the origin with a radius of 5.

Arithmetic of Complex Numbers—Adding and subtracting complex numbers are combined using like terms—real parts are combined with real parts, and imaginary parts are combined with imaginary parts. For example, the sum of 3 + 4i and –2 + 5i is 1 + 9i. 3 + (–2) = 1, and 4 + 5 = 9.

Subtract 3 + 4i from –2 + 5i to get –5 + 1i, or –5 + i. –2 – 3 = –5, and 5 – 4 = 1.

Multiplying complex numbers is the equivalent of multiplying binomials, with the exception that i^2 simplifies to be –1. For example, $(3 + 4i)(-2 + 5i) = -6 + 15i - 8i + 20i^2 = -6 + 7i + (-20) = -26 + 7i$.

You need to be careful, however, when faced with the seemingly "easy" problem $(\sqrt{-8})(\sqrt{-18})$. The temptation is to keep the radical, multiply –8 and –18 to get 144, and state that the square root of 144 is 12. This would be wrong.

When performing operations with negative numbers with square roots, you must first factor out the square root of –1 and then go about the rest of the problem. That is,

$$(\sqrt{-8})(\sqrt{-18}) = (i\sqrt{8})(i\sqrt{18}) = i^2\sqrt{144} = -12$$

Counting

The *Fundamental Theorem of Counting* tells you how to count the number of possible outcomes from a scenario in which a number of decisions must be made. According to the Fundamental Theorem, the number of possible outcomes for the entire scenario is equal to the product of the number of options that exists in each step of the scenario.

Example: A four-course meal consists of an appetizer, a salad, an entrée, and a dessert. Today's menu has 6 appetizers, 7 salads, 10 entrées, and 5 desserts.

The number of different possible meals is equal to $6 \times 7 \times 10 \times 5 = 2100$.

Example: A license plate number is to be formed from 3 letters followed by 3 numbers. To avoid confusion between 0 and O and 1 and *I*, the letters O and *I* cannot be used.

The number of different license plates which can be made is equal to the product of the number of ways in which each of the six characters can be chosen. Repetition of letters and numbers is allowed, so there are 24 choices for each of the letters and 10 choices for each of the numbers. The number of possible license plates equals $24 \times 24 \times 24 \times 10 \times 10 \times 10 = 13,824,000$.

Example: A Personal Identification Number (PIN) for the Northeast Moon Bank consists of 6 numbers with the following restrictions—no digit may be repeated, the first digit must be an even number greater than 0, and the last digit must be 1 more than the first digit.

There are 4 choices for the first digit (2, 4, 6, 8). Once the first digit is selected, there is only 1 choice for the last digit (that number which is 1 more than the first digit). This leaves 8 choices for the second digit, 7 choices for the third, 6 for the fourth, and 5 for the fifth digit. The number of different PINs is $4 \times 8 \times 7 \times 6 \times 5 \times 1 = 6720$.

Example: A tee ball coach has twelve players and needs to create a batting order for all twelve. She chooses the line-up for each game in the same manner. She writes each name on a piece of paper, puts each piece of paper into a hat, and draws names. The order in which she draws them is the batting order for that night. There are $12 \times 11 \times 10 \times 9 \times 8 \times 7 \times 6 \times 5 \times 4 \times 3 \times 2 \times 1$, or 479,001,600 different orders.

Writing the factors from 12 down to 1 is tedious. The notation for this product is 12!, read "12 factorial." By definition, when n is a positive integer, $n!$ = the product of the first n positive integers. An addition to this definition is that $0! = 1$. Why that is will be explained shortly.

An arrangement in which order matters is called a *permutation*. Typical examples are codes and roles with titles (e.g., president vs vice president). The number of permutations of n items taken r at a time is written $_nP_r = \dfrac{n!}{(n-r)!}$. Arrangements in which order does not matter are called *combinations*. The number of combinations of n items taken r at a time is written $_nC_r = \dfrac{n!}{(n-r)!r!}$.

Example: Eight students are running for the positions of class president, vice president, treasurer, and secretary. The winner of each position will be determined by the number of votes received. That is, the student with the highest total will be president, second most vice president, etc. Jamie as president and Alice as vice president is different from Alice as president and Jamie as vice president. This is a permutation. The number of different election results is $_8P_4 = \dfrac{8!}{(8-4)!} = \dfrac{8!}{4!} = \dfrac{8 \cdot 7 \cdot 6 \cdot 5 \cdot 4}{4!} = 8 \cdot 7 \cdot 6 \cdot 5 = 1680$.

Example: Sarah is the chair of the prom committee. Eight students are running for the remaining 4 positions on the committee. Because the

4 positions being voted on have no designated roles, there is no difference whether Jamie receives the most votes or the fourth most votes.
Therefore, this is an example of a combination. The number of different
election results is $_8C_4 = 70$.

Example: Determine the number of arrangements of the letters in
the word ARNOLD. From the 6 letters, pick the 6 letters to get $_6P_6 = \frac{6!}{(6-6)!} = \frac{6!}{0!} = 720$. Note that $0! = 1$. Thus, you simply calculate $6!$, as
with a regular counting problem.

A special situation occurs when the letters in the word are repeated.
For example, two arrangements of the word YANKEES are YANK*E*E*S*
and YANK*E*E*S*. The font change is for you to see the "differences."
Without the font change, there is no difference. Therefore, the number of arrangements in the seven-letter word needs to be adjusted for
the ease with which the two E's can be interchanged. The number of
arrangements of the letters in the word YANKEES is $\frac{7!}{2!} = 2520$.

Example: Determine the number of arrangements of the letters
in MISSISSAUGA. Of the 11 letters in the word, there are 4 S's, 2
I's, and 2 A's. The number of different arrangements of the letters is
$\frac{11!}{4!2!2!} = 415,800$

Venn diagrams are a good way to display the results of a survey.
A rectangle is used to encompass the total number of participants in
the survey.

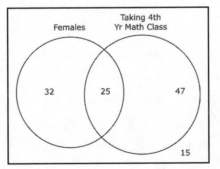

For example, the diagram above illustrates the results of a survey of
the senior class. There are 57 females (32 + 25) in the class and 62 males

(47 + 15). Twenty-five of the females and 47 males are taking a fourth-year math class, while 47 students (32 + 15) are not.

Example: A survey of the senior class who indicated an interest in pursuing further education in engineering is displayed in the Venn diagram below.

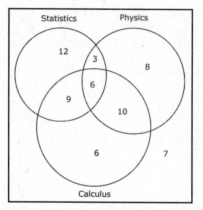

How many of these seniors are taking physics? 27 (that is, 3 + 6 + 10 + 8).

How many of these seniors are taking calculus? 31 (that is, 9 + 6 + 10 + 6).

How many of these seniors are taking exactly two of the three courses? 22 (that is, 9 + 3 + 10).

How many of these students are taking statistics but not physics? 21 (that is, 12 + 9).

Matrices

A matrix is a rectangular array of numbers. Matrices have application to any number of fields—from solving systems of linear equations to determining the value of a business's inventory to modeling a communications network. With the exception of solving a system of linear equations, these applications are outside of the realm of testing topics for the Math Level 1 or Level 2 exams.

The dimensions of a matrix are given as "number of rows" by "number of columns." For example, the matrix $A = \begin{bmatrix} a & b & c \\ d & e & f \end{bmatrix}$ has 2 rows and

3 columns. The element in first row, third column is $A_{1,3} = c$.

A matrix with an equal number of rows and columns is a square matrix. A square matrix with 1 in the positions along the main diagonal (where the row number = the column number) and zeroes everywhere else is the identity matrix. There are infinitely many identity matrices, one for each positive integer. For example,

$$I_2 = \begin{bmatrix} 1 & 0 \\ 0 & 1 \end{bmatrix} \qquad I_3 = \begin{bmatrix} 1 & 0 & 0 \\ 0 & 1 & 0 \\ 0 & 0 & 1 \end{bmatrix}$$

Matrices with the same dimensions can be added or subtracted by combining the elements in the same position in the matrix.

$$\begin{bmatrix} 1 & 2 \\ 8 & -1 \end{bmatrix} + \begin{bmatrix} 3 & 5 \\ 2 & -4 \end{bmatrix} = \begin{bmatrix} 4 & 7 \\ 10 & -5 \end{bmatrix}$$

Scalar multiplication means multiplying each element in the matrix by a constant.

$$2 \begin{bmatrix} 3 & 5 \\ 2 & -4 \end{bmatrix} = \begin{bmatrix} 6 & 10 \\ 4 & -8 \end{bmatrix}$$

Matrix multiplication is a bit more tricky. An example which may help you get a better handle on the process is this: imagine a car dealership with lots in two towns, Central Lake and North Lake. At each of these dealerships, four kinds of cars are sold, SubCompax, Compax, Sporty, and Guzzler. The number of each type of car at each location is given in the table below.

	Subcompax	Compax	Sporty	Guzzler
Central Lake	5	4	9	4
North Lake	6	7	5	2

The invoice value for each of these cars is

	Invoice Value
SubCompax	$12,500
Compax	$15,000
Sporty	$19,000
Guzzler	$21,000

The total value of the inventory for each location is the sum of the products of the number of cars of each model multiplied by that model's inventory value. That is, the value of the cars at Central Lake is $5 \cdot 12,500 + 4 \cdot 15,000 + 9 \cdot 19,000 + 4 \cdot 21,000 = \$377,500$, and the inventory value for North Lake is $6 \cdot 12,500 + 7 \cdot 15,000 + 5 \cdot 19,000 + 2 \cdot 21,000 = \$317,000$.

The matrix product is expressed as

$$\begin{bmatrix} 5 & 4 & 9 & 4 \\ 6 & 7 & 5 & 2 \end{bmatrix} \begin{bmatrix} 12500 \\ 15000 \\ 19000 \\ 21000 \end{bmatrix} = \begin{bmatrix} 377500 \\ 317000 \end{bmatrix}$$

The key to matrix multiplication is that the number of columns in the left-hand factor must be the same as the number of rows in the right-hand factor. As a consequence, *matrix multiplication is not commutative*.

Division of matrices does not exist. The multiplication inverse is used instead. Rather than have $\frac{B}{A}$, you would have $A^{-1}B$. Computing the inverse is most easily done on your graphing calculator.

Sequences

A sequence is a listing in which there is a discernible pattern. Common patterns are

- Arithmetic—the difference of consecutive terms is constant

- Geometric—the ratio of consecutive terms is constant

- Fibonacci—1, 1, 2, 3, 5, 8, 13, ... beginning with the third term, each term is the sum of the two previous terms

- Triangular Numbers—1, 3, 6, 10, 15, 21, ... the difference between consecutive terms increases by 1

There are formulas for computing arithmetic and geometric sequences.

If a_1 represents the first term and d represents the common difference in the arithmetic sequence, the nth term is given by the formula $a_n = a_1 + (n-1)d$.

If a_1 represents the first term and r represents the common ratio in the geometric sequence, the nth term is given by the formula $a_n = a_1(r)^{n-1}$.

The nth term in the triangular numbers is given by the formula $a_n = \dfrac{n(n+1)}{2}$.

The only formula for the Fibonacci sequence is given recursively. A *recursive formula* gives an initial value (or values) and then gives a rule for finding all other terms as a function of prior terms. The recursive formula for the Fibonacci sequence is

$$a_1 = 1 \qquad a_2 = 1 \qquad a_n = a_{n-1} + a_{n-2} \text{ for } n \geq 3$$

Example: Determine the 27th term of the sequence 3, 9, 15, 21, 27, ...

Observe that the difference between each term is 6, so this is an arithmetic sequence. Since the first term is 3, you can write $a_{27} = 3 + 6(27-1) = 159$.

Example: Find the 27th term of the sequence defined recursively as $a_1 = 3$ and $a_n = a_{n-1} + 6$.

The second term of the sequence $a_2 = 3 + 6 = 9$, and the third term is $a_3 = 9 + 6 = 15$, and you can see that this is the same arithmetic sequence from the previous example. In fact, the recursive definition identifies that consecutive terms differ by 6.

Example: Determine the 12th term in the sequence 4, 12, 36, 108, ...

Each term in the sequence is 3 times the previous term, so this is a geometric sequence with an initial value 4 and common ratio 3. The twelfth term is $a_{12} = 4(3)^{11} = 708{,}588$. The recursive definition for this problem would be $a_1 = 4$ and $a_n = 3a_{n-1}$.

Example: Find the 7th term of the sequence defined by $a_1 = 2$, $a_2 = 3$, and $a_n = 2a_{n-1} + 3a_{a-2}$ for $n \geq 3$.

This recursive definition does not appear anything as simple as an arithmetic or geometric sequence, so you will have to go term by term.

$a_3 = 2a_2 + 3a_1 = 2(3) + 3(2) = 12$

$a_4 = 2a_3 + 3a_2 = 2(12) + 3(3) = 33$

$a_5 = 2a_4 + 3a_3 = 2(33) + 3(12) = 102$

$a_6 = 2a_5 + 3a_4 = 2(102) + 3(33) = 303$

$a_7 = 2a_6 + 3a_5 = 2(303) + 3(102) = 712$

**Series

The sum of the terms of a sequence is called a series. There are formulas for the sum of arithmetic and geometric series.

Arithmetic Series: $S_n = \dfrac{n}{2}(a_1 + a_n)$

Finite Geometric Series: $S_n = \dfrac{a_1(1-r)^n}{1-r}$

When $|r| < 1$, you can compute the sum of the infinite geometric series as $S_\infty = \dfrac{a_1}{1-r}$.

Example: Find the sum of the first 100 terms in the series 4 + 11 + 18 + 25 + ...

You know $n = 100$ and $a_1 = 4$. All you need to compute the sum is a_{100}. Use the formula for the terms in an arithmetic sequence to get $a_{100} = 4 + 7(99) = 697$. $S_{100} = \dfrac{100}{2}(4 + 697) = 35050$.

Example: Compute $\sum\limits_{n=1}^{75} 3n - 2$

The Greek letter Σ, sigma, is used to indicate addition. You begin with the value below the sigma as your starting value and count by 1 until you reach the value above the sigma. In this case, the first term is $3(1) - 2 = 1$ and the 75th term is $3(75) - 2 = 223$. Therefore, $S_{75} = \dfrac{75}{2}(1 + 223) = 8400$.

Example: Compute 5 + 13 + 21 + ... + 197.

The series is arithmetic with first term 5 and common difference of

8. The questions to be answered before computing the sum is the number of terms. Use the formula for sequences to solve for n.

$197 = 5 + 8(n - 1)$

$192 = 8(n - 1)$

$24 = n - 1$

$n = 25$

Therefore, $S_{25} = \dfrac{25}{2}(5 + 197) = 2525$.

Example: Compute $\displaystyle\sum_{n=1}^{25} 12\left(\dfrac{3}{2}\right)^n$

The first term is 12 (3/2) = 18, and the common ratio is 3/2.

Therefore, $S_{25} = \dfrac{18\left(1 - \dfrac{3}{2}\right)^{25}}{1 - \dfrac{3}{2}}$

$= 909006.06$

Example: Compute $24 + 12 + 6 + 3 + 3/2 + 3/4 + \ldots$

The first term of this infinite geometric series is 24 and the common ratio is 1/2. The sum is $S_\infty = \dfrac{24}{1 - \frac{1}{2}} = 48$.

Example: Given $a_1 = 4$ and $a_n = 3a_{n-1} + 1$. Find the sum of the first 20 terms.

This problem will require too much time to solve by hand. You can use your calculator to compute the terms, though.

The TI-83/84 series has a sequence function which can be accessed through the Mode option.	Normal Sci Eng Float 0123456789 Radian Degree Func Par Pol Seq Connected Dot Sequential Simul Real a+bi re^θi Full Horiz G-T ↓NEXT↓
Press Y= to access the equation editor. The default variable is now n. The function u can be accessed with the 2nd 7 key. The braces for the set notation can be found above the parentheses keys.	Plot1 Plot2 Plot3 nMin=1 \u(n)■3u(n-1)+1 u(nMin)■{4} \v(n)= v(nMin)= \w(n)= w(nMin)=

QUIT to the home screen. The formula for computing this sum of the sequence starts with SUM (found at 2nd STAT, left arrow to MATH, and option 5).	NAMES OPS **MATH** 1∎min(2:max(3:mean(4:median(5:sum(6:prod(7↓stdDev(
Next is the seq(command. 2nd STAT, right arrow, option 5).	NAMES **OPS** MATH 1∎SortA(2:SortD(3:dim(4:Fill(5:seq(6:cumSum(7↓ΔList(
The parameters for the sequence command are: seq (function, variable, start, stop)	seq(u(n),n,1,20)
Be sure to close the parentheses for both the seq(command and the sum(command. It will take the calculator a little time to compute the sum.	sum(seq(u(n),n,▶ 7845264890

The TI-Nspire can solve this problem with its spreadsheet feature. Open a spreadsheet, label the first two columns for convenience.

In the first column, enter the formula seq(n,n,1,20) to fill in the first column with the numbers 1–20.	
Enter 4 in cell B1. Move to cell B2, type a 3, move the cursor to B1, press enter, add 1. The editing line at the bottom of the screen will read B2=3*B1+1. Repeat this for cell B3=3*B2+1.	
Highlght cells B2 and B3. Go to MENU–Statistics–Data–Fill Down. A marquee (dotted rectangle) will be drawn around the two cells. Scroll down to line 20 (the bottom of the rectangle will drag with you) and press ENTER.	
The cells should look like the picture.	

Go to the calculator page and type sum(outputs) to get the answer.	1.1 1.2 ▶ *Unsaved ▾ sum(outputs) 7845264890 1/99

One might think to do all series problems this way. This might not be a good idea, as it takes time to enter the information into the calculator, and you can use a known formula much more quickly.

Exercises

1.   The price of a student ticket to a high school production is $4, and the price for an adult is $8. If the total receipts for the sale of 225 tickets are $1600, how many student tickets were sold?

   (A) 50   (B) 60   (C) 75   (D) 85   (E) 100

2.   If $\dfrac{a}{b} = \dfrac{2}{5}$, what is the value of $\dfrac{b}{a + 3b}$?

   (A) $\dfrac{5}{17}$ (B) $\dfrac{5}{7}$ (C) 1   (D) $\dfrac{7}{5}$ (E) $\dfrac{17}{5}$

3.   If $(5 + 7i)^2 = a + bi$, then $a + b =$

   (A) –24   (B) 11   (C) 46   (D) 74   (E) 109

4.   Given: $a_1 = 1$
                        $a_n = 3a_{n-1} - 2$

   The 8th term of this sequence is

   (A) –128   (B) –13   (C) 1   (D) 256   (E) 6561

**5. Given: $a_1 = 40$

                 $a_n = \dfrac{1}{2} a_{n-1}$

   Find $\displaystyle\sum_{n=2}^{\infty} a_n$

   (A) 20   (B) 40   (C) 80   (D) 160   (E) ∞

Explanations

1. (A) A system of equations can be set up to solve this problem. Using the choices to determine the solution to this problem will also be quick. If 50 student tickets are sold, then 175 adult tickets need to be sold. Use your calculator to compute $4(50) + 8(175)$. Know that if you initially chose 60, for example, then the number of adult tickets would be 165 and the receipts would total $4(60) + 8(165) = 1560$. Since this number is too small, you can deduce that you need more adult tickets and fewer student tickets to reach $1600.

2. (A) If $\dfrac{a}{b} = \dfrac{2}{5}$, then adding 3 to each side of the equation gives

$\dfrac{a}{b} + 3 = \dfrac{2}{5} + 3 = \dfrac{a + 3b}{b} = \dfrac{17}{5}$. You were asked to determine the value

of $\dfrac{b}{a + 3b}$, the reciprocal of this number. Choices (B) and (D) are there in case you added 1 to each side and did not take into account the coefficient of b.

3. (C) $(5 + 7i)^2 = 25 + 2(5)(7i) + (7i)^2 = 25 + 70i + 49i^2 = -24 + 70i$. With $a = -24$ and $b = 70$, $a + b = 46$. The choices (A), (B), and (D) are there in case you expand the binomial incorrectly, and choice (E) is present should you not include that $i^2 = -1$.

4. (C) The recursive definition has the first term, $a_1 = 1$. $a_2 = 3a_1 - 2 = 3(1) - 2 = 1$. This will result in all terms being 1. The remaining choices are given should you ignore part of the recursive definition. Choice (B) comes from the arithmetic sequence defined by $a_n = a_{n-1} - 2$, choice (E) by the geometric sequence $a_n = 3a_{n-1}$. Choices (A) and (D) are there in case you misread the definition to be $a_n = (a_{n-1})(-2)$ and miscount the number of terms.

5. (B) The recursive definition $a_n = \dfrac{1}{2}a_{n-1}$ defines a geometric sequence. The notation $\sum\limits_{n=2}^{\infty} a_n$ directs you to find an infinite sum, **beginning with the second term.** The second term of the series is $1/2(40) = 20$. The sum for the infinite series is $S_\infty = \dfrac{20}{1 - \frac{1}{2}} = 40$.

Topic 2: Algebra and Functions

Expressions

Combining like terms such as $3a + 4a$ to be equal to $7a$ is a simple application of the distributive property, because $3a + 4a = (3 + 4)a = 7a$. Terms such as $3a^2b + 5ab^2$ cannot be simplified because the variable terms are not identical.

Example: Simplify $4a^2b + 3ab^2 - 5ab^2 + 6a^2b$

$4a^2b + 6a^2b$ can be simplified to $10a^2b$, while $3ab^2 - 5ab^2$ becomes $-2ab^2$. Therefore, $4a^2b + 3ab^2 - 5ab^2 + 6a^2b = 10a^2b - 2ab^2$.

Multiplication does not require like terms. Multiplying monomials such as $6a^2b$ and $5ab^3$ is done by multiplying the coefficients and then terms with common bases using the properties of exponents. So $(6a^2b)(5ab^3) = 30a^3b^4$.

Multiplying polynomials requires multiple applications of the distributive property. Many students learn the mnemonic FOIL (First Outside Inside Last) for multiplying two binomials.

Example: Multiply $(2x + 7)(5x - 4)$

$$(2x + 7)(5x - 4) = 2x(5x - 4) + 7(5x - 4) = 10x^2 - 8x + 35x - 28$$
$$= 10x^2 + 27x - 28.$$

Example: Multiply $(2x + 7)(3x^2 + 5x - 4)$

$$(2x + 7)(3x^2 + 5x - 4) = 2x\,(3x^2 + 5x - 4) + 7(3x^2 + 5x - 4)$$
$$= 6x^3 + 10x^2 - 8x + 21x^2 + 35x - 28$$
$$= 6x^3 + 31x^2 + 27x - 28$$

There are certain multiplication formulas that should be known in order to speed up your ability to solve problems and also help with factoring.

Difference of Squares:	$(a + b)(a - b) = a^2 - b^2$
Square Trinomials:	$(a + b)^2 = a^2 + 2ab + b^2$
	$(a - b)^2 = a^2 - 2ab + b^2$
Sum and Difference of Cubes:	$(a - b)(a^2 + ab + b^2) = a^3 - b^3$
	$(a + b)(a^2 - ab + b^2) = a^3 + b^3$

Algebraic fractions, or rational algebraic expressions, behave in the same way constant fractions do.

- The denominator cannot be equal to zero.

- Addition and subtraction require common denominators.

- Multiplication and division do not require common denominators.

- Fractions are reduced by finding common factors in both the numerator and denominator.

Example: $\dfrac{4}{x + 3} + \dfrac{7}{x + 3} = \dfrac{1}{x + 3}$

Example: Simplify $\dfrac{4}{x + 3} + \dfrac{7}{x - 3} = \left(\dfrac{4}{x + 3}\right)\left(\dfrac{x - 3}{x - 3}\right) + \left(\dfrac{7}{x - 3}\right)\left(\dfrac{x + 3}{x + 3}\right)$

$$= \dfrac{4(x - 3) + 7(x + 3)}{(x + 3)(x - 3)}$$

$$= \dfrac{4x - 12 + 7x + 21}{(x + 3)(x - 3)} = \dfrac{11x + 9}{(x + 3)(x - 3)}$$

Example: Simplify $\dfrac{x + 1}{x^2 - x - 6} + \dfrac{x - 3}{x^2 + 5x + 6}$

Factor the denominators to determine the common denominator. $x^2 - x - 6 = (x - 3)(x + 2)$ and $x^2 + 5x + 6 = (x + 2)(x + 3)$. Since $x + 2$ is a common factor of the denominators, the common denominator for this problem is $(x + 2)(x - 3)(x + 3)$. Rewrite the problem with the common denominator while creating equivalent fractions.

$$\frac{x+1}{x^2-x-6} + \frac{x-3}{x^2+5x+6} = \frac{x+1}{(x-3)(x+2)}\left(\frac{x+3}{x+3}\right) + \frac{x-3}{(x+2)(x+3)}\left(\frac{x-3}{x-3}\right)$$

$$= \frac{(x+1)(x+3) + (x-3)^2}{(x-3)(x+2)(x+3)}$$

$$= \frac{x^2+4x+3+x^2-6x+9}{(x-3)(x+2)(x+3)}$$

$$= \frac{2x^2-2x+12}{(x-3)(x+2)(x+3)}$$

Example: Simplify $\dfrac{3x^2-5x-2}{9x^2-1} \div \dfrac{2x^2-3x-2}{6x^2-11x+3}$

Division of fractions is accomplished by multiplying by the multiplicative inverse of the divisor (the reciprocal). After factoring the terms, this problems becomes

$$\frac{(3x+1)(x-2)}{(3x-1)(3x+1)} \cdot \frac{(3x-1)(2x-3)}{(2x+1)(x-2)}$$

Dividing common factors—reducing—this problem simplifies to $\dfrac{2x-3}{2x+1}$.

Equations

You will not be asked to solve a straightforward linear equation or system of linear equations as part of the Level 1 or Level 2 exams. You will be asked to do so in some context.

Example: For what values of x is the fraction $\dfrac{3x^2-5x-2}{9x^2-1}$ undefined?

Since the denominator of the fraction cannot equal zero, solve $9x^2 - 1 = 0$ to get $x = \pm 1/3$.

Example: For what values of x does the fraction $\dfrac{3x^2-5x-2}{9x^2-1} = 0$?

Fractions are equal to zero when the numerator is equal to zero. Solve $3x^2 - 5x - 2 = 0$ by factoring and solving $(3x + 1)(x - 2) = 0$ so $x = -1/3$ or 2. This is *not* the correct answer, because you just saw that the fraction is not defined when $x = \pm1/3$. $-1/3$ is not in the domain of the problem, so the correct answer, as to which numbers solve $3x^2 - 5x - 2 = 0$, is $x = 2$.

Example: Given $3x - 6y = 17$

$$5x + 2y = 23$$

What is the value of $x - \frac{1}{2}y$?

You could solve for x and y and then compute the value of $x - \frac{1}{2}y$, or you could add the two equations together to determine that $8x - 4y = 40$, and when you divide by 8, find that $x - \frac{1}{2}y = 5$.

Quadratic Equations: $ax^2 + bx + c = 0$

As already shown, quadratic equations can be solved by factoring, completing the square, using the quadratic formula $x = \dfrac{-b \pm \sqrt{b^2 - 4ac}}{2a}$, or finding a graphical solution with your graphing calculator using the Zero feature.

Completing the square is something you might use to rewrite the equation of a circle in standard form or to write the equation of a parabola in vertex form on the Level 1 exam (or to write the equations of any of the conic sections in standard form on the Level 2 exam). Completing the square to solve a quadratic usually requires more time than is necessary.

Given the roots of a quadratic equation, you can most easily determine the original equation by using the relationship between the coefficients and the sum $(S = -b/a)$ and product $(P = c/a)$.

Example: Write the quadratic equation whose roots are $-2/3$ and $5/6$.

The sum, $\dfrac{-2}{3} + \dfrac{5}{6} = \dfrac{1}{6} = \dfrac{-b}{a}$, and the product, $\left(\dfrac{-2}{3}\right)\left(\dfrac{5}{6}\right) = \dfrac{-5}{9} = \dfrac{c}{a}$, have different denominators. Use a common denominator of 18 to get $\dfrac{3}{18} = \dfrac{-b}{a}$ and $\dfrac{-10}{18} = \dfrac{c}{a}$. You now have $a = 18$, $b = -3$, and $c = -10$. The equation is $18x^2 - 3x - 10 = 0$.

You may want to argue (correctly) that it would be faster to "work the problem backwards."

If the roots are $-2/3$ and $5/6$, then $x = -2/3$ or $x = 5/6$.

$$3x = -2 \text{ or } 6x = 5$$
$$3x + 2 = 0 \text{ or } 6x - 5 = 0$$
$$(3x + 2)(6x - 5) = 0$$
$$18x^2 - 3x - 10 = 0$$

The first three lines of this process can be done mentally and will save you a great deal of time for more involved questions.

Example: Write the quadratic equations with roots $\dfrac{4}{3} \pm \dfrac{3\sqrt{2}}{4}i$.

"Working backwards" will be very difficult. The sum of the roots is $8/3$, and the product of the roots is

$$\left(\frac{4}{3} + \frac{3\sqrt{2}}{4}i\right)\left(\frac{4}{3} - \frac{3\sqrt{2}}{4}i\right) = \left(\frac{4}{3}\right)^2 - \left(\frac{3\sqrt{2}}{34}i\right)^2 =$$

$$\frac{16}{9} - \frac{18}{16}i^2 = \frac{16}{9} + \frac{18}{16} = \frac{209}{72}.$$

Given that $\dfrac{8}{3} = \dfrac{192}{72}$, you have $a = 72$, $b = -192$, and $c = 209$. The equation is $72x^2 - 192x + 209 = 0$.

Polynomial Equations with Degree > 2

If asked to solve a higher-order polynomial whose factors are not obvious (e.g., "Look for a common factor"), use the Zero feature of your graphing calculator to determine the roots.

Absolute Value

The absolute value of a number n, written as $|n|$, is computed as the distance from n to the origin, 0, on a number line. For example, $|-4| = 4$ and $|4| = 4$.

What is the solution to the equation $|n| = 5$? The numbers 5 units from the origin on a number line are 5 and -5.

What is the solution to $|n - 2| = 5$? From the last problem, you know that the expression inside the absolute value bars must be 5 or –5. That is, $n - 2 = 5$ or $n - 2 = -5$. Solve each of these equations to get $n = 7$ or $n = -3$. Take a moment to place these solutions on a number line. Midway between these solutions is the number 2, and the distance from each solution to 2 is 5. That is, the solution to the equation $|n - 2| = 5$ represents those numbers that are 5 units from 2. The solution to $|n - 2| = 5$ is the result of taking the problem $|n| = 5$ and translating it to the right 2 units.

Example: Solve $|n + 3| = 7$

Algebraically: $n + 3 = 7$ or $n + 3 = -7$

$$n = 4 \text{ or } n = -10$$

Graphically: $n + 3$ slides the graph 3 units to the left, so the solutions are the points where the line, $y = 7$, and the absolute value function, $y = |n + 3|$, intersect.

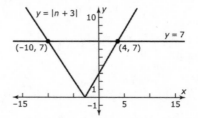

A more challenging problem for a graphical approach is $|3n - 5| = 8$. Solving the problem algebraically, you get

$$3n - 5 = 8 \text{ or } 3n - 5 = -8.$$

$$3n = 13 \quad \text{or} \quad 3n = -3$$

$$n = \frac{13}{3} \text{ or } n = -1.$$

What point is midway between –1 and 13/3? The answer is 5/3. How far is 13/3 from 5/3? 8/3. How far is –1 from 5/3? 8/3.

If the coefficient of the variable in an absolute value equation is not 1, factor it from the problem.

$$|3n - 5| = 8$$

$$3\left|n - \frac{5}{3}\right| = 8$$

Divide $\left|n - \frac{5}{3}\right| = \frac{8}{3}$

The points 8/3 from 5/3 on a number line are 5/3 − 8/3 on the left and 5/3 + 8/3 on the right.

Because $|ab| = |a| \, |b|$, this process will also work when the coefficient of the variable is a negative number.

Example: Solve $|9 − 4n| = 12$

Factor $|(−4)(n − 9/4)| = 12$

$\qquad |{-4}| \, |n − 9/4| = 12$

$\qquad\qquad 4|n − 9/4| = 12$

$\qquad\qquad\quad |n − 9/4| = 3$

The points 3 units from 9/4 are −3/4 and 21/4.

Exponential Equations

Equations involving exponential statements are solved by getting the bases common when possible. One then sets the exponents equal to each other.

Example: Solve for a: $25^{2a+3b} = \left(\sqrt{5}\right)^{4a-8b}$

Since both bases can written as powers of 5, the equation becomes

$$5^{2(2a+3b)} = 5^{1/2(4a-8b)}$$

Setting the exponents equal: $2(2a + 3b) = \dfrac{1}{2}(4a − 8b)$

$\qquad\qquad\qquad\qquad\qquad\qquad 4a + 6b = 2a − 4b$

$\qquad\qquad\qquad\qquad\qquad\qquad\qquad 2a = −10b$

$\qquad\qquad\qquad\qquad\qquad\qquad\qquad\; a = −5b$

When common bases cannot be found easily, you can use a graphical approach (provided there is only one variable and no literal constants), or you can use logarithms. (Logarithms will appear on the Level 2 exam only.)

Example: Solve for a: $5^{a+3} = 119$

Graph the functions $y = 5^{a+3}$ and $y = 119$ to find the point of intersection for the two graphs.

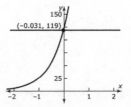

Inequalities

The most important fact to remember when solving inequalities is that you need to re-orient the inequality whenever you multiply or divide both sides of the inequality by a negative number.

Example: Solve $4 - 5x > 11$

Subtract 4: $-5x > 7$

Divide by -5: $x < -7/5$

Compound inequalities come in two types, an interval (such as $-1 < x < 3$) or distinct separate sets (e.g., $x < -1$ or $x > 3$). It is possible to have more involved sets for answers (e.g., $x < -3$ or $1 < x < 3$ or $x > 4$). Answers such as this last one may come from solving a polynomial inequality.

Example: Solve $-4 < 3 - 2x \leq 19$

Rewrite as the compound inequality $-4 < 3 - 2x$ and $3 - 2x \leq 19$

Subtract 3 $-7 < -2x$ and $-2x \leq 16$

Divide by -2 $7/2 > x$ and $x \geq -8$

Answer: $-8 \leq x < 7/2$

Because the steps in solving the inequality are the same, there is no need to separate the inequalities. $-4 < 3 - 2x \leq 19$

Subtract $-7 < -2x \leq 16$

Divide $7/2 > x \geq -8$

Two special cases that you must know how to solve are quadratic and absolute value inequalities. Both can be done with a graphing calculator as well as algebraically and mentally.

Example: Solve $x^2 - x - 6 \geq 0$

Factor $(x + 2)(x - 3) \geq 0$.

You should know that the graph of a quadratic is a parabola and that the direction in which the parabola opens depends on the quadratic coefficient. In this case, the coefficient of the x^2 term is 1, so the parabola opens up. Further, you know from the factors that the graph crosses the x-axis at $x = -2$ and 3. Therefore, the parabola is above the x-axis when $x < -2$ or $x > 3$. The solution to this problem is $x \leq -2$ or $x \geq 3$.

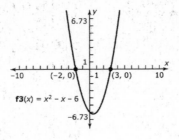

Example: Solve $|2x - 3| > 7$

Factor $\left|2\left(x - \dfrac{3}{2}\right)\right| = 7$

$$2\left|x - \frac{3}{2}\right| = 7$$

$$\left|x - \frac{3}{2}\right| = \frac{7}{2}$$

Those points which are *exactly* 7/2 from 3/2 are –2 and 5. Because this problem has a greater-than symbol rather than an equal sign, you are looking for those points that are farther than 7/2 units from 3/2. The solution to this problem is $x < -2$ or $x > 5$.

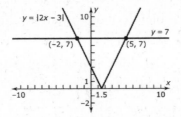

Example: Solve $|x - 1| + |3x - 2| > 4$

This is a difficult problem to do algebraically and can be solved quickly and efficiently with the graphing calculator.

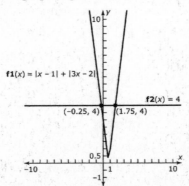

The solution is $x < -1/4$ or $x > 7/4$.

Properties of Functions

A *relation* is any set of ordered pairs. The following represents three relations:

   A = {(2,3), (–4,2), (2,7), (0,1)}
   B = {(1,1), (–1,1), (3,2), (2,3), (5,4)}
   C = {(1,–1), (2,3), (–4,5), (7,–2), (0,4)}

The *domain* of a relation is the set of all possible first elements (*abscissas*), or input values. The domain of A is {–4, 0, 2}, the domain of B is {–1, 1, 2, 3, 5}, and the domain of C is {–4, 0, 1, 2, 7}. (Please note that although it is convenient to write the domains in increasing order, as these ones are written, it is not required. Further, the number 2 is used twice as the abscissa in relation A, but only needs to be written once in the domain.)

The *range* of a relation is the set of all possible second elements (*ordinates*), or output values. The range of A is {1, 2, 3, 7}, the range of B is {1, 2, 3, 4}, and the range of C is {–2, –1, 3, 4, 5}.

The *inverse* of a relation is found by interchanging the first and second elements. The inverse of A is denoted by A^{-1}. (Do not confuse this with the notation used with variables to represent reciprocals.) A^{-1} = {(3,2), (2,–4), (7,2), (1,0)}, B^{-1} = {(1,1), (1,–1), (2,3), (3,2), (4,5)}, and C^{-1} = {(–1,1), (3,2), (5,–4), (–2,7), (4,0)}.

A *function* is a special relation in which each first element is matched with **exactly** one second element. The relation A is not a function, because the input value 2 is associated with both 3 and 7. A^{-1} is a function. The relation B is a function, but B^{-1} is not a function, because the value 1 is associated with 1 and –1. C and C^{-1} are both functions. As can be seen from this simple example, it is possible for a relation to be a function though its inverse is not, for a relation not to be a function though its inverse is, for both a relation and its inverse to be functions, and, although not demonstrated here, for both a function and its inverse not to be functions. In a *one-to-one (1–1) function*, both the relation and its inverse are functions—that is, for each input there is only one output, AND for each output there is only one input.

A graphical representation about functions and their inverses involves the *vertical line test* and the *horizontal line test*. If a vertical line can be drawn somewhere on a graph, and the line intersects the graph at more than one point, then the graph does not represent a function. If a horizontal line can be drawn on a graph so that the horizontal line intersects the graph at more than one point, then the inverse does not represent a function.

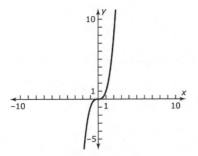

Passes vertical line test

Passes horizontal line test

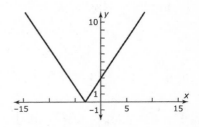

Passes vertical line test

Fails horizontal line test

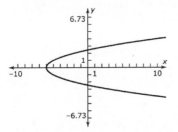

Fails vertical line test

Passes horizontal line test

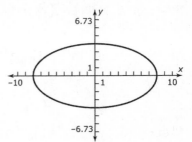

Fails vertical line test

Fails horizontal line test

Functions are usually named with the letter f (for function) or a letter near f, but this is not a requirement. In addition, the variable used to represent the domain is included in the name of the function. The notation $f(x)$, read as "f of x," tells you that the function name is f and the domain variable is x.

The notation is very efficient for directions. For example, one could write, "find the value of y in the equation $y = 3x + 7$ when $x = 4$" or "given $f(x) = 3x + 7$, find $f(4)$." In either case, the answer is 19. You could also be asked to "find the sum of the results of substituting $x = 4$ into $y = 3x + 7$ and substituting $x = -3$ into $y = -5x + 9$" or " given $f(x) = 3x + 7$ and $g(x) = -5x + 9$, find $f(4) + g(-3)$." $f(4) = 19$ and $g(-3) = -5(-3) + 9 = 24$. So, $f(4) + g(-3) = 43$.

Example: Given $f(x) = 7x - 2$, solve $f(x) = 33$.

Replace $f(x)$ with the rule that defines it, $7x - 2 = 33$, and solve to get $x = 5$.

Example: Given $f(x) = 7x - 2$, find $f(2a - 1)$.

In this problem, you are told to use $x = 2a - 1$ to evaluate the function.

$$f(2a - 1) = 7(2a - 1) - 2 = 14a - 7 - 2 = 14a - 9.$$

Functions can be combined by any of the operations as well as by substitution in a process called composition. For example, given $f(x) = 7x - 2$ and $g(x) = -5x + 9$.

Add: $f+g(x) = f(x) + g(x) = 7x - 2 + (-5x) + 9 = 2x + 7$

Subtract: $f-g(x) = f(x) - g(x) = 7x - 2 - (-5x + 9) = 7x - 2 + 5x - 9$
$= 12x - 11$

Multiply: $fg(x) = (f(x))(g(x)) = (7x - 2)(-5x + 9) = -35x^2 + 73x - 18$

Divide: $\dfrac{f}{g}(x) = \dfrac{f(x)}{g(x)} = \dfrac{7x - 2}{-5x + 9}$

Composition: $f \circ g(x) = f(g(x)) = f(-5x + 9) = 7(-5x + 9) - 2 =$
$-35x + 63 - 2 = -35x + 61$

Example: Given $f(x) = 3x - 2$ and $g(x) = 4x + 5$, find $f \circ g(x)$, $g \circ f(x)$, and $g \circ g(x)$.

$f \circ g(x) = f(g(x)) = f(4x + 5) = 3(4x + 5) - 2 = 12x + 15 - 2 = 12x - 13$

$g \circ f(x) = g(f(x)) = g(3x - 2) = 4(3x - 2) + 5 = 12x - 8 + 5 = 12x - 3$

$g \circ g(x) = g(g(x)) = g(4x + 5) = 4(4x + 5) + 5 = 16x + 20 + 5 = 16x + 25$

Linear

Linear functions take the form $f(x) = mx + b$.

Example: Given the linear function $f(x)$ with $f(2) = 9$ and $f(5) = 3$, find $f(28)$.

With $f(x)$ a linear function, $f(2) = 9$, and $f(5) = 3$, you know that the points (2,9) and (5,3) lie on the line. The slope of the line is $\dfrac{3-9}{5-2} = -2$.

Therefore, $f(x) = -2x + b$. Using $f(5) = 3$, $3 = -2(5) + b$, or $b = 13$. $f(x) = -2x + 13$ so $f(28) = -2(28) + 13 = -43$.

Polynomial

Functions of the form $f(x) = a_n x^n + a_{n-1}x^{n-1} + \ldots + a_2 x^2 + a_1 x + a_0$ are called polynomial functions of degree n, the largest exponent in the problem. Aside from quadratics and certain cubic functions, the work with polynomials is limited to the Level 2 test.

Example: Solve $96x^4 - 144x^2 - 6x^2 + 9x > 0$

Although there is a common factor of x in this quartic polynomial, you are advised to graph the function on you calculator to find the answer. As tempting as it is to try to have all of the turning points of the graph displayed (as shown),

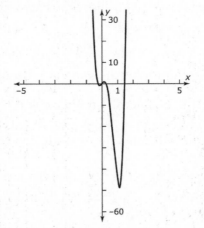

the image you want is the one which allows you to clearly see where the graph crosses the x-axis and which enables you to use the zero feature.

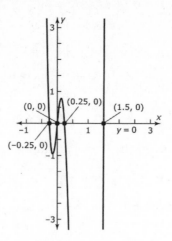

The solution to the inequality represents the intervals for which the graph is above the x-axis. The solution is $x < -0.25$ or $0 < x < 0.25$ or $x > 1.5$.

The **Fundamental Theorem of Algebra** states that when the coefficients of the polynomial are real numbers, the number of roots to the equation $a_n x^n + a_{n-1} x^{n-1} + \ldots + a_2 x^2 + a_1 x + a_0 = 0$ from the set of complex numbers is n. Keep in mind that when the coefficients are real, complex roots always appear in conjugate pairs.

Other useful items to know about polynomial functions are:

Remainder Theorem: If $f(x)$ is divided by $x - a$, the remainder is $f(a)$.

An immediate consequence of this is the **Factor Theorem**. If $f(a) = 0$, then $x - a$ is a factor of $f(x)$.

The relationship between the coefficients and the roots can be extended from the quadratic to the general polynomial functions. The sum of the roots of the polynomial function is $\dfrac{-a_{n-1}}{a_n}$. The product of the roots is $\dfrac{a_0}{a_n}$. The coefficients between a_{n-1} and a_0, when divided by a_n, represent the sum of the roots taken two at a time, three at a time, etc. The ratio alters between $+$ and $-$ as the number of terms increases.

Example: Find the roots of the equation $f(x) = 0$ if $f(x) = 6x^5 - 13x^4 + 6x^3 - 9x^2 + 4$.

Graphing the function shows that the real zeroes are $\frac{-1}{2}$, $\frac{2}{3}$, and 2. The Fundamental Theorem of Algebra guarantees that there are two more roots, and these must be complex, because they cannot be found as x-intercepts of the graph of $y = f(x)$. Dividing $f(x)$ by $2x + 1$, $3x - 2$, and $x - 2$ in succession shows that $f(x) = (2x + 1)(3x - 2)(x - 2)(x^2 + 1)$, so that the remaining roots are $\pm i$.

The sum of the roots is $\frac{-1}{2} + \frac{2}{3} + 2 + i + -i = \frac{13}{6}$, which is consistent with the rule from quadratics. The product of the roots is $\left(\frac{-1}{2}\right)\left(\frac{2}{3}\right)(2)(i)(-i) = \frac{4}{6}$.

The sum of the roots *taken two at a time* is

$$\left(\frac{-1}{2}\right)\left(\frac{2}{3}\right) + \left(\frac{-1}{2}\right)(2) + \left(\frac{-1}{2}\right)i + \left(\frac{-1}{2}\right)(-i) + \left(\frac{2}{3}\right)(2) + \left(\frac{2}{3}\right)i +$$

$$\left(\frac{2}{3}\right)(-i) + 2i + 2(-i) + (i)(-i) = \frac{-1}{3} - 1 - \left(\frac{1}{2}\right)i + \left(\frac{1}{2}\right)i + \frac{4}{3} +$$

$$\left(\frac{2}{3}\right)i - \left(\frac{2}{3}\right)i + 2i - 2i - 1 = -1 = \frac{-6}{6} = \frac{-a_3}{a_5}.$$

The sum of the roots *taken three at a time* is

$$\left(\frac{-1}{2}\right)\left(\frac{2}{3}\right)(2) + \left(\frac{-1}{2}\right)\left(\frac{2}{3}\right)i + \left(\frac{-1}{2}\right)\left(\frac{2}{3}\right)(-i) + \left(\frac{-1}{2}\right)(2i) + \left(\frac{-1}{2}\right)(-2i)$$

$$+ \left(\frac{-1}{2}\right)(-i^2) + \left(\frac{2}{3}\right)(2i) + \left(\frac{2}{3}\right)(-2i) + \left(\frac{2}{3}\right)(-i^2) + 2i(-i) = \frac{-9}{6} = \frac{a_2}{a_5}.$$

It will be left to you to show that the sum of the roots *taken four at a time* is $0 = \frac{-a_1}{a_5}$.

Rational Functions

The graph of the function $f(x) = \dfrac{3x - 4}{2x + 1}$ is shown.

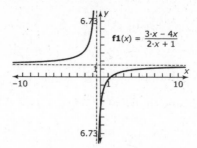

The domain of the function is $x \neq -1/2$. This is represented by the vertical dotted line. Notice that the graph cannot cross this vertical asymptote. The graph of $f(x)$ crosses the x-axis at $x = 4/3$. As the magnitude of the values of x get very large, you can see that the graph begins to level out and gets closer to the horizontal asymptote of $y = 3/2$. It is no coincidence that 3/2 is the ratio of the leading coefficients of the linear expressions that make up the function.

The function $f(x) = \dfrac{4x - 8}{x^2 + 2}$ is graphed below.

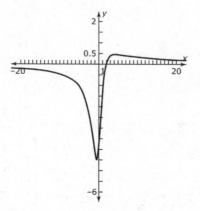

There is no vertical asymptote for this rational function because there is no real value of x that causes the denominator to equal 0. For large values of x, the numerator stays much smaller than the denominator. This is represented in the graph as the graph gets closer to the x-axis

($y = 0$). Pay note to the fact that the graph can cross a horizontal asymptote for small values of x, but not for large values of x.

The function $f(x) = \dfrac{3x^2 - 5x - 2}{9x^2 - 1}$ is sketched below. You read earlier in this chapter that the domain of the function is $x \neq \pm\dfrac{1}{3}$. Because the fraction $\dfrac{3x^2 - 5x - 2}{9x^2 - 1}$ reduces to $\dfrac{x - 2}{3x - 1}$, the graph of $f(x)$ has a vertical asymptote at $x = \dfrac{1}{3}$ and a horizontal asymptote at $y = \dfrac{1}{3}$. There is something occurring at $x = -\dfrac{1}{3}$ that the calculator does not show—there is a hole in the graph! The hole occurs at the point $\left(-\dfrac{1}{3}, \dfrac{7}{6}\right)$. A graph will always have a hole in it whenever the rational expression that defines the graph can be reduced.

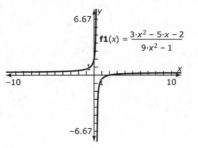

Irrational Functions

Expressions of the form $\sqrt[n]{f(x)}$ are called irrational. The term $f(x)$ is the radicand, and n is the index. For functions with an even index, the domain can be found by solving $f(x) \geq 0$, while functions with an odd index have the set of real numbers as their domain. For example, in the functions $f(x) = \sqrt{x}$ and $g(x) = \sqrt[3]{f(x)}$, the domain of $f(x)$ = is $x \geq 0$, while the domain of $g(x)$ = is the set of real numbers.

Questions in which the radicand is a rational expression and the index is even present special challenges for determining the domain algebraically. So long as the rational expression does not reduce, domains can be found graphically with some ease.

Example: Determine the domain and range of the function $f(x) = \sqrt{\dfrac{3x^2 - 5x - 2}{9x^2 - 1}}$.

No index is indicated, so this is a square root function.

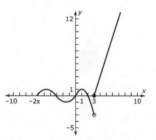

The graph reveals that the range of the function is $y \geq 0$. The graph seems to have two vertical asymptotes, one each at $x = -2$ and $x = 3$, the restrictions from the denominator of the radicand.

**Piecewise Functions

The definition of a function requires that for each input value there must be a unique output value. There is no stipulation which says that the output values come from a single rule. Examine the graph of $y = f(x)$ in the following figure.

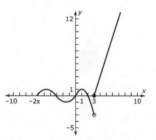

The graph is formed from three functions: $y = \sin(x)$ for the interval from $-2\pi \leq x < 0$; $y = -(x - 1)^2 + 1$ from $0 \leq x < 3$, and $y = 3(x - 3)$ for $x \geq 3$. $f(3) = 0$. You know this to be true because the point $(3,0)$ is a closed circle, while the point $(3,-3)$ is an open circle, as is consistent with what you have learned about graphing inequalities on a number line.

The evaluation of piecewise functions is a matter of looking at the domain of each of the defining functions (which is why piecewise functions are also known as split-domain functions). The function $f(x)$ that defines the graph above is written as

$$f(x) = \begin{cases} \sin(x) & -2\pi \leq x < 0 \\ -(x-1)^2 & 0 \leq x < 3 \\ 3(x-3) & x \geq 3 \end{cases}$$

Example: Sketch the graph of $f(x) = \begin{cases} x^2 & -2 \leq x < 1 \\ -(x-2)^2 + 2 & 1 \leq x < 4 \\ \sqrt{x-4}-2 & x \geq 4 \end{cases}$

Sketch the parabola $y = x^2$ from $(-2,4)$ to $(1,1)$. Because the second piece of the function begins at $(1,1)$, there is no issue of open and closed circles. The parabola $-(x-2)^2 + 2$ ends at the point $(4,-2)$, which is where the graph of the square-root function in the third piece of the definition begins.

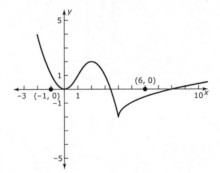

Exercises

1. $\dfrac{2x+1}{x^2 - x - 2} - \dfrac{x+4}{x^2 + x - 6} =$

(A) $\dfrac{x-1}{(x-2)(x+1)(x+3)}$

(B) $\dfrac{x+7}{(x-2)(x+1)(x+3)}$

(C) $\dfrac{x^2 + 2x - 1}{(x-2)(x+1)(x+3)}$

(D) $\dfrac{x^2 + 2x + 7}{(x-2)(x+1)(x+3)}$

(E) $\dfrac{x^2 + 12x + 7}{(x-2)(x+1)(x+3)}$

2. If $f(x) = 4x + 3$ and $g(x) = \dfrac{2x - 1}{x - 4}$, $f \circ g(x) =$

(A) $\dfrac{11x - 8}{x - 4}$ (B) $\dfrac{11x - 16}{x - 4}$ (C) $\dfrac{8x + 7}{4x - 1}$

(D) $\dfrac{20x - 44}{4x - 16}$ (E) $\dfrac{20x - 12}{4x - 16}$

3. Which statement about the graph below is correct?

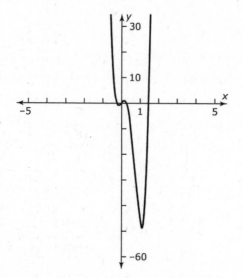

(A) It represents a function, and its inverse is also a function.

(B) It represents a function, and its inverse is not a function.

(C) It does not represent a function, and its inverse is a function.

(D) It does not represent a function, and its inverse is also not a function.

(E) It represents a function, but there is not enough information to make a determination about its inverse.

4. What is the domain of the function $f(x) = \sqrt{\dfrac{x^2 - 4x - 5}{x^2 - 4}}$?

(A) $x \neq \pm 2$ (B) $x < -2$ or $x > 2$ (C) $x < -1$ or $x > 5$

(D) $x < -2$ or $-1 < x < 2$ or $x > 5$ (E) $x < -5$ or $-1 < x < 2$ or $x > 4$

**5. Which of the following statements is true about the graph of $f(x) = \dfrac{x^3 - 2x^2 - 3x}{x^3 + 3x^2 - 4x}$?

   I. It has vertical asymptotes at $x = -4$, $x = 0$, and $x = 1$.

   II. It has a horizontal asymptote at $y = 1$.

   III. It has a hole at the point $(0,0)$.

     (A) I only   (B) II only   (C) III only

     (D) I and II only   (E) II and III only

Explanations

1. (C) The denominator of the first fraction factors to be $(x - 2)(x + 1)$, and the denominator of the second fraction factors to be $(x - 2)(x + 3)$. Therefore, the common denominator will be the product $(x - 2)(x + 1)(x + 3)$. Get equivalent fractions and simplify. Be careful with the distribution of the negative sign through the second numerator.

$$\frac{2x + 1}{x^2 - x - 2} - \frac{x + 4}{x^2 + x - 6} = \frac{2x + 1}{(x - 2)(x + 1)}\left(\frac{x + 3}{x + 3}\right) - \frac{x + 4}{-2(x + 3)}\left(\frac{x + 1}{x + 1}\right)$$

$$= \frac{2x^2 + 7x + 3}{(x - 2)(x + 1)} - \frac{x^2 + 5x + 4}{(x - 2)(x + 3)}$$

$$= \frac{2x^2 + 7x + 3 - (x^2 + 5x + 4)}{(x - 2)(x + 1)}$$

$$= \frac{2x^2 + 7x + 3 - x^2 - 5x - 4}{(x - 2)(x + 1)}$$

$$= \frac{2x^2 + 2x - 1}{(x - 2)(x + 1)}$$

2. (B) $f \circ g(x) = f(g(x)) = f\left(\dfrac{2x - 1}{x - 4}\right) = 4\left(\dfrac{2x - 1}{x - 4}\right) + 3 = \dfrac{8x - 4}{x - 4} + \dfrac{3(x - 4)}{x - 4}$

$$= \frac{8x - 4 + 3x - 12}{x - 4} = \frac{11x - 16}{x - 4}.$$

3. (B) The graph passes the vertical line test (identifying it as a function) but fails the horizontal line test (indicating that the inverse is not a function).

4. (D) Enter the function into your calculator and read the intervals for which the function is defined.

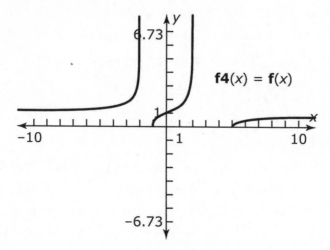

5. (B) The function $f(x) = \dfrac{x^3 - 2x^2 - 3x}{x^3 + 3x^2 - 4x}$ can be rewritten as

$f(x) = \dfrac{x(x-3)(x+1)}{x(x+4)(x-1)}$. The common factor of x reduces the function

to $f(x) = \dfrac{(x-3)(x+1)}{(x+4)(x-1)}$. Because the common factor of x dropped from the problem, there will be a hole in the graph, but the hole will be at (0,3/4), the output from the reduced function when $x = 0$ is substituted. Additionally, because the common factors of x reduced, there is not a vertical asymptote at $x = 0$ (although there are vertical asymptotes at $x = -4$ and $x = 1$). The degree of the numerator and denominator in the reduced fraction is 2, and the leading coefficient for each is 1. Therefore, there is a horizontal asymptote at $y = 1$.

Topic 3: Geometry and Measurement

While you will not be asked to write a proof on the SAT Level 1 Mathematics test, you will be expected to know many of the properties from your Geometry class. A summary of many of the items from that class follows.

Triangles, Angle Measurement, and More

If the sum of the measures of two angles is 90°, the angles are *complementary*, and if the sum is 180°, the angles are *supplementary*.

The sum of the measures of the interior angles of a triangle is 180°. The sum of the interior angle measurements for a *convex* polygon (a polygon that does not "cave in" on itself) is found by breaking the figure into non-overlapping triangles. A convex polygon with n sides can be divided into $n - 2$ triangles, so the sum of the measures of the interior angles of a convex polygon is $180(n - 2)$. If the polygon is *regular* (all sides are congruent and all angles are congruent), the measure of one interior angle is $\frac{180(n - 2)}{n}$. The sum of the measures of the exterior angles of all convex polygons is 360°.

The base angles of an isosceles triangle (the angles opposite the congruent sides) are congruent, while the angle between the legs is the vertex angle. The median and altitude to the base of an isosceles triangle are the same segment.

The *median* of a triangle is the segment joining a vertex to the midpoint of the opposite side. The medians are *concurrent* at the centroid, G (i.e., the three medians intersect at a common point), and the *centroid* is 2/3 of the way from the vertex to the midpoint of the opposite side.

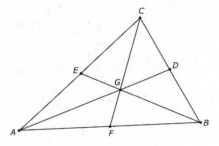

AG = 2/3 AD or AG = 2GD. The areas of △AGC, △AGB, and △BGC are all equal. For that reason, the centroid is also called the center of gravity. In coordinate geometry, the coordinates of G are the average of the coordinates for the vertices A, B, and C.

Every triangle can be circumscribed about a circle. The center of the circle, called the circumcenter, is the intersection of the perpendicular bisectors of the three sides. (** The diameter of the circumscribed circle is the ratio of the length of a side of the triangle to the sine of the opposite angle. This is the constraint ratio gained from the Law of Sines.)

The inscribed circle of a triangle is centered at the intersection of the angle bisectors of the triangle.

Example: Suppose the measure of an interior angle of a regular polygon measures 12° more than six times the measure of an exterior angle. Determine the number of sides in the polygon.

Letting x represent the measure of the exterior angle, $x + 6x + 12 = 180$ becomes $7x = 168$, and $x = 24$. If the measure of an exterior angle of a regular polygon is 24°, the number of sides is $\frac{360}{24} = 15$.

Example: In isosceles △HGY, $\overline{HG} \cong \overline{GY}$, $m\angle H = 6t + 20$, and $m\angle G = 4t + 60$. Find t.

If, $\overline{HG} \cong \overline{GY}$, then $m\angle H = m\angle Y$. The sum of the measures of the angles of the triangle is 180°, so $2(6t + 20) + 4t + 60 = 180$. This becomes $16t + 100 = 180$, or $16t = 80$. Therefore, $t = 5$.

The segment joining the midpoints of two sides of a triangle is parallel to the third side of the triangle, and is half as long as the third side.

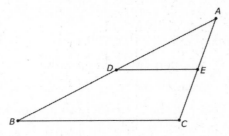

D and E are midpoints of the sides of the triangle, $DE = .5\ BC$ and $\overline{DE} \parallel \overline{BC}$.

Parallel and Perpendicular Lines

There are a number of relationships involving parallel lines and a transversal that cuts them. A number of these statements are biconditionals—that is, the statement and its converse are both true. For example, the statement "If two parallel lines are cut by a transversal, then alternate interior angles are congruent," and the converse, "If two lines are cut by a transversal so that alternate interior angles are congruent, then the lines are parallel." Another way to write this is "Two lines are parallel if and only if alternate interior angles are congruent."

Other biconditionals to note are:

- Two lines are parallel if and only if corresponding angles are congruent.

- Two lines are parallel if and only if they are coplanar and perpendicular to the same line.

- Two lines are parallel if and only if same side interior angles are supplementary.

A line is perpendicular to a plane if it is perpendicular to every line in the plane that intersects it.

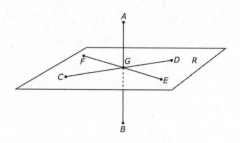

$\overline{AB} \perp plane$ ℜ if and only if $\overline{AB} \perp \overline{CD}$ and $\overline{AB} \perp \overline{EF}$.

If two planes are each perpendicular to a third plane, you cannot be sure about the relationship of the two planes. Look at a wall in the room you are in. The ceiling and the floor are both perpendicular to this wall. The floor and the ceiling are (hopefully) parallel. However, the floor and the vertical wall adjacent to the common wall are not parallel. Be careful about extending what you know from plane geometry into spacial relationships.

Quadrilaterals

Properties about parallelograms and trapezoids lead to interesting questions for the exam writers. All parallelograms have the properties that

- opposite sides are congruent and parallel,

- opposite angles are congruent,

- consecutive angles are supplementary, and

- the diagonals bisect each other.

Special parallelograms such as the rectangle, rhombus, and square have additional properties. In a rectangle, the diagonals are also congruent, and the angles are right angles.

In a rhombus, the sides are all congruent, the diagonals are perpendicular to each other, and the diagonals bisect opposite angles of the quadrilateral.

Since a square is both a rectangle and a rhombus, it has all of the properties of both rectangles and rhombuses.

If a quadrilateral has perpendicular diagonals, the area of the quadrilateral is one-half the product of the diagonals. An example of a quadrilateral with perpendicular diagonals that is not a rhombus or a square is a deltoid (kite).

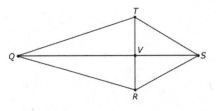

$$\overline{QS} \perp \overline{RT}, QS = QT, RS = RT$$

Congruence

Figures are congruent if a rigid transformation (reflection, rotation, translation, or a composition of these) allows for one figure to lie exactly on top of the other. The notation for congruent figures identifies corresponding vertices by the order in which the vertices are written. That is why it is critical to write the correspondence correctly when identifying congruent figures. It identifies which pieces must have the same measure.

Similarity

Triangles that are a result of a dilation of one another are similar. Although their shapes are unchanged (therefore, corresponding angles have the same measure), corresponding sides will be proportional. For example, doubling the length of the side of one triangle to create a similar triangle demands that all sides be double for the larger triangle.

The minimum criteria necessary to guarantee that two triangles are similar is the AA matchup (the third angles will automatically agree). When a line parallel to a side of a triangle intersects the remaining two sides, those sides are cut proportionally.

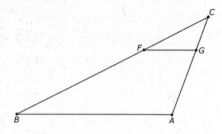

$\overline{FG} \parallel \overline{AB}$

$\triangle ABC \sim \triangle GFC$, so $\dfrac{FG}{AB} = \dfrac{FC}{BC} = \dfrac{GC}{AC}$. You can use the properties of proportions, discussed in the chapter Numbers and Operations, to get $\dfrac{FC}{FB} = \dfrac{GC}{GA}$.

All linear measurements (perimeters, lengths of medians, lengths of altitudes, etc) are in the same ratio as the lengths of any pair of corresponding sides.

The ratio of the areas of similar figures is the square of the ratio of the lengths of any pair of corresponding sides.

Example: In $\triangle ABC$, Q is on $\overline{AB}$ and R is on $\overline{BC}$ so that $\overline{QR} \parallel \overline{AC}$. If $BQ = 8$, $QA = 10$, and $QR = 6$, find (a) AC and (b) the ratio of the areas of $\triangle ABC$ to $\triangle BQR$.

The two triangles are similar to each other, so the sides are in the ratio $\dfrac{QB}{AB} = \dfrac{QR}{AC}$. Substitute to get $\dfrac{8}{18} = \dfrac{6}{AC}$ so that $8AC = 108$ and $AC = 13.5$. The ratio of the areas of the two triangles is the square of the

ratio of the corresponding sides. Area $\triangle ABC$: area $\triangle BQR = (18:8)^2 = (9:4)^2 = 81 : 16$.

Similarity in a Right Triangle

An important application occurs when the altitude is dropped to the hypotenuse of a right triangle.

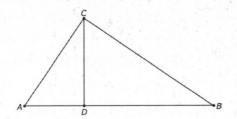

In $\triangle ABC$, $\angle C$ is a right angle, and $\overline{CD} \perp \overline{AB}$. $\triangle ABC \sim \triangle ACD$, $\triangle ABC \sim \triangle CBD$, and $ACD \sim \triangle CBD$. The important relation involves the proportions with the segments common to each pair of triangles: $\dfrac{AB}{AC} = \dfrac{AC}{AD}$, $\dfrac{AB}{BC} = \dfrac{BC}{AD}$, and $\dfrac{AD}{CD} = \dfrac{CD}{BD}$. These proportions, in turn, become $AC^2 = (AB)(AD)$, $BC^2 = (AB)(BD)$, and $CD^2 = (AD)(BD)$. These form the basis for one proof of the Pythagorean Theorem.

   Example: In $\triangle ABC$, $\angle C$ is a right angle, and $\overline{CD} \perp \overline{AB}$. If $AC = 12$, and $AD = 8$, find (a) AB; (b) CD; (c) BC.

   $AC^2 = (AB)(AD)$, so $12^2 = 8(AB)$, and $AB = 18$. DB must equal 10, so $CD^2 = (8)(10) = 80$, and $CD = \sqrt{80} = 4\sqrt{5}$. The third relationship or the Pythagorean Theorem can be used to find BC. $BC^2 = (10)(18) = 180$, so $BC = \sqrt{180} = 6\sqrt{5}$.

   The Pythagorean Theorem ("In a right triangle, the sum of the squares of the legs is equal to the square of the hypotenuse") is one of the most used theorems in all of mathematics. Pythagorean triples are three integers that satisfy the condition of this theorem. 3-4-5 is the most commonly used primitive Pythagorean triple (primitive because the greatest common factor of the three numbers is 1). Other primitive Pythagorean triples that you should know are 5-12-13, 8-15-17, and 7-24-25. They, or their multiples, appear often in mathematics.

   Example: A 25-foot ladder is leaning against a building so that the foot of the ladder is 7 feet from the base of the building. If the foot of the ladder slides to a point 8 feet further from the building, how many feet does the top of the ladder slide down?

The ladder forms the hypotenuse of a right triangle. The distance from the base of the building is one leg, while the height of the ladder above the ground is the other leg. In its original position, the top of the ladder will be 24 feet above the ground (7-24-25). When the base of the ladder slides another 8 feet from the wall, the base will be 15 feet from the wall, so the top of the ladder will be 20 feet above the ground (5 times 3-4-5 is a 15-20-25 triangle). The top of the ladder slides down 4 feet.

The initial study of trigonometry is the ratio of the sides of a right triangle. For any right triangle, the ratio of the length of a side opposite an acute angle θ to the length of the hypotenuse is called the sine of the angle, and is abbreviated sin(θ). The ratio of the length of the adjacent leg to the length of the hypotenuse is the cosine (complement of the sine), or cos(θ), and the ratio of the length of the opposite leg to the length of the adjacent leg is the tangent, tan(θ). You are probably familiar with the mnemonic SOHCAHTOA, the first letters from each of the key words, to remember the ratios.

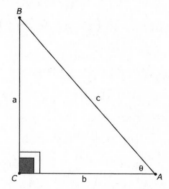

$$\sin(A) = \frac{opposite}{hypotenuse} = \frac{a}{c} \quad \cos(A) = \frac{adjacent}{hypotenuse} = \frac{b}{c} \quad \tan(A) = \frac{opposite}{adjacent} = \frac{a}{b}$$

$$\sin(B) = \frac{opposite}{hypotenuse} = \frac{b}{c} \quad \cos(B) = \frac{adjacent}{hypotenuse} = \frac{a}{c} \quad \tan(B) = \frac{opposite}{adjacent} = \frac{b}{a}$$

In any right triangle, if sin(A) = cos(B) then $A + B = 90$.

Example: Find the length of *AB* in the following diagram.

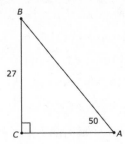

The acute angle is 50, the opposite leg is 27, and the hypotenuse is not known. Use the sine function to solve the problem.

$\sin(50) = \dfrac{27}{c}$ becomes $c \sin(50) = 27$. Therefore, $c = \dfrac{27}{\sin(50)} = 35.2$

The functions $\sin^{-1}(A)$, $\cos^{-1}(A)$, and $\tan^{-1}(A)$ are the inverse functions. Given a trig ratio, use of one of these functions enables you to find the angle.

Example: In right $\triangle DEF$ with a right angle at *D*, $DF = 25$ and $EF = 40$. Find, to the nearest degree, the measure of $\angle E$.

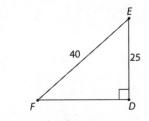

$\cos(E) = \dfrac{25}{40}$ so $E = \cos^{-1}\left(\dfrac{25}{40}\right) = 51.3°$.

Example: The sides of a regular decagon are each 40 cm. Find, to the nearest integer, the area of the decagon.

Each exterior angle of the 10 sided decagon is 36°, making each interior angle 144°. A partial drawing of the decagon is shown below.

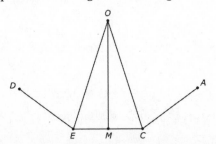

The decagon is made up of 10 isosceles triangles, each with a base of 40 cm. Use trigonometry to find the height of one triangle, and you will then be able to compute the area of the decagon. The altitude from central point O is dropped to side $\overline{EC}$. Because the triangle is isosceles, M is the midpoint of $\overline{EC}$. The measure of $\angle ECA$ is 144°, so the measure of $\angle ECO$ is 72°. MC = 20. $\tan(72) = \dfrac{OM}{20}$, so OM = 20tan(72). Do not compute the decimal value at this time because it will increase the chance of having a round off error. The area of $\triangle ECO$ is $\frac{1}{2}$(OM)(EC) = $\frac{1}{2}$(20 tan(72))(40) = 400 tan(72). The area of the decagon is 10 times this value or 4000 tan(72). Enter this expression into your calculator to get 12,311 sq cm.

The ratio of the sides of the isosceles right triangle (45-45-90) and the 30-60-90 triangle are used repeatedly in trigonometry. The sides of the 45-45-90 triangle are in the ratio 1-1-$\sqrt{2}$, while the sides of the 30-60-90 triangle are in the ratio 1-$\sqrt{3}$-2.

Example: In $\triangle WTV$, $m\angle W = 45$, $m\angle T = 30$, and V is 20 cm from $\overline{WT}$. What is the perimeter of $\triangle WTV$?

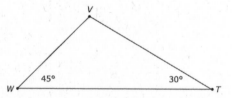

Drop the altitude from V to $\overline{WT}$ and call the foot of the altitude S. $VS = 20$, and $\triangle WSV$ is a 45-45-90 triangle, so $WS = 20$ and $WV = 20\sqrt{2}$. $\triangle TSV$ is a 30-60-90 triangle, so $TS = 20\sqrt{3}$ and $TV = 40$. The perimeter of $\triangle WTV$ is 60 + 20$\sqrt{2}$ + 20$\sqrt{3}$.

Circles

By definition, the circle is the set of all points in a plane equidistant from a fixed point.

A line tangent to a circle intersects the circle at one point and is perpendicular to the radius that ends at that point.

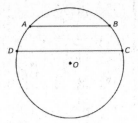

If two chords are parallel, as above, they form congruent arcs. $\overline{CD} \parallel \overline{AB}$ implies that $m\overset{\frown}{BC} = m\overset{\frown}{AD}$. It can also be shown that $\overline{BC} \cong \overline{AD}$.

A central angle is formed by two radii, and its measure is equal to the measure of the arc it encloses. An inscribed angle is formed by two chords that intersect on the circle, and the measure of an inscribed angle is one-half the measure of the arc it encloses.

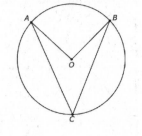

$$m\angle AOB = m\overset{\frown}{AB} \text{ and } m\angle ACB = \frac{1}{2}m\overset{\frown}{AB}.$$

The measure of an angle formed by a tangent line and a chord intersecting at a point on the circle is equal to one-half the measure of the enclosed arc.

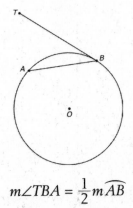

$$m\angle TBA = \frac{1}{2}m\overset{\frown}{AB}$$

If the vertex of an angle formed by two chords is in the interior of the circle but not the center, the measure of the angle is the average of the measures of the arcs enclosed by the vertical angles.

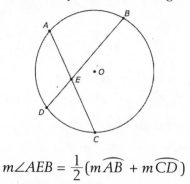

$$m\angle AEB = \frac{1}{2}(m\widehat{AB} + m\widehat{CD})$$

If the angle is formed by two tangents, its measure will be the supplement of the minor arc contained inside the angle.

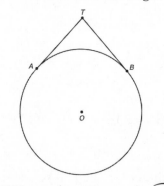

$$\angle ATB \text{ supplementary to } m\widehat{AB}$$

If the angle is formed by two secants or by a tangent and a secant, then the measure of the angle formed is one-half the difference of the two arcs contained within the angle.

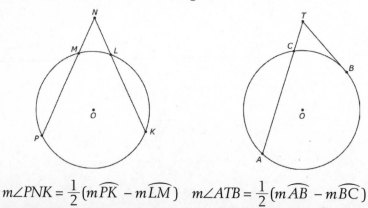

$$m\angle PNK = \frac{1}{2}(m\widehat{PK} - m\widehat{LM}) \quad m\angle ATB = \frac{1}{2}(m\widehat{AB} - m\widehat{BC})$$

A diameter perpendicular to a chord bisects the chord.

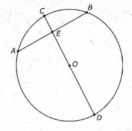

$$\overline{AB} \perp \overline{COD} \leftrightarrow \overline{AE} \cong \overline{EB}$$

Two tangents drawn to a circle from the same external point are equal in length.

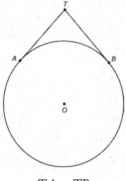

$$TA = TB$$

There are relationships about the segments formed in a circle that are derived from the similar triangles. With two secants, the product of the external segment of the secant and the length of the secant segment is constant.

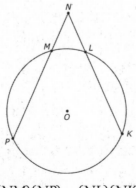

$$(NM)(NP) = (NL)(NK)$$

If a secant and tangent are drawn from the same external point, the square of the tangent is equal to the product of the external segment of the secant and the length of the secant segment.

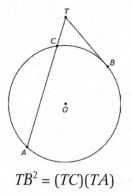

$$TB^2 = (TC)(TA)$$

Exercises

1. $\overline{AB} \parallel \overline{CD}$, $m\widehat{AB} = 82$ and $m\widehat{CD} = 118$. $m\angle ABD =$

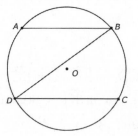

    (A) 40   (B) 41   (C) 59   (D) 80   (E) 82

2. In $\triangle KLP$, $KL = LP$, $m\angle K = 3x + 17$, and $m\angle L = 5x + 9$. $m\angle P =$

    (A) 4   (B) 12.45   (C) 29   (D) 54.36   (E) 74.75

3. $\overline{AB} \perp \overline{BD}$ and $\overline{DE} \perp \overline{BD}$. If $AB = 12$, $CE = 34$, and $DE = 30$, $BC =$

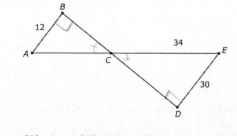

    (A) 6.4   (B) 8   (C) 16   (D) 30   (E) 40

4. In rhombus QHDG, diagonals HG and QD intersect at Z. If $m\angle QHD = 130$ and $QD = 40$, the perimeter of QHDG, to the nearest tenth, is

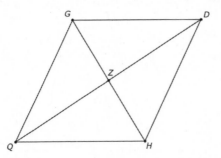

(A) 88.3   (B) 104.4   (C) 176.5   (D) 189.3   (E) 208.9

5. A regular hexagon has an area of $600\sqrt{3}$. The perimeter of the hexagon is

(A) $100\sqrt{3}$ (B) 120   (C) $120\sqrt{3}$ (D) $100\sqrt{6}$ (E) $120\sqrt{6}$

Explanations

1. (A) Because $\overline{AB} \parallel \overline{CD}$, $m\overset{\frown}{AD} = m\overset{\frown}{BC}$. Given $m\overset{\frown}{AB} = 82$ and $m\overset{\frown}{CD} = 118$, then $m\overset{\frown}{AD} = m\overset{\frown}{BC} = 80$. Inscribed $\angle ABD$ measures half this number.

2. (D) $KL = LP$ implies that $m\angle K = m\angle P$. Add the sum of the measures of the angles of the triangle to get $2(3x + 17) + 5x + 9 = 180$. $11x + 43 = 180$ so $11x = 137$ and $x = 137/11$. $m\angle P = 3(137/11) + 17 = 54.36$.

3. (A) $\triangle ABC \sim \triangle EDC$, so $\dfrac{AB}{ED} = \dfrac{BC}{DC}$. Use the Pythagorean Theorem $(CD^2 + 30^2 = 34^2)$ in $\triangle EDC$ to find that $CD = 16$. $\dfrac{12}{30} = \dfrac{BC}{16}$ becomes $30\,BC = 192$ and $BC = 6.4$.

4. (A) The measure of $\angle QHZ = 65$ and $QZ = 20$. Use trigonometry to find QH. $\sin(65) = \dfrac{20}{QH}$. Solve this to get $QH \sin(65) = 20$ and $QH = \dfrac{20}{\sin(65)}$. The perimeter of the rhombus is $4QH = 88.3$.

5. (B) The hexagon consists of 6 equilateral triangles, each with area $100\sqrt{3}$. Because the area of an equilateral triangle can be computed with the formula $\frac{s^2\sqrt{3}}{4}$, where s is the length of a side of the triangle, solve to find $s = 20$. The perimeter of the hexagon is 120.

Topic 4: Coordinate Geometry

Lines

There are three forms for the equation of a line that are used more than any other: slope-intercept ($y = mx + b$), point-slope ($y - y_1 = m(x - x_1)$), and standard ($Ax + By = C$, with A, B, and C being integers). The slope of a line given in standard form is $-A/B$ (think about solving the standard equation for y). In general, the slope of a line is the ratio of the change in y-values to the change in x-values, written as $m = \dfrac{y_2 - y_1}{x_2 - x_1}$.

Parallel lines have equal slopes, while the slopes of perpendicular lines are negative reciprocals (with the exception of a vertical-horizontal pair of lines). When you are working with lines whose equations are given in standard form, parallel lines will take on the same $Ax + By$ form but the constant on the right will change. With perpendicular lines, you will switch the A and B, change the sign between the terms, and determine the new value of the constant on the right. That is, the equation of a line perpendicular to $Ax + By = C$ will be of the form $Bx - Ay = D$.

Example: Find the equation of the line through the point $(2,-5)$ that is parallel to $3x - 4y = 7$.

The equation of the line will be of the form $3x - 4y = C$. Substitute for x and y to get $3(2) - 4(-5) = 26$. The equation of the line is $3x - 4y = 26$.

Example: Find the equation of the line through the point (2,–5) that is perpendicular to $3x - 4y = 7$.

The equation of the line must be of the form $4x + 3y = C$. Substitute for x and y to get $4(2) + 3(-5) = -7$. The equation of the line is $y = -\dfrac{4}{3}x - \dfrac{7}{3}$.

Example: $\triangle ABC$ has coordinates $A(2,5)$, $B(-1,7)$ and $C(-3,-1)$. Write an equation in standard form for the altitude to side BC.

The altitude is a line perpendicular to a side of the triangle that passes through the vertex opposite that side. The slope of side BC is $\dfrac{-1-7}{-3-(-1)} = \dfrac{-8}{-2} = 4$. The slope of the perpendicular line is $-1/4$. This tells you that the equation for the altitude must be of the form $x + 4y = C$. Substituting the coordinates of vertex A for x and y gives $2 + 4(5) = C$, so the equation of the altitude is $x + 4y = 22$.

Parabolas

The two most commonly used equations for the parabola are the standard form $(f(x) = ax^2 + bx + c)$ and the vertex form $(y - k = a(x - h)^2)$.

In the vertex form, the vertex is the point (h,k), and the axis of symmetry is the line $x = h$.

In the standard form, the equation for the axis of symmetry is $x = \dfrac{-b}{2a}$ and the vertex is at the point $\left(\dfrac{-b}{2a}, f\left(\dfrac{-b}{2a}\right)\right)$.

The quadratic coefficient, a, indicates the direction in which the parabola will open. If $a > 0$, the parabola opens up, and if $a < 0$, the parabola opens down.

If two points on the parabola have the same y-coordinate, the axis of symmetry must be the perpendicular bisector of the segment joining these points.

Example: A parabola passes through the points $(-2,5)$, $(6,5)$ and $(4,-1)$. Determine the equation of the parabola.

The axis of symmetry must be $x = 2$, since the average of -2 and 6 is 2. The equation of the parabola is of the form $y - k = a(x - 2)^2$. Substitute $(6,5)$ and $(4,-1)$ into this equation to get the system $5 - k = a(6 - 2)^2$ or $5 - k = 16a$ or $k = 5 - 16a$.

$$-1 - k = a(4 - 2)^2 \text{ or } -1 - k = 4a \text{ or } k = -4a - 1.$$

Solve for a to get $a = 1/2$. Substitute into one of the above equations to find $k = -3$. The equation of the parabola is $y + 3 = \frac{1}{2}(x - 2)^2$. This can be expanded to get the standard form $y = 1/2x^2 - 2x - 1$.

Circles

A circle is the set of all points in a plane equidistant from a fixed point. The equations for the circle are center-radius $[(x - h)^2 + (y - k)^2 = r^2]$ and standard $[x^2 + y^2 + Ax + By + C = 0]$.

Example: Determine the equation of the circle with a diameter whose endpoints are at $(-3,5)$ and $(9,-7)$.

The center of the circle is at the midpoint of the diameter $(3,-1)$. Therefore, the equation of the circle takes on the form $(x - 3)^2 + (y + 1)^2 = r^2$. Substitute the coordinates for one of the endpoints of the diameter (e.g., $(-3,5)$) to get $(-3 - 3)^2 + (5 + 1)^2 = r^2$ so $r^2 = 72$. Therefore, $(x - 3)^2 + (y + 1)^2 = 72$.

Example: Determine the coordinates of the center of the circle and the length of its radius if the circle has equation $x^2 + y^2 + 8x - 12y + 10 = 0$.

Complete the square in x and y to get $x^2 + 8x + \underline{16} + y^2 - 12y + \underline{36} = -10 + \underline{16} + \underline{36}$.

Factor to get $(x + 4)^2 + (y - 6)^2 = 42$. The center of the circle is $(-4,6)$, and the radius has length $\sqrt{42}$.

Symmetry

The parabola will always have an axis of symmetry. Other graphs may or may not be symmetric about some line.

Example: The following picture shows a section of the graph of a function that is symmetric to the y-axis. Sketch the rest of the graph.

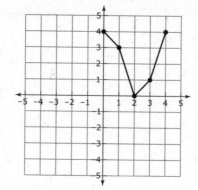

Reflect the points (1,3), (2,0), (3,1), and (4,4) across the y-axis to give you a guide for sketching the function.

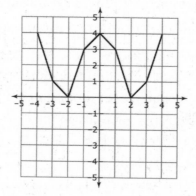

Example: The accompanying picture shows a section of the graph of a function that is symmetric to the origin. Sketch the remainder of the graph.

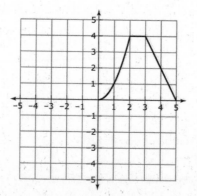

Symmetry with respect to the origin means that for each point (x,y) on the original graph, $(-x,-y)$ is a point on the graph as well. Graph the images of $(2,4)$, $(3,4)$ and $(5,0)$ to get the new graph. Be careful with curvature of the parabola.

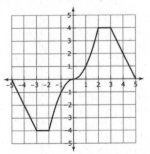

Example: The accompanying picture shows a section of the graph of a relation that is symmetric to the x-axis. Sketch the remainder of the graph.

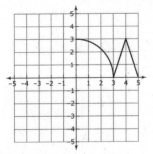

If a graph is symmetric with respect to the x-axis, then for each ordered pair (x,y) on the graph, $(x,-y)$ is also on the graph. Use the points $(0,3)$ and $(4,4)$ to sketch the image.

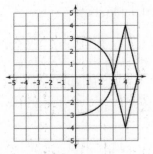

Clearly, this is not the graph of a function.

Example: The accompanying picture shows a section of the graph of a relation that is symmetric to the line $y = x$. Sketch the remainder of the graph.

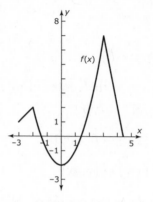

Whenever a point (x,y) is on a graph that is symmetric to the line $y = x$, the point (y,x) is also on the graph. Use the points $(-4,0)$, $(0,2)$, and $(5,3)$ to sketch the image.

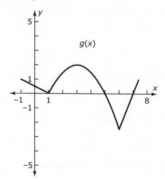

Transformations of Figures

The basic transformations in the Euclidean plane are line reflection, translation, rotation, and dilation. On the SAT Math test, for expedience, these transformations are usually applied to a line segment, triangle, or quadrilateral.

Transformation formulas that you should know are:

Line Reflections

- across the x-axis, r_x: $(x,y) \rightarrow (x,-y)$

- across the y-axis, r_y: $(x,y) \rightarrow (-x,y)$

- across the line $y = x$, $r_{y=x}$: $(x,y) \rightarrow (y,x)$

- reflections over any other line (such as $x = 2$ or $y = -1$) are best done with a picture.

Translations
- $T_{a,b}(x,y) \rightarrow (x + a, y + b)$

Rotations with the origin as the center of rotation
- rotate 90°, R_{90}: $(x,y) \rightarrow (-y,x)$

- rotate 180°, R_{180}: $(x,y) \rightarrow (-x,-y)$

- rotate 270°, R_{270}: $(x,y) \rightarrow (y,-x)$

Dilations with the origin as the center of dilation
- $D_k(x,y) \rightarrow (kx,ky)$

Line reflections, translations, and rotations are rigid motions. This means that the image and pre-image will be congruent figures. Dilations create similar figures, as the sizes will change due to the multiplication by the scale factor, k.

Example: Find the coordinates of the image of $\triangle ABC$ with A (1,0), B (-1,4), and C (4,1) under R_{90}.

$A(1,0) \rightarrow A'(0,1)$ $B(-1,4) \rightarrow B'(-4,-1)$ $C(4,1) \rightarrow C'(-1,4)$

More than one transformation can be applied to a pre-image through a composition. Remember that *compositions are executed from right to left.*

Example: Find the coordinates of the image of $\triangle ABC$ with $A(1,0)$, $B(-1,4)$, and C (4,1) under $r_x \circ T_{-2,3} \circ R_{270}$.

$$\begin{array}{cccc} & R_{270} & T_{-2,3} & r_x \\ A(1,0) & \rightarrow A'(0,-1) & \rightarrow A''(-2,2) & \rightarrow A'''(-2,-2) \\ B(-1,4) & \rightarrow B'(-4,-1) & \rightarrow B''(-6,4) & \rightarrow B'''(-6,-4) \\ C(4,1) & \rightarrow C'(-1,4) & \rightarrow C''(-3,7) & \rightarrow C'''(-3,-7) \end{array}$$

Transformations of Functions
Transformations of functions behave in a slightly different manner. Translations might seem to be in the reverse order of what you expect.

If h is a positive number, $y = f(x - h)$ translates the graph of $y = f(x)$ to the right, while $y = f(x + h)$ moves the graph of $y = f(x)$ to the left. However, if you realize that the translation definitions move the transformed graph back to the parent graph, the notation becomes clearer.

For example, the graphs of $f(x) = x^2$ and $g(x) = f(x - 3) = (x - 3)^2$ are drawn below.

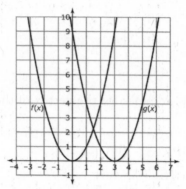

You can see that you need to move $g(x)$ to the left 3 units so that it coincides with the parent function $y = x^2$.

Vertical translations are consistent with the translations from the Euclidean figures. If k is a positive number, the graph of $y = f(x) - k$ translates the graph down, while $y = f(x) + k$ translates the graph up. **Beware:** $y = f(x) - k$ is the same as $y + k = f(x)$, and the graph of $f(x)$ is still translated down k units!

Dilations of functions occur with respect to an axis, not with respect to a point as with Euclidean figures. For example, the graph of $y = 2x^2$ takes each y-coordinate from the graph of $y = x^2$ and multiplies it by 2. The impact is that the graph of $y = x^2$ is stretched from the x-axis by a factor of 2. If k is a positive number, then the graph of $y = kf(x)$ stretches the graph from the x-axis by a factor of k. If k is negative, the graph is also reflected over the x-axis.

**If k is a positive number, the graph of $y = f(kx)$ dilates the graph of $y = f(x)$ from the y-axis by a factor of $1/k$. For example, the graphs of $f(x) = \sin(x)$ and $g(x) = f(2x) = \sin(2x)$ are drawn on the following axes. The period for $f(x)$ is 2π, while the period for $g(x)$ is π.

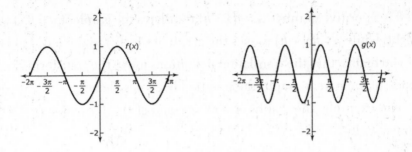

Exercises

1. Determine the coordinates for the vertex of the parabola $y = -2x^2 + 4xb + 3$.

    (A) (1,5) (B) (2,3) (C) (–1,–3)
    (D) (–2,–13) (E) (0.5,4.5)

2. What is the image of point $A(-4,5)$ under the transformation $r_{x^\circ}R_{90}$?

    (A) (4,5) (B) (5,–4) (C) (4,–5) (D) (–5,4) (E) (–4,–5)

3. What are the coordinates of the circumcenter for the triangle with coordinates $A(2,-1)$, $B(5,2)$, and $C(-1,2)$?

    (A) (2,–1) (B) (2,1) (C) (2,2) (D) (5,2) (E) (–1,2)

4. The circle with equation $x^2 + y^2 - 12x + 10y - 60 = 0$ has

    (A) center (6,5); radius 1   (B) center (6,–5); radius 1
    (C) center (6,5); radius 11   (D) center (6,–5); radius 11
    (E) center (6,–5); radius $\sqrt{61}$

**5. The graph of $f(x) = -3\sin\left(\frac{2\pi}{3}\left(x + \frac{\pi}{6}\right)\right) + 1$ is the graph of $y = \sin(x)$ with the properties

    I. amplitude = period

    II. phase shift right $\frac{\pi}{6}$

    III. vertical translation up 1

    (A) I and II only   (B) II and III only   (C) I and III only
    (D) I, II, and III   (E) None of these properties

Explanations

1. (A) The equation for the axis of symmetry for the parabola is $x = \frac{-b}{2a}$. With $b = 4$ and $a = -2$, the axis has the equation $x = 1$. Substitute this value into the equation to determine that $y = 5$.

2. (D) R_{90} takes $(-4,5)$ and sends it to $(-5,-4)$. Reflecting this point over the x-axis gives the answer $(-5,4)$. Keep in mind that compositions are done from left to right.

3. (C) The triangle is a right triangle. The circumcenter of a right triangle is always the midpoint of the hypotenuse.

4. (D) Complete the square on $x^2 + y^2 - 12x + 10y - 60 = 0$ to get $(x - 6)^2 + (y + 5)^2 = 121$, so the center is at $(6,-5)$ and the radius is 11.

5. (C) The amplitude of this function is $|-3| = 3$. The period is $\frac{2\pi}{\left(\frac{2\pi}{3}\right)} = 3$. The phase shift is left $\frac{\pi}{6}$, and the vertical translation is up 1.

Topic 5: Three-Dimensional Geometry

Solids

Three-dimensional figures which connect the vertices of congruent polygons with perpendicular line segments are called *right prisms*. They are prisms because of the congruent polygons (the *bases*) and right because the line segments connecting the vertices form a right angle with the planes containing the base. The line segments connecting the vertices and the sides of the polygons are called the edges.

A *cylinder* is similar to a prism, except that the base is a circle rather than a polygon. (Some people choose to think of a circle as a polygon with an infinite number of sides. In this case, a cylinder can be thought of as a circular prism.)

A *pyramid* is a three-dimensional figure with one base. The lateral (non-base) edges meet at a common point, the vertex, in a different plane. If the segment from this common point that is perpendicular to the base passes through the center of the base, the pyramid is a *right pyramid*. A pyramid with a circular base is a *cone*.

A *sphere* is a solid with the property that all points on the solid are equidistant from a central point. A plane that cuts through a sphere and contains the center of the sphere creates hemispheres (half spheres). The base of a hemisphere is called a *great circle*.

Volume

The volume of a prism is given by the formula $V = bh$, where b represents the area of a base and h represents the height of the prism. The volume of a pyramid is one-third of this amount. That is, for a pyramid, $V = \frac{1}{3}bh$. These formulas also cover the cylinder, the prism formed when the base is a circle.

The volume of a sphere, which is given to you on the test, is $V = \frac{4}{3}\pi r^3$.

Example: Cylindrical tubes filled with sand are poured into a prism with height 40 cm and square base measuring 7 cm per side. If each cylinder has a radius of 3 cm and a height of 12 cm, how many cylinders are needed to completely fill the prism?

The volume of one cylinder is $\pi(3^2)(12) = 108\pi$ cm^3. The volume of the prism is $(7^2)(40) = 1960$ cm^3. $\frac{1960}{108\pi} = 5.78$ cylinders.

Surface Areas

The lateral surface area (LSA) of a prism or pyramid is the area of the faces of the solid, excluding the bases. For a prism, this would be the sum of the areas of the rectangles that form the sides, and for the pyramid, the sum of the areas of the triangles. The total surface area (TSA) is the sum of the LSA and the base(s).

Computing the area of the triangular face of a pyramid involves a language issue. You know that the area of a triangle is computed with the formula one-half base times height, $\frac{1}{2}bh$. The height of the pyramid is the distance from the vertex to the plane containing the base of the pyramid. Therefore, the height of the side of the pyramid is called the *slant height* (after all, it does slide down the side of the pyramid).

Example: In the accompany diagram, pyramid $VABCD$ has rectangular base $ABCD$ with $AB = 40$ cm and $BC = 16$ cm. If the altitude of the pyramid, VG, has length 15, find the total surface area and volume of the pyramid.

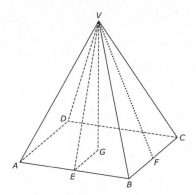

If $BC = 16$, then $GE = 8$ (the foot of the altitude of the pyramid will be at the center of the rectangle). $GE^2 + VG^2 = VE^2$ becomes $8^2 + 15^2 = VE^2$ so $VE = 17$ cm.

GF (not drawn) will have a length of 20. $GF^2 + VG^2 = VF^2$ becomes $20^2 + 15^2 = VF^2$ so $VF = 25$ cm.

The area of the base $ABCD$ is (16 cm)(40 cm) = 640 cm². The area of face VAB is 1/2(40 cm)(17 cm) = 340 cm². This is also the area of face VCD.

The area of face VBC is 1/2(16 cm)(25 cm) = 200 cm². This is also the area of face VAD. The number of square centimeters in the total surface area of the pyramid is 640 + 340 + 340 + 200 + 200 = 1720.

The volume of the pyramid is $\frac{1}{3}$(640 cm²)(15 cm) = 3200 cm³.

The slant height, l, for the cone can also be computed from the Pythagorean Theorem when you know the radius and height of the cone. The LSA for the cone is $\pi r l$.

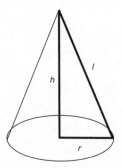

Example: If the radius of the circle is 6 and the height of the cone is 8, find the length of the slant height and the LSA for the cone.

Use the Pythagorean Theorem to determine the length of the slant height is 10. The LSA for this cone is $\pi r l = (6)(10)\pi$ or 60π.

The surface area of a sphere is given by the formula $A = 4\pi r^2$.

Example: Find the volume and total surface area of a cone with radius 5 cm and height 12 cm.

$$V = \frac{1}{3}bh = \frac{1}{3}(5^2\pi)(12) = 100\pi \text{ cm}^3.$$

To compute the LSA, you first need to determine that $l = 13$ cm (5-12-13 right triangle). Therefore, LSA $= \pi(5)(13) = 65\pi$ cm^2. The total surface area is equal to the sum of the LSA and the area of the circle. Therefore, TSA $= 90\pi$ cm^2.

Example: When the figure in the accompanying diagram is rotated about the vertical axis, what is the volume of the solid formed?

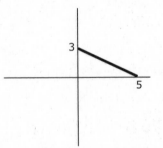

The figure formed will be a cone r with radius 5 and height 3. The volume will be 25π.

The volume of a sphere, which is given to you on the test, is $V = \frac{4}{3}\pi r^3$.

The surface area of a sphere is given by the formula $A = 4\pi r^2$.

Example: Determine the surface area of a sphere which has a volume of 288π cm^3.

Solve $V = \frac{4}{3}\pi r^3 = 288\pi$ to determine that the radius of the sphere is 6 cm. The surface area of a sphere with radius 6 cm is $= 4\pi(6)^2 = 144\pi$ cm^2.

**Coordinates in Three Dimensions

In the coordinate plane, points are identified with ordered pairs (x,y). In rectangular space, points are located with ordered triples (x,y,z). As in plane geometry, midpoints are found by computing the average of the coordinates of the endpoints.

The distance formula is also an extension of the Pythagorean Theorem. Given the ordered triples (x_1,y_1,z_1) and (x_2,y_2,z_2), the distance between these points is $\sqrt{(x_2 - x_1) + (y_2 - y_1)^2 + (z_2 - z_1)^2}$.

Example: Given the points A (2,4,–1) and B (–4,8,5), determine the coordinates of the midpoint of $\overline{AB}$ and the length of $\overline{AB}$.

The midpoint is $\left(\dfrac{2 + -4}{2}, \dfrac{4 + 8}{2}, \dfrac{-1 + 5}{2}\right)$ = (–1,6,2). AB = $\sqrt{(2 - (-4))^2 + (4 - 8)^2 + (-1 - 5)^2}$ = $\sqrt{88}$ = $2\sqrt{22}$.

Exercises

1. A rectangular prism measures 5 cm × 10 cm × 12 cm. If each dimension is increased by 10%, what is the percent change in the volume of the prism?

    (A) 10   (B) 30   (C) 33.1   (D) 66.9   (E) 133.1

2. The quarter circle in the accompanying diagram is rotated about the x-axis. Determine the total surface area of the solid formed.

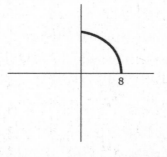

    (A) 16π (B) 64π (C) 128π (D) 192π (E) 256π

3.   Find, to the nearest square centimeter, the total surface area of a cone with base diameter of 48 cm and height 45 cm.

(A) 3,845   (B) 5,655   (C) 9,922   (D) 17,160   (E) 27,143

4.   A spherical water balloon with radius 15 cm is punctured after being placed in a rectangular prism 20 cm × 20 cm × 45 cm. To what percent will the water fill the prism?

(A) 5   (B) 15.7   (C) 25   (D) 75   (E) 78.5

**5. Find the distance between the points (–3,5,1) and (1,2,–12).

(A) 12.5   (B) 13.0   (C) 13.5   (D) 13.9   (E) 14.0

Explanations

1. (C) The dimensions of the new prism are 5.5, 11, and 13.2. The ratio of the new volume to the old volume is $\dfrac{(5\times1.1)(10\times1.1)(12\times1.1)}{5\times10\times12}$ = $(1.1)^3$ = 1.331. Therefore, the increase in volume is 0.331, or 33.1%, of the original prism. Notice that 33.1% would have been the answer no matter what the original measurements were. Choice (E) is present in case you did not subtract the volume of the original prism. Choice (D) is the difference between 100 and 33.1, should someone overthink the problem. Choice (A) is the answer students who are guessing might pick. Choice (B) is also a choice a student might guess, as it is 3×10.

2. (D) The figure formed is a hemisphere. The total area of the figure is the area of the base circle (64π) plus the surface area of the hemisphere (128π). Choice (C) does not include the base circle. Choice (B) is only the base circle. Choice (E) is the area of the full sphere. Choice (A) is the circumference of a circle with radius 8.

3. (B) The radius of the base is 24 cm. Use the Pythagorean Theorem to determine that the slant height of the cone is 51 cm. The total surface area is 1800π cm^2, or approximately 5,655 cm^2. Choice (A) is the LSA of the cone without the base. Choice (C) is the LSA computed with a

radius of 48 rather than 24 and choice (E) is the TSA of the same cone. Choice (E) is the volume of the cone with radius 24 cm.

4. (E) The volume of the water balloon is 4500π cm^3 and the volume of the prism is 18,000 cm^3. Compute $\frac{4500\pi}{18000} \times 100$ to get the correct percentage. Choice (C) forgets to use π in the computation of the volume of the sphere. Choice (B) uses the area of the sphere rather than its volume. Choice (C) uses the area and forgets to include π. Choice (E) is the consequence of calculator misusage.

5. (D) The distance is computed by $\sqrt{(-3-1)^2 + (5-2)^2 + (1-(-12))^2}$ $= \sqrt{194} = 13.9$. The other choices are consequences of arithmetic errors with signed numbers.

Topic 6: Trigonometry

Right Triangles

For any right triangle, the ratio of the length of a side opposite an acute angle θ to the length of the hypotenuse is called the sine of the angle, and is abbreviated $\sin(\theta)$. The ratio of the length of the adjacent leg to the length of the hypotenuse is the cosine (complement of the sine), or $\cos(\theta)$, and the ratio of the length of the opposite leg to the length of the adjacent leg is the tangent, $\tan(\theta)$. You are probably familiar with the mnemonic SOHCAHTOA; the first letters form each of the key words, to remember the ratios.

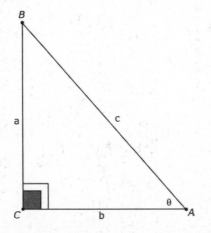

$$\sin(A) = \frac{opposite}{hypotenuse} = \frac{a}{c} \quad \cos(A) = \frac{adjacent}{hypotenuse} = \frac{b}{c} \quad \tan(A) = \frac{opposite}{adjacent} = \frac{a}{b}$$

$$\sin(B) = \frac{opposite}{hypotenuse} = \frac{b}{c} \quad \cos(B) = \frac{adjacent}{hypotenuse} = \frac{a}{c} \quad \tan(B) = \frac{opposite}{adjacent} = \frac{b}{a}$$

In any right triangle, if $\sin(A) = \cos(B)$, then $A + B = 90$.

Example: Find the length of AB in the accompanying diagram.

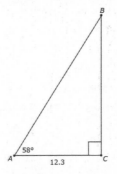

The acute angle is 58, the adjacent leg is 12.3, and the hypotenuse is not known. Use the cosine function to solve the problem.

$$\cos(58) = \frac{12.3}{c} \text{ becomes } c\cos(58) = 12.3. \text{ Therefore, } c = \frac{12.3}{\cos(58)} = 23.2.$$

Example: In right $\triangle DEF$ with a right angle at D, $DF = 15$ and $DE = 24$. Find, to the nearest degree, the measure of $\angle E$.

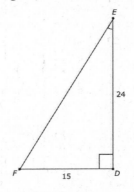

$$\tan(E) = \frac{15}{24}.$$

The functions $\sin^{-1}(A)$, $\cos^{-1}(A)$, and $\tan^{-1}(A)$ are the inverse functions. Use these when you are given the value of the trigonometric ratio and need to find the angle. In this example, the value for $\tan(E)$ is known.

Use the inverse tangent function to find the measure of angle E.

$$E = \tan^{-1}\left(\frac{15}{24}\right) = 32°.$$

Angles of Elevation and Depression

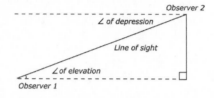

The diagram above illustrates two observers looking at each other. Observer 1 is at a lower height than observer 2, and the parallel dotted lines indicate their lines of vision when they look forward from their respective positions. However, when they look at each other, the lines of vision change. Observer 1 must elevate/raise his line of vision, while observer 2 must lower her line of vision. It is important to observe that the angle of elevation lies within the right triangle, while the angle of depression is outside of the triangle, and its complement makes up the third angle of the right triangle. The angles of elevation and depression are always equal, as they represent alternate interior angles for the set of parallel lines.

Example: Jackie and her sister Eileen are looking at each other from two points—Jackie from the top of a cliff and Eileen from a point 1500 yards from the foot of the cliff. If Jackie's angle of depression to see Eileen is 29.4°, determine, to the nearest yard, the height of the cliff that Jackie is standing on.

Eileen's angle of elevation is also 29.4°. If h is the height of the cliff,

$$\tan(29.4) = \frac{h}{1500}, \text{ so } h = 1500\tan(29.4) = 845 \text{ yds.}$$

The three basic functions also have reciprocal functions. The reciprocal of the sine function is the cosecant function; the reciprocal of the cosine function is the secant function; the reciprocal of the tangent function is the cotangent function. Do not confuse $\sin^{-1}(A)$, the inverse sine function, with $\csc(A)$, the reciprocal of the $\sin(A)$.

Example: Find the value of $\csc(A)$ if $\sin(A) = \dfrac{3}{5}$.

The cosecant (csc) is the reciprocal of the sine function. Therefore, $\csc(A) = \dfrac{5}{3}$.

[Notice how this is different from $\sin^{-1}\left(\dfrac{3}{5}\right) \approx 36.9°$.]

Beyond the Right Triangle

The study of trigonometry extends beyond the right triangle using coordinates and symmetries. The acute angles studied in right-triangle trigonometry serve as reference angles for the rest of the plane.

The reference angle for an angle outside of the first quadrant is the acute angle made by the terminal ray with the *x*-axis.

Ratios are now determined by the coordinates of a point on the terminal ray and the distance of that point from the origin.

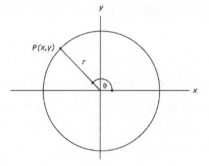

$$\sin(\theta) = \frac{y}{r} \qquad \cos(\theta) = \frac{x}{r} \qquad \tan(\theta) = \frac{y}{x}$$

$$\csc(\theta) = \frac{r}{y} \qquad \sec(\theta) = \frac{r}{x} \qquad \cot(\theta) = \frac{x}{y}$$

The implications of these definitions are that $\sin(\theta)$ and $\csc(\theta)$ are positive in quadrant II, $\tan(\theta)$ and $\cot(\theta)$ are positive in quadrant III, and that $\cos(\theta)$ and $\sec(\theta)$ are positive in quadrant IV. All six functions are positive in quadrant I.

The unit circle, the circle centered at the origin with a radius of 1, is used as a guide for all other circles (since a dilation by an appropriate factor will give the correct coordinates without changing the ratios). The special angles 30°, 45°, and 60°, as well as the quadrantal angles 0°, 90°, 180°, and 270°, are studied from the unit circle. These are numbers that you should know to help speed you through many questions involving trigonometry.

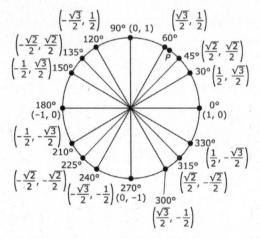

The angles 60°, 120°, 240°, and 300° are all 60° from the x-axis. The difference between the coordinates for each of these points is the presence or absence of a negative sign, determined by the quadrant in which the angle terminates. The same can be said for the other special angles and is true for all angles and their reference angles.

**Radian Measure

Just as length and temperature can be measured in different units, so, too, can angle measurement. A mathematical definition for the measure of an angle comes from the relationship between the arc of a circle and the angle that creates it. This measure is called the *radian* measure of the angle.

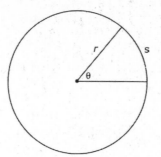

The radian value of angle θ is defined as the ratio of the length of the arc, s, to the radius of the circle, r. That is, $\theta = \frac{s}{r}$, so that you get the formula for arc length as $s = r\theta$.

The circumference of the unit circle is 2π, and the length of the arc formed, s, is a proportional piece of that circle. The relationship between the degree measure of an angle θ_d and the radian measure of an angle θ_r is given by the proportion $\frac{\theta_d}{360} = \frac{\theta_r}{2\pi}$ or $\frac{\theta_d}{180} = \frac{\theta_r}{\pi}$.

Example: Determine the number of revolutions made by a wheel with diameter 26 inches when it travels a distance of 1 mile.

The radius of the wheel is 13 inches, and in one revolution the wheel would travel a distance of 26π inches. There are 5280 feet in a mile and 12 inches in a foot, so the number of inches in 1 miles is $12 \cdot 5280 = 63360$. Therefore, the number of revolutions is $\frac{63360}{26} = 775.7$.

Example: Find the perimeter and area of the sector of a circle with radius 20 cm formed by an angle of $\frac{\pi}{5}$ radians.

The length of the arc is $20\left(\frac{\pi}{5}\right) = 4\pi$ cm, so the perimeter of the sector is $40 + 4\pi$ cm. The area of the sector is a proportional piece of the area of the circle. The area of the circle is 400π so the area of the sector is $\frac{\frac{\pi}{5}}{2\pi} \cdot 400\pi = 40\pi$ cm^2. (There is a formula for the area of a sector in terms of the radian angle and radius, $A_s - \frac{1}{2}r^2\theta$ should you feel the need to memorize it. But it is probably just as easy to use proportions with the area of the circle to do problems such as these.)

Identities

Angles that rotate counterclockwise are given positive measurement, while angles formed from a clockwise rotation are given a negative measurement. Consequently,

$$\sin(-\theta) = -\sin(\theta) \qquad \cos(-\theta) = \cos(\theta) \qquad \tan(-\theta) = \tan(\theta)$$

The cosine of an angle is, by definition, the same as the sine of the angle's complement, so

$$\cos(\theta) = \cos(90 - \theta) \text{ and } \sin(\theta) = \cos(90 - \theta)$$

$$\cos(\theta) = \sin\left(\frac{\pi}{2} - \theta\right) \text{ and } \sin(\theta) = \cos\left(\frac{\pi}{2} - \theta\right)$$

A rotation across the y-axis does not change the sign of the y-coordinate but it does the x-coordinate.

$$\sin(\theta) = \sin(180 - \theta) \text{ and } \cos(\theta) = -\cos(180 - \theta)$$

$$\sin(\theta) = \sin(\pi - \theta) \text{ and } \cos(\theta) = -\cos(\pi - \theta)$$

Example: If $\sin(A) = -3/5$, determine $\sin(-A)$, $\cos(90 - A)$, and $\sin(180 - A)$.

Using the identities from the last paragraphs:

$\sin(-A) = -\sin(A) = -3/5$

$\cos(90 - A) = \sin(A) = 3/5$

$\sin(180 - A) = \sin(A) = 3/5$.

Because $\sin(\theta) = \frac{y}{r}$, $\cos(\theta) = \frac{x}{r}$, and $\tan(\theta) = \frac{y}{x}$, $\tan(\theta) = \frac{\sin(\theta)}{\cos(\theta)}$.

The equation of the unit circle is $x^2 + y^2 = 1$. For each point on the unit circle, the (x,y) coordinates can be replaced by $(\cos(\theta), \sin(\theta))$. Substituting into the equation of the circle gives the first of the three Pythagorean Identities:

$\sin^2(\theta) + \cos^2(\theta) = 1$

Divide by $\cos^2(\theta)$. $\dfrac{\sin^2(\theta)}{\cos^2(\theta)} + \dfrac{\cos^2(\theta)}{\cos^2(\theta)} = \dfrac{1}{\cos^2(\theta)}$, which becomes

$\tan^2(\theta) + 1 = \sec^2(\theta)$.

Divide $\sin^2(\theta) + \cos^2(\theta) = 1$ by $\sin^2(\theta)$.

$$\frac{\sin^2(\theta)}{\sin^2(\theta)} + \frac{\cos^2(\theta)}{\sin^2(\theta)} = \frac{1}{\sin^2(\theta)} \text{ or } \cot^2(\theta) + 1 = \csc^2(\theta).$$

Example: If $\sin(A) = 3/5$ and $\cos(A) < 0$, find $\cos(A)$ and $\tan(A)$.

$\sin^2(\theta) + \cos^2(\theta) = 1$ becomes $\left(\dfrac{3}{5}\right)^2 + \cos^2(\theta) = 1$ or

$$\cos^2(\theta) = 1 - \left(\frac{3}{5}\right)^2 = \frac{16}{25}$$

Because $\cos(A) < 0$, $\cos(A) = -4/5$. $\tan(A) = \dfrac{\sin(A)}{\cos(A)} = \dfrac{\dfrac{3}{5}}{-\dfrac{4}{5}} = -\dfrac{3}{4}$.

$\sin(90°) = \sin(30° + 60°) = 1$. However, $\sin(30°) + \sin(60°)$ is greater than 1. This illustrates an important aspect of trigonometry: $\sin(A + B) \neq \sin(A) + \sin(B)$ unless one of the angles is 0.

The sum and difference identities are

$\sin(A+B) = \sin(A)\cos(B) + \sin(B)\cos(A)$

$\sin(A–B) = \sin(A)\cos(B) - \sin(B)\cos(A)$

$\cos(A+B) = \cos(A)\cos(B) - \sin(A)\sin(B)$

$\cos(A–B) = \cos(A)\cos(B) + \sin(A)\sin(B)$

$$\tan(A + B) = \frac{\sin(A + B)}{\cos(A + B)} = \frac{\tan(A) + \tan(B)}{1 - \tan(A)\tan(B)}$$

$$\tan(A - B) = \frac{\sin(A - B)}{\cos(A - B)} = \frac{\tan(A) - \tan(B)}{1 + \tan(A)\tan(B)}$$

If A and B are the same numbers, you get the double-angle formulas.

$\sin(2A) = 2\sin(A)\cos(A)$

$\cos(2A) = \cos^2(A) - \sin^2(A)$

$\qquad = 2\cos^2(A) - 1$

$\qquad = 1 - 2\sin^2(A)$

$\tan(2A)\dfrac{2\tan(A)}{1 - \tan^2(A)}$

Example: Given $\sin(A) = -5/13$ with $180 < A < 270$ and $\cos(B) = 15/17$ with $270 < B < 360$, find $\sin(A + B)$, $\cos(B - A)$, $\tan(A + B)$, and $\cos(2A)$.

With A in quadrant III, $\cos(A) < 0$. Use the Pythagorean Identity $\left(-\dfrac{5}{13}\right)^2 + \cos^2(A) = 1$ to get $\cos(A) = \left(-\dfrac{12}{13}\right)$ and $\tan(A) = \left(\dfrac{5}{12}\right)$.

With B is quadrant IV, $\sin(B) < 0$. Use the Pythagorean Identity $\sin^2(B) + \left(\dfrac{15}{17}\right)^2 = 1$ to get $\sin(B) = -\dfrac{8}{17}$ and $\tan(B) = -\dfrac{8}{15}$.

$\sin(A + B) = \sin(A)\cos(B) + \sin(B)\cos(A) =$
$$\left(\frac{-5}{13}\right)\left(\frac{15}{17}\right) + \left(\frac{-8}{17}\right)\left(\frac{-12}{13}\right) = \frac{21}{221}$$

$\cos(B - A) = \cos(A - B) = \cos(A)\cos(B) + \sin(A)\sin(B) =$
$$\left(\frac{-12}{13}\right)\left(\frac{15}{17}\right) + \left(\frac{-8}{17}\right)\left(\frac{-5}{13}\right) = \frac{-140}{221}$$

$$\tan(A + B) = \frac{\tan(A) + \tan(B)}{1 - \tan(A)\tan(B)} = \frac{\dfrac{5}{12} + \dfrac{-8}{15}}{1 - \left(\dfrac{5}{12}\right)\left(\dfrac{-8}{15}\right)} = \frac{-21}{220}$$

$$\cos(2A) = 1 - 2\sin^2(A) = 1 - 2\left(\frac{-5}{13}\right)^2 = \frac{119}{169}.$$

**Law of Sines

The area of a triangle is given by the formula $A = \dfrac{1}{2}ab\sin(C)$. A consequence of looking at the variation of this area from the different angles of a triangle is the Law of Sines.

The Law of Sines states that the ratio of the length of a side of a triangle to the sine of the opposite angle is always a constant. That is, in

$\triangle ABC$, $\dfrac{a}{\sin(A)} = \dfrac{b}{\sin(B)} = \dfrac{c}{\sin(C)}$. The Law of Sines can be applied when two sides and two angles of a triangle are involved in a problem. From a geometric perspective, this means that ASA, AAS, and SSA information can be used to attempt to find the remaining information about the triangle. It is important to keep in mind that (1) in any triangle, the larger side is opposite the larger angle; and (2) SSA does not always guarantee the existence of a triangle.

Example: In $\triangle ABC$, $m\angle A = 50°$, $m\angle B = 75°$, and $AB = 12$. Find AC and the area of the triangle. The $m\angle C = 55°$. Use the Law of Sines to determine the length of AC. $\dfrac{b}{\sin(75)} = \dfrac{12}{\sin(55)}$ becomes $b = \dfrac{12\sin(75)}{\sin(55)}$

$= 14.150$. The area of the triangle is $A = \dfrac{1}{2}(12)(14.150)\sin(50) = 65.04$.

Example: In $\triangle DEF$, $DE = 15$, $EF = 20$, and $m\angle F = 42$. Find $m\angle D$ to the nearest degree. This is an example of SSA information. Use the Law of Sines to get the proportion $\dfrac{15}{\sin(42)} = \dfrac{20}{\sin(D)}$ and solve this to get $\sin(D) = \dfrac{20\sin(42)}{15} = 0.8921741418$. Because $\angle D$ is larger than $\angle F$, there is no way to know if $\angle D$ is an acute angle or obtuse angle. This is what makes the *ambiguous case*. The $\sin^{-1}(0.8921741418) = 63.1$. Therefore, $m\angle D = 63.1$ or 116.9.

**Law of Cosines

The Law of Cosines, $k^2 = m^2 n^2 - 2mn\cos(K)$, can be used when the information presented fits either the SAS or SSS pattern. It is important to remember that the angle indicated at the end of the right side of the equation must be opposite the side listed on the left side of the equation.

Example: Find the measure of the largest angle of the triangle with sides 23, 34, and 42.

The largest angle will be opposite the side with length 42. Therefore, the equation is

$$42^2 = 23^2 + 34^2 - 2(23)(34)\cos(K)$$
$$1764 = 529 + 1156 - 1564\cos(K)$$
$$1764 = 1685 - 1564\cos(K)$$

$$79 = -1564\cos(K)$$
$$\frac{-79}{1564} = \cos(K)$$
$$K = \cos^{-1}\left(\frac{-79}{1564}\right) = 92.3$$

Example: Two forces of 40N and 60N act on an object with an angle of 40.2° between the forces. Determine the magnitude of the resultant of the forces.

The resultant is the length of the diagonal of the parallelogram with two sides of lengths 40 and 60, with an included angle of measure 40.2°.

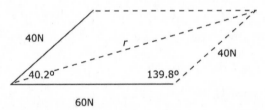

The triangle containing the resultant has an angle of measure 139.8°. Use the Law of Cosines to compute $r^2 = 40^2 + 60^2 - 2(40)(60)\cos(139.8)$. $r^2 = 8866.221$, so $r = 94.2N$.

**Periodic Functions

The tides, a normal heartbeat, and a pendulum (over a short time span) are periodic phenomena because they repeat themselves over some interval—the period. Once the period is known, future (or past) values can be determined based on any observed interval.

Example: The following graph shows 2 cycles of a periodic function $y = f(x)$ that has a period of 5 units. What is $f(127)$? What is $f(-17)$?

Because the period of the function is 5, you know that $f(0) = f(5) = f(10)$, etc. Therefore, what you need to do is to find the closest multiple of 5 that is less than 127 (i.e., 125) and work from there. $f(127) =$ $f(125+2) = f(2) = 2$. To evaluate $f(-17)$, be careful that you work from $f(-20)$ rather than $f(-15)$, as you want to find the closest multiple of 5 that is <u>less</u> than -17. $f(-17) = f(-20 + 3) = f(3) = -1$.

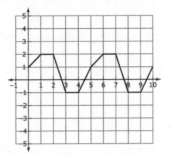

**Graphs of Trigonometric Functions

The graphs of the trigonometric functions are periodic. The graphs of the $y = \sin(x)$, $y = \cos(x)$, $y = \csc(x)$, and $y = \sec(x)$ functions have a period of 2π while the graphs of $y = \tan(x)$ and $y = \cot(x)$ have a period of π.

For the functions $y = A \sin(B(x - C)) + D$ and $y = A \cos(B(x - C)) + D$:

- the period of the function is computed as $\dfrac{2\pi}{|B|}$,

- the horizontal translation, called phase shift, is C (right if C > 0; left if C < 0),

- the amplitude (the distance from the average—center—of the function to an extreme value) is $|A|$,

- the vertical translation is D (up if D > 0; down if D < 0).

Example: Write an equation for the function whose graph is

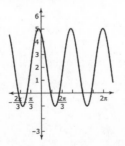

The points $-\pi/3$ and $2\pi/3$ are helpful to draw your eye to the begin-ning and end of a cycle of the curve. The period of this function is π, so the value of B must be 2. The maximum value of the function is 5 and the minimum is -1. This puts the average at 2 (the value of D) and the amplitude is 3. A cycle of the graph begins at the point $(-\pi/3, 2)$, so the phase shift is $-\pi/3$. Finally, as the graph starts at the center (average) of the graph, this is a sine graph, and the equation is $y = 3\sin\left(2\left(x + \dfrac{\pi}{3}\right)\right) + 2$.

Inverse Trigonometric Functions

Reflecting any of the trigonometric functions across the line $y = x$ will produce graphs of relations that are not functions. As the reflection of the parabola must be restricted to create the square root function, the domains of the inverse trigonometric functions need to be restricted to create functions. Looking at the graphs of the three primary functions, $\sin(x)$, $\cos(x)$, and $\tan(x)$ over the interval from -4π to 4π, for example, you can see that there are many continuous intervals for the function that can be 1–1 and can cover the full range of the function. While there are many choices for the intervals to meet the conditions for an inverse function, the intervals that are commonly used have the property that they all contain zero.

Function	Restricted Domain	Range	Inverse-Function	Domain	Range
$y=\sin(x)$	$-\pi/2 \le x \le \pi/2$	$-1 \le y \le 1$	$y = \sin^{-1}(x)$	$-1 \le x \le 1$	$-\pi/2 \le y \le \pi/2$
$y= \tan(x)$	$-\pi/2 < x < \pi/2$	$-\infty < y < \infty$	$y = \tan^{-1}(x)$	$-\infty < x < \infty$	$-\pi/2 < y < \pi/2$
$y= \cos(x)$	$0 \le x \le \pi$	$-1 \le y \le 1$	$y = \cos^{-1}(x)$	$-1 \le x \le 1$	$0 \le y \le \pi$

Knowing these domains and ranges will help you avoid many of the incorrect choices that will be present on the test when trig equations and graphs are involved.

Example: Evaluate $\sin^{-1}\left(\sqrt{\dfrac{3}{2}}\right)$.

Know that when $\sin^{-1}(x)$ is less than zero, then $-\pi/2 \le x < 0$ to determine that the answer is $-\pi/3$. (You could type $\sin^{-1}\left(\dfrac{-\sqrt{3}}{2}\right)$ into your calculator to find the answer. If your calculator does not give exact answers, realize that with π approximately equal to 3.14, $\pi/3$ is approximately 1.05.)

Example: Solve $3\sin^2(\theta) - 1 = 0$ for $0 \le \theta \le 2\pi$.

Solve this equation to determine $\sin(\theta) = \pm\dfrac{1}{\sqrt{3}}$. Use your calculator to get an estimate for $\sin^{-1}\left(\dfrac{1}{\sqrt{3}}\right) = 0.61548$, which will serve as the reference angle for finding all the solutions. Compute $\pi - 0.61548$, $\pi + 0.61548$, and $2\pi - 0.61548$ to find that $\theta = 0.61548$, 2.52611, 3.5707, 5.66771.

Example: Evaluate $\cos\left(\sin^{-1}\left(\dfrac{x}{2}\right)\right)$.

Define $\theta = \sin^{-1}\left(\dfrac{x}{2}\right)$. You are being asked to determine $\cos(\theta)$, knowing that $\sin(\theta) = x/2$. Draw a right triangle with acute angle θ, hypotenuse 2, and leg opposite θ equal to x. Use the Pythagorean Theorem to find the leg adjacent to θ is $\sqrt{4-x^2}$. Then,

$$\cos\left(\sin^{-1}\left(\frac{x}{2}\right)\right) = \cos(\theta) = \frac{\sqrt{4-x^2}}{2}.$$

**Equations

It is not unusual for students to have trouble when solving trigonometric equations because of uncertainty with the inverse trigonometric functions. An algebraic analogy to this problem is the difference between solving the equation $x^2 = 4$ and evaluating $\sqrt{4}$. With $x^2 = 4$, you are being asked to find all values of x for which the equation is true. The answer, of course, is $x = \pm 2$. The expression $\sqrt{4}$ is a function, and the function can have only one output for a given input. You have learned that the output is 2.

With trigonometric equations, you could be asked to *solve* $\sin(A) = 1/2$ as opposed to *evaluating* $\sin^{-1}(1/2)$. You might know that $\sin^{-1}(1/2) = \pi/6$ or you could compute it with your calculator. However, it also true that $\sin\left(\frac{5\pi}{6}\right)$, $\sin\left(\frac{13\pi}{6}\right)$, $\sin\left(\frac{17\pi}{6}\right)$, $\sin\left(\frac{-7\pi}{6}\right)$, and $\sin\left(\frac{-11\pi}{6}\right)$ also equal 1/2. In fact, there are an infinite number of solutions to $\sin(A) = 1/2$. You need to pay attention to the interval stated in the problem for the answers that are to be found.

It is common, but not necessary, that the solution to trigonometric equations is limited by some condition stated in the problem.

Example: Solve $4\cos^2(A) - 3 = 0$ for $0 \leq A \leq 2\pi$.

Add 3, divide by 4, and take the square root to get $\cos(A) = \pm\frac{\sqrt{3}}{2}$, so that $A = \pi/6$, $5\pi/6$, $7\pi/6$, or $11\pi/6$.

Example: Solve $8\cos^2(A) - 3 = 0$ for $0 \leq A \leq 2\pi$.

Add 3, divide by 8, and take the square root to get $\cos(A) = \pm\sqrt{\frac{3}{8}}$. Use your calculator to get a reference angle for A, and then you can go about finding the solution to the problem. The reference angle, θ, is $\cos^{-1}\left(\sqrt{\frac{3}{8}}\right) = .9117$.

Therefore, $A = .9117$, $\pi - \theta = 2.2299$, $\pi + \theta = 4.0533$, and $2\pi - \theta = 5.3714$.

Example: Solve $2\sec^2(A) - 5\sec(A) - 3 = 0$.

Factor the quadratic to get $(2\sec(A) + 1)(\sec(A) - 3) = 0$ and solve, so that $\sec(A) = -1/2$, 3. Because the range of the secant function is $|\sec(A)| \geq 1$, reject $-1/2$ as a solution.

$\sec(A) = 3$ is the same as $\cos(A) = 1/3$. $\cos^{-1}(1/3) = 1.2310$, so $A = 1.2310$, or $2\pi - .2310 = 5.0522$.

**Vectors

Vector addition and subtraction, as done geometrically, use the *tail-to-head approach*. The first vector is drawn from the origin, and the second vector is drawn from the end (head) of the first vector. For example,

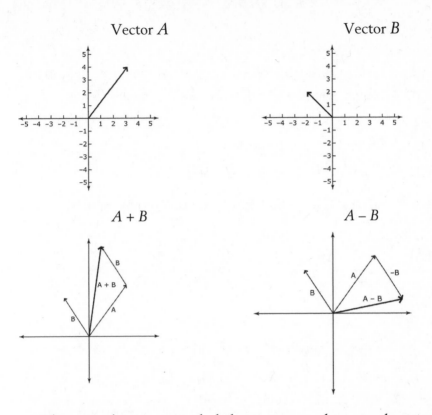

When coordinates are included, you can see how much easier this process becomes. The head of vector A is at $(3,4)$ and the head of vector B is at $(-2,3)$. Vector $A + B$ ends at $(1,7)$, while vector $A - B$ ends at $(5,1)$. What are traditionally referred to as the x- and y-coordinates of an ordered pair are called the horizontal and vertical components of the vector. To add vectors, add the horizontal components together and add the vertical components together. Subtraction is done in a like manner.

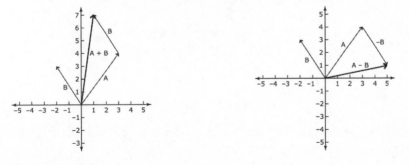

Exercises

1. Alex is looking through a telescope in a park that is at the top of a cliff 2340 feet high. Seeing a friend, he looks at the angle of the telescope and notes that the angle of depression is 63°. How far is his friend from the base of the cliff?

   (A) 4593   (B) 1192   (C) 1062   (D) 2085   (E) 2626

2. Given $\cot(K) = \frac{-1}{3}$ with $90 < K < 180$, find the value of $\tan\left(\frac{\pi}{3} + K\right)$.

   (A) $\dfrac{4\sqrt{3} + 3}{3}$ (B) $\dfrac{4\sqrt{3} - 3}{3}$ (C) $\dfrac{3\sqrt{3} - 3}{13}$

   (D) $\dfrac{6 + 5\sqrt{3}}{13}$ (E) $\dfrac{6 - 5\sqrt{3}}{13}$

**3. Solve $4\tan^2(\theta) - \tan(\theta) - 9 = 3\sec^2(\theta)$ for $0 \le \theta \le 2\pi$.

   (A) {1.2490, 1.8158, 4.3906, 4.9574}
   (B) {1.2490, 1.3258, 4.3906, 4.4674}
   (C) {1.3258, 1.8925, 4.4674, 5.0341}
   (D) {1.8158, 1.8925, 4.9574, 5.0341}
   (E) {1.3258, 1.8925, 4.3906, 4.9574}

**4. A portion of the graph of $y = f(x)$ is sketched below.

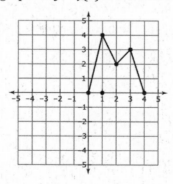

   If $f(x)$ is symmetric to the origin and has a period of 8 units, evaluate $f(53)$.

   (A) –4   (B) –3   (C) 0   (D) 3   (E) 4

**5. $\sec\left(\sin^{-1}\left(\dfrac{x+1}{3}\right)\right) =$

(A) $\dfrac{x+1}{3}$ (B) $\dfrac{3}{x+1}$ (C) $\dfrac{3}{\sqrt{8-2x-x^2}}$

(D) $\dfrac{3}{\sqrt{8-2x+x^2}}$ (E) $\dfrac{\sqrt{8-2x-x^2}}{3}$

Explanations

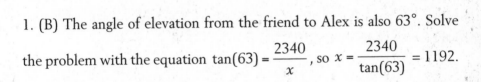

1. (B) The angle of elevation from the friend to Alex is also 63°. Solve

the problem with the equation $\tan(63) = \dfrac{2340}{x}$, so $x = \dfrac{2340}{\tan(63)} = 1192.$

2. (E) If $\cot(K) = \dfrac{-1}{3}$, then $\tan(K) = -3$. $\tan\left(\dfrac{\pi}{3} + K\right) = \dfrac{\tan\left(\dfrac{\pi}{3}\right) + \tan(K)}{1 - \tan\left(\dfrac{\pi}{3}\right)\tan(K)}$

$= \dfrac{\sqrt{3}-3}{1-(\sqrt{3})(-3)} = \left(\dfrac{\sqrt{3}-3}{1+3\sqrt{3}}\right)\left(\dfrac{1-3\sqrt{3}}{1-3\sqrt{3}}\right) = \dfrac{10\sqrt{3}-12}{-26} = \dfrac{6-5\sqrt{3}}{13}$

3. (C) $4\tan^2(\theta) - \tan(\theta) - 9 = 3\sec^2(\theta)$ becomes $4\tan^2(\theta) - \tan(\theta) - 9 = 3(\tan^2(\theta) + 1)$. Combining terms, $4\tan^2(\theta) - \tan(\theta) - 12 = 0$, or $(\tan(\theta) - 4)(\tan(\theta) + 3) = 0$, so that $\tan(\theta) = 4$ or -3. $\tan^{-1}(4) = 1.3258$, and $\tan^{-1}(3) = 1.2490$. $\tan(\theta) = 4$ when $\theta = 1.3258$ or 4.4674 (that is, $1.3258 + \pi$) and $\tan(\theta) = -3$ when $\theta = 1.8925$ (that is, $\pi - 1.2490$) or 5.0341 (that is, $2\pi - 1.2490$).

4. (B) The period of the function is 8. $f(53) = f(56 - 3) = f(\,(8 \cdot 7) - 3)$ $= f(-3) = -f(3) = -3$.

5. (D). The inverse sine of an expression represents an angle. If you refer to $\sin^{-1}\left(\dfrac{x+1}{3}\right) = \theta$, then $\sin(\theta) = \dfrac{x+1}{3}$. Draw a picture of the triangle with hypotenuse 3 and the side opposite the angle as $x + 1$.

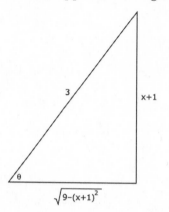

Use the Pythagorean Theorem to determine the adjacent leg has length $\sqrt{8 - 2x + x^2}$. The secant value is the ratio of the adjacent leg to the hypotenuse (that is, the secant is the reciprocal of the cosine).

Topic 7: Exponents and Logarithms

Exponential Functions

Exponential functions are of the form $f(x) = b^x$, where $b > 0$ and $b \neq 1$. When $b > 1$, the functions increases as x moves from left to right and when $0 < b < 1$, the functions decreases. All functions of the form $y = b^x$ pass through the point $(0,1)$.

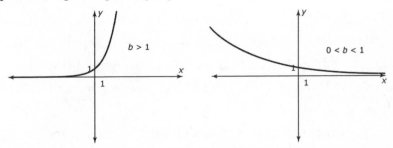

Exponential functions are used to model many important phenomena—compound interest, population growth, and radioactive decay, to name a few.

Example: The amount of money in an account earning 4% interest compounded quarterly is given by the equation $c(t) = 1000(1.01)^{4t}$, where t is the number of years that the $1,000 has been invested. To the nearest dollar, how much money will be in the account after 5 years?

With $t = 5$, $c(5) = 1000(1.01)^{20} = \$1,220$.

Example: How many years must the money be in the account before the money doubles in value?

"The money doubles in value" is asking you to double the $1,000. The equation is $2000 = 1000(1.01)^{4t}$, or $2 = (1.01)^{4t}$. This problem can be solved by graphing the exponential function as well as the linear equation $y = 2$.

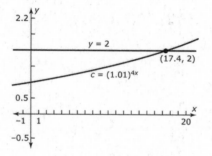

The graphs intersect at the point (17.4,2). Since this is an example of money being compounded quarterly, the interest will not be charged to the account until the quarter has ended, so it will take 17.5 years before the money will double.

Example: An automobile that cost $31,000 when it was new depreciates in value by 18% per year. What is the value of the car after 4 years?

Each year the car loses 18% of its value. This also means that the car maintains 82% of its value from year to year. After 4 years, the value of the car will be $31,000(.82)^4 = $14,016$ (answer rounded to the nearest dollar).

Exponential regression is a process in which an equation is sought to describe a set of data that appear to grow or decay exponentially. For example, the data collected from measuring the maximum heights of a bouncing ball are shown in the table. The input value is the number of bounces, and the output value is the height of the ball, in meters, above the floor.

Bounce	1	2	3	4	5	6
Height (m)	1.07254	0.85644	0.72244	0.57169	0.49838	0.43138

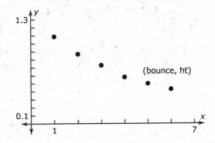

Even without seeing the table, you can see that the points indicate that the heights are decreasing and that there is a bend to the points, indicating that the behavior is not linear. Perform an exponential regression to determine that the equation that models this experiment is $h(n) = 1.25044(0.832595)^n$, where n represents the number of bounces. The ball is maintaining approximately 83.3% of its height from the previous bounce.

**An important exponential function uses the number e (approximately equal to 2.71828). The graph of $y = e^x$ grows more quickly than the graph of $y = 2^x$ but not as quickly as $y = 3^x$.

**Logarithmic Functions

The logarithmic functions are the inverses of the exponential function. The most commonly used logarithmic functions are the common log, base 10, $\log(x)$, and the natural log, base e, $\ln(x)$. Whenever the ordered pair (a,c) is on the graph of $y = b^x$, the point (c,a) is on the graph of $y = \log_b(x)$. In other words, the equations $c = b^a$ and $a = \log_b(c)$ are equivalent.

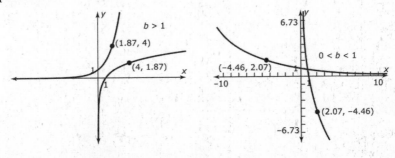

Example: Evaluate $\log_6 (36 \sqrt[5]{6})$.

Set $\log_6 (36 \sqrt[5]{6}) = c$ and rewrite the problem to be $6^c = 36 \sqrt[5]{6} = (6^2)$ $(6^{1/5}) = 6^{11/5}$. Therefore, $c = 2\frac{1}{5}$.

There are six basic rules to know for logarithms:

I. $\log_b(AC) = \log_b(A) + \log_b(C)$

II. $\log_b(A/C) = \log_b(A) - \log_b(C)$

III. $\log_b(A^n) = n \log_b(A)$

IV. $\log_b(1) = 0$

V. $\log_b(b) = 1$

VI. $\log_A(C) = \dfrac{\log_b(C)}{\log_b(A)}$

**Example: Solve for a: $25^{2a+3} = 119$

Take the log of both sides of the equation: $\log(25^{2a+3}) = \log(119)$

Use property III to get: $(2a + 3) \log(25) = \log(119)$

Divide: $2a + 3 = \log(119)/\log(25)$

Subtract 3 and divide by 2 to get $a = -0.758$.

**Example: If $b^c = 3$, what is the value of $\log_3(b)$?

$\log_3(b)$ is equal to $\dfrac{\log_b(b)}{\log_b(3)} = \dfrac{1}{\log_b(3)}$. $b^c = 3$ is equivalent to $\log_b(3) = c$

so $\log_3(b) = \dfrac{1}{\log_b(3)} = \dfrac{1}{c}$.

**Example: Solve $\log_6(x-2) + \log_6(5x-4) = 3$.

Combine the terms on the left side of the equation to get $\log_6((x-2)(5x-4)) = 3$. Changing the logarithmic equation to an exponential equation to get $(x - 2)(5x - 4) = 6^3$ or $5x^2 - 14x + 8 = 216$.

Set the right-hand side of the equation to zero: $5x^2 - 14x - 208 = 0$. Solve using the quadratic formula:

$$x = \frac{14 \pm \sqrt{(-14)^2 - 4(5)(-208)}}{2(5)} = \frac{14 \pm \sqrt{4356}}{10}$$

$$= \frac{14 \pm 66}{10} = \frac{14+66}{10}, \frac{14-66}{10}$$

or $x = 8, -5.2$. Since $-5.2 - 2 < 0$, and the argument for a logarithm must be a positive number, reject $x = -5.2$ and get the answer $x = 8$.

Example: Solve $105e^{2.1x} = 4100$

Divide by 105 to get $e^{2.1x} = \dfrac{4100}{105}$. Take the natural logarithm of both sides of the equation to get $2.1x = \ln\left(\dfrac{4100}{105}\right)$ or $x = \dfrac{\ln\left(\dfrac{4100}{105}\right)}{2.1} = 1.745$.

Exercises

1. If $8^{2x+3y} = 32^{3x-4y}$, $y =$

    (A) $\dfrac{x}{7}$
    (B) $\dfrac{9x}{7}$
    (C) $\dfrac{x-4}{7}$
    (D) $\dfrac{9x}{29}$
    (E) $\dfrac{21x}{29}$

**2. Evaluate $\log_{27}\left(9\sqrt[5]{81}\right)$

    (A) $\dfrac{14}{15}$
    (B) $\dfrac{4}{5}$
    (C) $1\dfrac{4}{5}$
    (D) $\dfrac{4}{3}$
    (E) $\dfrac{28}{15}$

3. Solve $23.4\,(1.08)^{5x} = 928.1$

    (A) -37.998
    (B) 0.423
    (C) 9.564
    (D) 17.691
    (E) 26.994

**4. Solve $\log_8(x+7) + \log_8(3x+5) = 3$

    (A) $-17.667, 9$
    (B) 9
    (C) $-0.446, -8.221$
    (D) 42.508
    (E) 9.284

5. According to Newton's Law of Cooling, the temperature of a sub-stance, such as a cup of coffee, will decrease at a rate proportional to the difference between the temperature of the coffee and the temperature of the room. If a cup of coffee with an initial temperature of 180°F is left standing in a room with constant temperature 70°F, the tempera-ture of the coffee is given by the equation $c(t) = 70 + 110e^{-.08t}$, where t is the number of minutes the coffee has been left standing. If the person

drinking the coffee will not drink the coffee if the temperature of the beverage drops below 115°F, how many minutes can the coffee be left standing before he will throw it away?

(A) 2.94   (B) 5.60   (C) 6.50   (D) 11.17   (E) 52.55

Explanations

1. (D) Rewrite the terms of the equation with the common base of 2. $8^{2x+3y} = 32^{3x-4y}$ becomes $2^{3(2x+3y)} = 2^{5(3x-4y)}$. Be sure to use parentheses around the original exponents. Use the distributive property to get $6x + 9y = 15x - 20y$. Combine like terms to get $29y = 9x$, so $y = 9x/29$.

2. (A) Set $\log_{27}(9\sqrt[5]{81}) = c$ and rewrite the problem as the exponential equation $27^c = (9)(\sqrt[5]{81})$. 9, 27, and 81 are all powers of 3. Rewrite the equation to $3^{3c} = (3^2)(3^{4/5}) = 3^{14/5}$. Set the exponents equal and solve to get $3c = 14/5$, or $c = 14/15$.

3. (C) Graph the two functions $y = 23.4(1.08)^{5x}$ and $y = 928.1$, being sure that the window on the graph screen goes as high as ymax = 1000. Find the point of intersection.

**Algebraically: Take $23.4\,(1.08)^{5x} = 928.1$ and divide by 23.4 to get $(1.08)^{5x} = \dfrac{928.1}{23.4}$. Take the log of both sides to get $\log(1.08)^{5x} = \log\left(\dfrac{928.1}{23.4}\right)$ or $5x\log(1.08) = \log\left(\dfrac{928.1}{23.4}\right)$. Divide to get $x = \dfrac{\log\left(\dfrac{928.1}{23.4}\right)}{5\log(1.08)} = 9.564$.

4. (B) $\log_8(x+7) + \log_8(3x+5) = 3$ becomes $\log_8((x+7)(3x+5)) = 3$ or $(x+7)(3x+5) = 8^3$. Expand the left side to $3x^2 + 26x + 35 = 512$ or $3x^2 + 26x - 477 = 0$. Use the quadratic formula to get $x = -17.667$ or 9. Reject -17.667 because $\log(-17.667 + 7)$ is not defined.

5. (D) Set $115 = 70 + 110e^{-.08t}$. Subtract 70 from both sides of the equation and then divide by 110 to get $e^{-.08t} = \dfrac{45}{110}$. Take the natural logarithm of both sides of the equation to get $-0.08t = \ln\left(\dfrac{45}{110}\right)$. Solve

$$t = \frac{\ln\left(\dfrac{45}{110}\right)}{-0.08} = 11.17 \text{ minutes.}$$

Topic 8: Conics, Parametric Equations, and Polar Coordinates

**Locus Definition of a Parabola

The parabola is the locus of points equidistant from a fixed point (the focus) and a fixed line (the directrix). The point midway between the focus and directrix is the vertex. This definition extends the parabola to open in any direction, but it is customary to limit the directrix to be a vertical or a horizontal line.

If the vertex is at (h,k) and the directed distance from the vertex to the focus (or the directrix to the vertex) is p, the equation of the parabola is $y - k = \frac{1}{4p}(x - h)^2$ when the directrix is horizontal and $x - h = \frac{1}{4p}(y - k)^2$ when the directrix is vertical.

Example: Determine the equation of the parabola with focus at $(2,1)$ and directrix at $x = 6$.

The directrix is a vertical line, the vertex is at the point $(4,1)$, and the directed distance from the vertex to the focus is -4. The equation of the parabola is $x - 4 = -\frac{1}{16}(y - 1)^2$.

**Ellipses

The locus of points that satisfy the condition that the sum of the distances to two fixed points is constant is called an ellipse. The fixed distance is called the length of the *major axis* and is designated with the value $2a$. The midpoint of the major axis is called the center of the ellipse. The two fixed points, the foci (plural of *focus*), lie on the major axis at a distance of c units from the center. Perpendicular to the major axis and passing through the center is the *minor axis*. The length of the minor axis is $2b$. The equation that relates these three lengths is $a^2 = b^2 + c^2$ (don't confuse this with the traditional statement of the Pythagorean Theorem!). The *eccentricity* of the ellipse, e, is defined as the ratio of the focal length to the length of the major axis. For the ellipse, $e = c/a$ and will always be smaller than 1.

For an ellipse centered at the point (h,k) whose major axis is horizontal, the equation is

$$\frac{(x-h)^2}{a^2} + \frac{(y-k)^2}{b^2} = 1$$

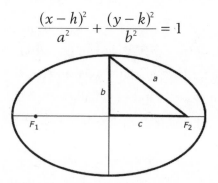

For an ellipse centered at the point (h,k) and whose major axis is vertical, the equation is

$$\frac{(x-h)^2}{b^2} + \frac{(y-k)^2}{a^2} = 1$$

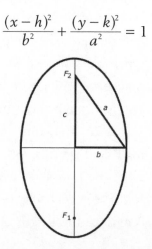

Notice that the larger denominator is always the value of a^2, and the variable in the corresponding numerator indicates the direction of the major axis.

The area of the ellipse is given by the formula $A = \pi ab$. There is no formula for the circumference of the ellipse.

Example: Determine the equation for the ellipse with foci at $(-2,4)$ and $(-2,-6)$ that has a major axis with endpoint $(-2,6)$.

The midpoint of the foci is $(-2,-1)$—this is the center of the ellipse. The distance to the foci from the center is 5, and the distance to the end of the major axis from the center is 7. Solving $7^2 = 5^2 + b^2$, you can find that $b^2 = 24$. The focal axis, and therefore the major axis, is vertical, so the equation for the ellipse is $\dfrac{(x+2)^2}{24} + \dfrac{(y+1)^2}{49} = 1$.

Example: An ellipse with center at $(1,4)$ and an endpoint on the major axis at $(9,4)$ has eccentricity .5. Write an equation for the ellipse.

The ellipse has a horizontal major axis, and $a = 8$. Since the eccentricity is .5 and is equal to c/a, you can calculate $c = 4$. Solve for $b^2 = 48$, and the equation of the ellipse is $\dfrac{(x-1)^2}{64} + \dfrac{(y-4)^2}{48} = 1$.

**Hyperbolas

A hyperbola is the locus of points that satisfy the condition that the absolute value of the difference of their distances to two fixed points is constant. The fixed distance is called the length of the *transverse axis* and is designated with the value $2a$. The midpoint of the major axis is called the center of the hyperbola. The two fixed points, the foci, lie on the transverse axis at a distance of c units from the center. Perpendicular to the major axis and passing through the center is the *conjugate axis*. The length of the minor axis is $2b$. The equation that relates these three lengths is $a^2 + b^2 = c^2$ (don't confuse this with the relationship for the ellipse!). The intersections of the transverse axis and the hyperbola are the *vertices* of the hyperbola. The eccentricity of the hyperbola is defined as the ratio of the focal length to the length of the major axis. For the hyperbola, $e = c/a$ and will always be greater than 1. As the graph of the hyperbola gets further from its center, the graph becomes asymptotic to lines that pass through the center. Use the diagrams to help determine the slope.

For a hyperbola centered at the point (h,k) whose transverse axis is horizontal, the equation is

$$\frac{(x-h)^2}{a^2} - \frac{(y-k)^2}{b^2} = 1$$

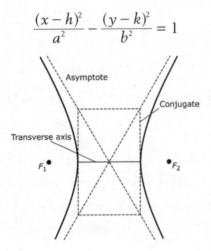

The slope of the asymptotes is $\pm b/a$.

For a hyperbola centered at the point (h,k) whose transverse axis is vertical, the equation is

$$\frac{(y-k)^2}{a^2} - \frac{(x-h)^2}{b^2} = 1$$

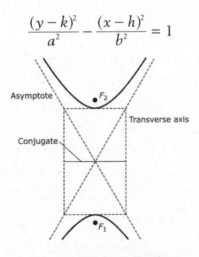

Notice that the first denominator is always a^2 and that the direction of the transverse axis is associated with the variable in the numerator.

The slope of the asymptotes is $\pm a/b$.

Example: The vertices of a hyperbola are $(-2,3)$ and $(8,3)$. There is a focus at $(10,3)$. Write an equation for the hyperbola.

The transverse axis is horizontal, so the equation will be of the form $\dfrac{(x-h)^2}{a^2} - \dfrac{(y-k)^2}{b^2} = 1$. The center of the hyperbola is the midpoint of the vertices, $(3,3)$, and a = 5. The distance from the center to the focus is 7, so $25 + b^2 = 49$ yields $b^2 = 24$. The equation is $\dfrac{(y+2)^2}{24} - \dfrac{(x+1)^2}{49} = 1$.

Example: Write the equations for the asymptotes of the hyperbola $\dfrac{(x-3)^2}{25} - \dfrac{(y-3)^2}{24} = 1$.

The easiest way to determine the equations of the asymptotes is to replace the 1 with a zero and solve for y. (The rationale behind this is that for points far enough from the center of the hyperbola, there will be very little difference between the distances to the foci.)

$\dfrac{(x-3)^2}{25} - \dfrac{(y-3)^2}{24} = 0$ becomes $\dfrac{(x-3)^2}{25} - \dfrac{(y-3)^2}{24}$. Solve for

$$y - 3 = \pm \frac{2\sqrt{6}}{5}(x-3).$$

Example: The equation $9y^2 - 16x^2 + 90y + 128x - 175 = 0$ represents a hyperbola. Find the coordinates of the foci.

You must complete the square to get the equation back to vertex form. **Warning**: the minus sign can wreak havoc here if you are not careful!

Gather terms in y and x together: $9y^2 + 90y - 16x^2 + 128x = 175$

Factor the quadratic coefficients: $9(y^2 + 10y) - 16(x^2 - 8x) = 175$

Complete the square inside the parentheses (remember the coefficients when compensating on the right side of the equation).

$$9(y^2 + 10y + 25) - 16(x^2 - 8x + 16) = 175 + 9(25) - 16(16)$$

$$9(y+5)^2 - 16(x-4)^2 = 144$$

$$\frac{(y+5)^2}{16} - \frac{(x-4)^2}{9} = 1$$

The center of the vertical hyperbola is $(4,-5)$. With $a^2 = 16$ and $b^2 = 9$, $c^2 = 25$ and $c = 5$. The foci are 5 units above and below center, so their coordinates are $(4,0)$ and $(4,-10)$.

**Parametric Functions

Rectangular functions usually take the form *output variable = Rule(input variable)*. $y = x^2$, $f(x) = \sin(x)$, and the implicit $x^2 + y^2 = 25$ are examples. There are rectangular functions for which the output value is dependent upon more than one input variable. For example, the volume of a cylinder depends upon the radius and height of the cylinder, so when written as a function (rather than a formula), the volume for the cylinder would look like $V(r,h) = \pi r^2 h$. $V(3,4) = \pi(3)^2 4 = 36\pi$, while $V(4,3) = 48\pi$.

With parametric functions, both the input and output variables are functions of a third variable—the parameter. Very often the parameter is t, because the common application is to think of the position of an object in the coordinate plane and the time at which the object is at that position. A traditional application is to think about the intersection of two roads and the graphs of the positions of two cars as each passes through the intersection. While it might look as though the graphs intersect, the reality is that most often the cars pass through the intersection at different times, and therefore the intersection, or accident, does not occur.

Example: Find the rectangular equation that corresponds to the parametric equation

$$x(t) = 4t^2 - 9 \qquad y(t) = 3t - 1$$

Solve the equation $y(t)$ for t, $t = (y+1)/3$. Substitute this for t in the equation in x to get

$$x = 4\left(\frac{y+1}{3}\right)^2 - 9 = \frac{4}{9}(y+1)^2 - 9$$

This is a parabola with vertex at $(-9,1)$, which opens to the right.

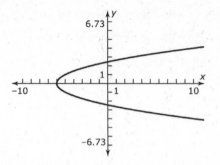

Example: Determine the rectangular equation for the parametric equations

$$x(t) = 5\cos(t) + 2 \qquad y(t) = 3\sin(t) - 1$$

Solving for t as was done in the last problem will not work easily. Rather, take advantage of the Pythagorean Identity $\cos^2(t) + \sin^2(t) = 1$. Solve each equation for the corresponding trigonometric function and then substitute these expressions into the identity.

$$\cos(t) = \frac{x-2}{5} \quad \text{and} \quad \sin(t) = \frac{y+1}{3} \quad \text{becomes} \quad \left(\frac{x-2}{5}\right)^2 + \left(\frac{y+1}{3}\right)^2 \text{ or}$$

$\dfrac{(x-2)^2}{25} + \dfrac{(y+1)^2}{9} = 1$, a horizontal ellipse centered at $(2,-1)$.

Example: Determine the rectangular equation for the parametric equations

$$x(t) = 2\tan(t) - 3 \qquad y(t) = 4\sec(t) - 2$$

The identity to apply for this problem is $1 + \tan^2(t) = \sec^2(t)$ or $\sec^2(t) - \tan^2(t) = 1$. Solving for the trigonometric functions and substituting into the identity gives the hyperbola $\dfrac{(y+2)^2}{16} - \dfrac{(x+3)^2}{4} = 1$.

**Polar Coordinates

The Cartesian coordinate plane is set up as a series of squares. Arbitrary axes are established, and the intersection of these axes is designated the origin. Points are identified first by their horizontal position from the origin and then by their vertical position. Points in the plane can also be identified by a set of concentric circles (center is called the *pole*) and the measure of an angle from an initial ray (*polar axis*) that lies horizontally to the right of the pole. This is called the *polar coordinate plane*. Points on this plane are identified by the radius and angle, (r,θ).

A quick picture will help you see the relationship between these two systems.

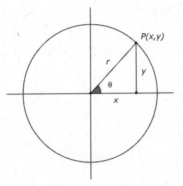

Point P with coordinates (x,y) is, in this case, x units to the right of the origin and y units above the origin. Point P is also on a circle centered at this same origin (pole) with a radius of r and at an angle of θ from the polar axis. The Pythagorean Theorem relates the Cartesian coordinates to the radius of the circle, $r = \sqrt{x^2 + y^2}$. Right triangle trigonometry tells you that $\tan(\theta) = \frac{y}{x}$, so that $\theta = \tan^{-1}\left(\frac{y}{x}\right)$. Converting from polar functions to rectangular functions is also done with trigonometry. Because $\sin(\theta) = \frac{y}{r}$ and $\cos(\theta) = \frac{x}{r}$, $x = r\cos(\theta)$ and $y = r\sin(\theta)$.

Care must be taken for a problem such as this:

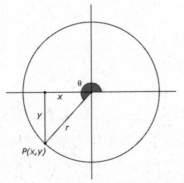

Computing $\theta = \tan^{-1}\left(\frac{y}{x}\right)$ with your calculator will give an answer that is a positive acute angle. You need to realize the limitations of your calculator so that you can determine the correct angle when converting to polar coordinates.

Unlike the rectangular coordinate system, in which each point has a unique pair of coordinates, each point in the polar plane has an infinite number of coordinates. For example, the points $(2,\pi)$, $(2,-\pi)$, and $(2,3\pi)$ are all the same point. In addition, the radius behaves as a vector—that is, positive direction is measured along the ray. The point $(2,\pi)$ can also be denoted by the coordinates $(-2,0)$ and $(-2,2\pi)$. The rays for an angle of 0 or 2π radians point to the right, but the negative radius uses the opposite ray of the terminal side of the angle.

Example: Find a set of polar coordinates that correspond to the Cartesian ordered pair $\left(-5\sqrt{3},5\right)$.

$r = \sqrt{(-5\sqrt{3})^2 + 5^2} = 10$. Ignoring the signs of the coordinates, the reference angle for this point is $\tan^{-1}\left(\dfrac{5}{5\sqrt{3}}\right) = \dfrac{\pi}{6}$. Because $\left(-5\sqrt{3},5\right)$ is in the second quadrant of the Cartesian plane, $\theta = \pi - \dfrac{\pi}{6} = \dfrac{5\pi}{6}$ $\theta = \pi - \dfrac{\pi}{6} = \dfrac{5\pi}{6}$. The polar coordinates are $\left(10,\dfrac{5\pi}{6}\right)$.

Example: Name two ordered pairs, one with a positive angle and negative radius and one with a negative angle and positive radius, that correspond to the point $(4,2\pi/3)$.

The angle with the ray opposite $2\pi/3$ is $5\pi/3$. So an answer for the first condition is $(-4,5\pi/3)$. A coterminal angle for $2\pi/3$ is $-4\pi/3$. An answer for the second condition is $(4,-4\pi/3)$. There are many other possible answers to this problem.

Multiplication, division, and powers of complex numbers are done more easily in polar mode than in rectangular mode. The point $a + bi$ in rectangular form becomes $r\cos(\theta) + ir\sin(\theta)$ (which is abbreviated to $r\operatorname{cis}(\theta)$; cis means cosine $+ i$ sine) in polar form.

Example: Convert $5 - 5i\sqrt{3}$ to polar form.

As before, the radius is $\sqrt{a^2 + b^2}$. The imaginary unit does not appear in the computation as this indicates the vertical direction. Therefore, $r = \sqrt{5^2 + (5\sqrt{3})^2} = \sqrt{25 + 75} = 10$. The angle is in the fourth quadrant and has a reference angle of $\tan^{-1}\left(\frac{5\sqrt{3}}{5}\right) = \frac{\pi}{3}$ so $\theta = \frac{5\pi}{3}$. We now have $5 - 5i\sqrt{3} = 10 \text{ cis}\left(\frac{5\pi}{3}\right)$.

The rules for multiplying, dividing, and raising powers of complex numbers in polar form are:

Multiplication: $(r_1 \text{cis}(\theta_1))(r_2 \text{cis}(\theta_2)) = r_1 r_2 \text{cis}(\theta_1 + \theta_2)$. Multiply the radii and add the angles.

Division: $\frac{r_1 \text{cis}(\theta_1)}{r_2 \text{cis}(\theta_2)} = \frac{r_1}{r_2} \text{cis}(\theta_1 - \theta_2)$ Divide the radii and subtract the angles.

Powers: $(r \text{ cis}(\theta))^n = r^n \text{cis}(n\theta)$ Raise the radius to the power and multiply the angle by the power.

Example: Given $G = 8 \text{ cis}\left(\frac{5\pi}{6}\right)$ and $K = 4 \text{ cis}\left(\frac{2\pi}{3}\right)$ in polar form. Write G and K in rectangular form.

$G = 8 \text{cis}\left(\frac{5\pi}{6}\right) = 8 \cos\left(\frac{5\pi}{6}\right) + 8i \sin\left(\frac{5\pi}{6}\right) = 8\left(\frac{-\sqrt{3}}{2}\right) + 8i\left(\frac{1}{2}\right) = -4\sqrt{3} + 2i$.

$K = 4 \text{cis}\left(\frac{2\pi}{3}\right) = 4 \cos\left(\frac{2\pi}{3}\right) + 4i \sin\left(\frac{2\pi}{3}\right) = 4\left(\frac{-1}{2}\right) + 4i\left(\frac{\sqrt{3}}{2}\right) = -2 + 2i\sqrt{3}$

Example: Given $G = 8 \text{ cis}\left(\frac{5\pi}{6}\right)$ and $K = 4 \text{ cis}\left(\frac{2\pi}{3}\right)$, compute GK, $\frac{G}{K}$, and K^3.

$GK = \left(8 \text{cis}\left(\frac{5\pi}{6}\right)\right)\left(4 \text{cis}\left(\frac{2\pi}{3}\right)\right) = 32 \text{cis}\left(\frac{5\pi}{6} + \frac{2\pi}{3}\right) = 32 \text{cis}\left(\frac{3\pi}{2}\right)$

which in rectangular form would be $32\cos\left(\frac{3\pi}{2}\right)+32i\sin\left(\frac{3\pi}{2}\right) = 32(0-1i) = -32i$.

$$\frac{G}{K} = \frac{8\,\text{cis}\left(\frac{5\pi}{6}\right)}{4\,\text{cis}\left(\frac{2\pi}{3}\right)} = 2\,\text{cis}\left(\frac{5\pi}{6}-\frac{2\pi}{3}\right) = 2\,\text{cis}\left(\frac{\pi}{6}\right)$$

which in rectangular form would be

$$2\cos\left(\frac{\pi}{6}\right)+2i\sin\left(\frac{\pi}{6}\right) = 2\left(\frac{\sqrt{3}}{2}\right)+2i\left(\frac{1}{2}\right) = \sqrt{3}+i.$$

$$K^3 = \left(4\,\text{cis}\left(\frac{2\pi}{3}\right)\right)^3 = 4^3\,\text{cis}\left(3\left(\frac{2\pi}{3}\right)\right) = 64\,\text{cis}(2\pi)$$

when the angle is represented between 0 and 2π. The rectangular form of this answer is 64.

Graphs of equations in polar coordinates can best be done on your calculator (make sure that the mode is polar and the angles are in radians).

Exercises

**1. The equation of the parabola with focus $(-3,2)$ and directrix $x = -7$ is

  (A) $y-2 = \frac{1}{8}(x+3)^2$ (B) $y-2 = \frac{1}{8}(x+5)^2$ (C) $x+5 = \frac{1}{8}(y-2)^2$

  (D) $x+3 = \frac{1}{8}(y-2)^2$ (E) $y = .125x^2 + 1.25x + 5.125$

**2. The polar equation $r = 5$ is equivalent to the rectangular equation

  (A) $x+y = 5$ (B) $x^2 + y^2 = 5$ (C) $x^2 + y^2 = 25$

  (D) $x+y = 25$ (E) $\sqrt{x+y} = 5$

**3. The equation of the hyperbola with asymptotes $y - 3 = \pm\, 2(x + 2)$ and with a vertex at $(-2,9)$ is

(A) $\dfrac{(y-3)^2}{4} - \dfrac{(x+2)^2}{1} = 1$ (B) $\dfrac{(y-3)^2}{36} - \dfrac{(x+2)^2}{9} = 1$

(C) $\dfrac{(x+2)^2}{4} - \dfrac{(y-3)^2}{1} = 1$ (D) $\dfrac{(x+2)^2}{36} - \dfrac{(y-3)^2}{9} = 1$

(E) $(y - 3)(x + 2) = 2$

**4. Which of the following polar coordinates represents the same point as the coordinates $\left(6, \dfrac{-2\pi}{3}\right)$?

(A) $\left(6, \dfrac{4\pi}{3}\right)$ (B) $\left(-6, \dfrac{2\pi}{3}\right)$ (C) $\left(6, \dfrac{-8\pi}{3}\right)$

(D) $\left(6, \dfrac{8\pi}{3}\right)$ (E) $\left(6, \dfrac{10\pi}{3}\right)$

**5. The parametric equations $\begin{cases} x = 3\cos(2t) + 1 \\ y = 4\sin(t) - 3 \end{cases}$ for $0 \le t \le 2\pi$ is equivalent to

(A) $\dfrac{(y+3)^2}{16} + \dfrac{(x-1)^2}{9} = 1;\ -7 \le y \le 1$ (B) $(x - 1)^2 + (y + 4)^2 = 9;$
$-7 \le y \le 1$

(C) $x - 4 = \dfrac{-3}{8}(y+3)^2;\ -2 \le x \le 4$ (D) $x - 4 = \dfrac{-2}{3}(y+4)^2;$
$-2 \le x \le 4$

(E) $x + 2 = \dfrac{3}{8}(y+3)^2;\ -2 \le x \le 4$

Explanations

1. (C) The vertex of the parabola is midway between the focus and the directrix. Therefore, the vertex is at $(-5,2)$, and the directed distance from the directrix to the vertex is 2 units. This parabola opens to the right.

2. (C) The conversion for the radius is $r = \sqrt{x^2 + y^2}$, so the problem becomes $\sqrt{x^2 + y^2} = 5$. Simplify this equation by squaring both sides to get $x^2 + y^2 = 25$.

3. (B) Use the equation of the asymptotes to determine the center of the hyperbola is at $(-2,3)$. Because the vertex is above the center, the hyperbola is vertical and is of the form $\dfrac{(y-k)^2}{a^2} - \dfrac{(x-h)^2}{b^2} = 1$. The distance from the center of the hyperbola to the vertex is $a = 6$. Use the slope of the asymptote to determine that $b^2 = 9$.

4. (D) All points but choice (D) lie on the line which contain the ray $\theta = \dfrac{-2\pi}{3}$ and have the appropriate positive radius when the angle overlays $\theta = \dfrac{-2\pi}{3}$ $\theta = \dfrac{-2\pi}{3}$ and a negative radius when the angle is the opposite ray to $\theta = \dfrac{-2\pi}{3}$.

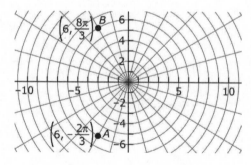

5. (C) $x = 3(1 - 2\sin^2(t)) + 1 = 4 - 6\sin^2(t)$. Use the equation $y = 4\sin(t) - 3$ to find $\sin(t) = \dfrac{y+3}{4}$. Substitute to get $x = 4 - 6\left(\dfrac{y+3}{4}\right)^2$ or $x = 4 - \dfrac{3}{8}(y+3)^2$. The range of $x = 3\cos(2t) + 1$ over the interval $0 \le t \le 2\pi$ is $-2 \le x \le 4$.

Topic 9: Data Analysis, Statistics, and Probability

Measures of Central Tendency

"What is the average?" For years, this probably meant to you that someone added up a bunch of numbers and then divided by the number of pieces of data. This average is called the *mean* of the data and is still the most widely used measure of where the center of the data in question can be found. However, there are two other measures of center. The *median*, the point in the middle when the data has been arranged from smallest to largest (or largest to smallest), and the *mode*, the data value that occurs with the highest frequency, are also measures of central tendency, although the mode is rarely used.

Example: Find the three measures of central tendency for data set 1.

6, 6, 6, 7, 8, 10, 12, 13, 15, 17

The mean is the sum of the data, 100, divided by the number of pieces of data, 10, to get 10.

The median requires that the data be arranged from smallest to largest (as it is here) or largest to smallest. Because there is an even number of terms, there is "no number in the middle." In this case, take the two terms in the middle, 8 and 10, and compute their mean. The median for this data set is 9.

The mode is the data value with the highest frequency. The data value 6 is repeated three times, so the mode for this data is 6. The problem with mode is that there are many sets of data that have no mode or have multiple modes. (There are some fields of study in which multiple modes are an important topic.)

Example: Find the three measures of central tendency for data set 2.

6, 6, 6, 7, 8, 10, 12, 13, 15, 17, 2210

This is the same set of data as before with one extra data value included. The mode is unchanged. The median is now 10, rather than 9. The mean, however, changes from 10 to an exorbitant 210.

This problem illustrates an important aspect of central tendency. The mean is impacted by large data values, while the median is impacted only by the number of pieces of data. As a single, stand-alone measure of central tendency, the median gives a better measure than does the mean. The mean is the most widely accepted measure of central tendency and is appropriate when there are not any extreme outliers in the data set. The development of statistics determined that the mean can be a good measure of central tendency for the purpose of prediction, provided one is provided with more information—a statement about how the data is spread out. This is why, with the power of the computer available to almost everyone today, the mean is still used as the measure of central tendency.

Example: Data can be given in a table with frequencies noted. For example, the following data represents the heights, in inches, of the male players in a suburban basketball league.

Heights	Frequency
68	2
69	13
71	9
72	23
74	18
75	5
77	4

There are 2 + 13 + 9 + 23 + 18 + 5 + 4 = 74 players in the league. This is an even number, so the median for this data is midway between the 37th and 38th pieces of data. Since both the 37th and 38th pieces of data are 72, the median for the data is 72. Seventy-two is also the data value with the highest frequency and thus represents the mode of the data. The mean is the sum of the heights of these 74 players divided by 74. You can use your calculator to enter the data into two lists and use the statistical menu to compute the mean, or you can do this on the home screen of your calculator.

$$68 \cdot 2 + 69 \cdot 13 + 71 \cdot 9 + 72 \cdot 23 + 74 \cdot 18 + 75 \cdot 5 + 77 \cdot 4 = 5343$$

The mean height of the players is $5343 \div 74 = 72.2$.

Measures of Spread

The easiest measure of how far spread a set of data is can be found taking the difference between the largest and smallest piece of data. This is called the *range*. The range of the data for the first preceding example is 11, while the range of the second set of data is 2204. The range of the heights of the basketball players is 9 inches. This gives you the idea that the data for one set are very close to one another, while the data for the second may be very far spread out or, as is the case the case with the second example, there may be a number that is very different from all the others. Given some thought, you can probably take the range of 2204 and arrive at a number of different distributions for the data.

The interquartile range examines the set of data that has been arranged in numerical order. The middle of the data is the median, as discussed in the section on central tendency. When the subset of the data from the minimum value to the median is examined, this set has a middle. While it is the median for the subset, it represents the one-quarter mark for the entire set of data. This point is the first quartile, Q1. Its counterpart in the subset from the median to the maximum value is the third quartile, Q3. The difference between the third and first quartiles is called the interquartile range, IQR.

Example: Find the interquartile range for data set 1.

With 10 pieces of data, the first subset covers data values 1–5, or, 6, 6, 6, 7, 8. The median of this subset, or the first quartile of the data, is 6. The third quartile is 13, the middle of 10, 12, 13, 15, and 17. The IQR = Q3 – Q1 = 7.

Example: Find the interquartile range for data set 2.

With 11 pieces of data, the first subset covers data values 1–5, or, 6, 6, 6, 7, 8. The median of this subset, or the first quartile of the data, is 6. The third quartile is 14, the middle of 12, 13, 15, 17, 2210. The IQR = Q3 – Q1 = 8.

Example: Find the interquartile range for the heights of the basketball players given in the section on Central Tendency. With 74 data points, the subsets will be data points 1–37 and 38–74. The midway point for 1–37 is data point 19. The 19th data point represents a player with height 71 inches. Q1 = 71. The midway point for data points 38–74 is data point 56. The height of the 56 player in the set is 74 inches. Q3 = 74. The IQR for this data is 3.

A summary of what is known about the three data sets is listed in the table.

	Mean	Median	Range	IQR
Data Set 1	10	9	11	2
Data Set 2	210	10	2204	8
Heights	72.02	72	9	3

Reading the table gives you the sense that there is something different about data set 2. The median and IQR indicate a set of numbers that are relatively close, yet the mean and range are fairly large.

**Standard Deviation

The most important measure of spread is the *standard deviation*. Mathematicians have shown that with this measure of spread, it is possible to make accurate inferences about a population from a sample of that population. The standard deviation gives a measure of the average (standard) difference (deviation) between the data points and the mean of the data. The formula for calculating the standard deviation, σ, for the population is

$$\sqrt{\frac{1}{n}\sum_{i=1}^{n}(x_i - x)^{-2}}$$

where x_i represents each of the data points and x is the mean of the data.

Use your calculator to determine the standard deviation for a set of data. Enter the data into a list and use the one-variable stat calculation tool to determine the value of σ. [Note: s is used to represent the standard deviation for a sample. Rather than dividing by n, the sum is divided by $n - 1$. This represents a non-biased measure of spread.]

	Data Set 1	Data Set 2	Heights
Standard Deviation	3.847	632.466	2.242
Mean	10	210	72.02

Again, statisticians can draw information from these two statistics about center and whether or not the measure is meaningful.

Graphical Representation of Data

The three most used graphical representations for discrete data are the box-and-whisker plot, the histogram, and the scatter plot. Box-and-whisker plots are used for one-variable representations of data, while the scatter plot is used with two-variable data. More will be done with the scatter plot in the next section.

The box-and-whisker plot makes use of five key numerical values— the minimum, first quartile, median, third quartile, and maximum—in its representation. The box is drawn from Q_1 to Q_3 and is divided at the median. Segments (whiskers) are drawn to the minimum and maximum.

Example: Given data set 3

29, 28, 5, 16, 13, 23, 2, 11, 30, 7, 24, 29, 7, 12, 1, 29, 4, 1, 17, 26

Sketch the box-and-whisker plot for this data.

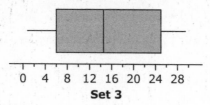

0   4   8   12 16 20 24 28

Set 3

The 1 on the graph is the minimum value. The left edge of the box is $Q_1 = 6$, the right edge is $Q_3 = 27$, the median is 14.5, and the maximum is 30. Use this graph (not the data values listed) to answer these questions:

Are there fewer data values between Q_1 and the median than between the median and Q_3?

Are the magnitudes of the numbers between Q_1 and the median less than the magnitudes between the median and Q_3?

Where would you estimate the mean of this data to be?

The answer to the first question is no—there are the same number of data points between Q_1 and the median as there are between the median and Q_3. The numbers between Q_1 and the median are closer in magnitude than are the numbers between the median and Q_3. This is verified by looking at the data. There are five data points between Q_1 and the median (7, 7, 11, 12, 13) and the difference between these data values is 6. There are five data points between the median and Q_3 (16, 17, 23, 24, 26) and the difference between these data values is 10. The minimum is further from Q_1 than the maximum is from Q_3, giving an indication of the density of the data values in the given interval. Since the higher numbers seem to be more spread out than the lower numbers, the mean of the data, 15.7, is greater than the median but not too far from it. The density of the smaller numbers does not offset the magnitude of the largest numbers in the set, which is why the mean is to the right of the median.

The box-and-whisker plot for data set 1 is

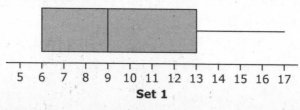

5   6   7   8   9   10 11 12 13 14 15 16 17

Set 1

There is no tail on the left because the minimum and the first quartile are the same numbers. This is a consequence of there being so few data points in the set.

The box-and-whisker plot for data set 2 is distorted because of the enormously large (in comparison to the rest of the data set) number 2210.

The box-and-whisker plot for the set of the heights of the basketball players is

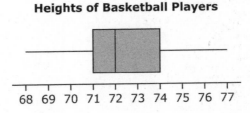

The median is left of center in the box, while the whiskers seem to be of comparable length. The number of taller players pulls the box to the right. Where is the mean for this data? 72.02 is a hair to the right of the median, 72.

A histogram for set of heights of the basketball players is

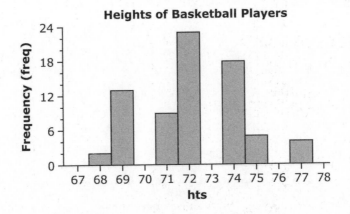

You can determine the minimum and maximum values as well as the mode from the graph. Determining the median and mean is not as easy.

Modeling with Data

A manufacturer examines data for a product she has been selling for the past year. The data for price per unit, in dollars, and volume sold is displayed in the table, and a scatter plot of this data is provided.

Price	Volume
19	5120
20	5400
22	4200
17	6000
24	4000
25	3300
28	2600
21	4900
31	2100
33	1000

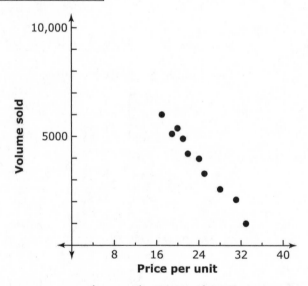

The data seems very close to linear, with a steep negative slope. As a member of the manufacturer's analysis team, you would most likely suggest performing a linear correlation to determine a model for volume sold as a function of the price per unit. Substituting your data into your calculator and performing the regression, you find that $v = -299.6p + 11052.4$ and that the correlation coefficient, r, is -0.989173.

What does this tell you? The slope indicates that for every $1 increase in price, almost 300 fewer units will be sold. If the items were given away for free, the demand would be a little over 11,000. The correlation coefficient of -0.989173 indicates that there is a strong relationship between the two variables. In general, the closer $|r|$ is to 1, the stronger the correlation between the variables. There is a lot more involved to regression equations, but this gives you a good rule of thumb.

You can gauge that a linear relationship is reasonable, as the points sit relatively tight to one another. The slope of this line is clearly negative. This indicates that r should be fairly close to -1. To estimate the slope, pick two points, one each from the left- and right-hand sides of the data. For example, the slope of the line joining (17,6000) to (33,1000) is -312.5.

You can use the regression equation to estimate an output value from a given input value in the interval containing the domain of the data points. For example, you can predict that the volume sold when the price is $23 is 4161.6. You may stretch the domain a little bit (in this case, possibly up to 35 or down to 15) but not too far beyond that.

Example: Given the scatter plot for two sets of data (x,y), estimate the value of the slope and the value of the correlation coefficient, r.

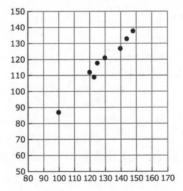

The data points are very close to linear and have a positive slope. The coordinates for two of the points are approximately (100,88) and (140,138). An estimate for the slope is $\dfrac{138 - 188}{140 - 100} = 1.2$. The correlation coefficient is close to 1, so guessing a number such as 0.9 is reasonable.

Using the actual data

L3	L4
100	87
120	112
123	109
125	118
130	121
140	127
144	133
148	138
150	151
160	155

yields a regression equation $y = 1.129x - 26.158$ with $r = 0.982$.

**Quadratic Regression

A motion detector was used to measure the height of a bouncing ball, in meters, as a function of the time, in seconds. The graph below shows the data collected.

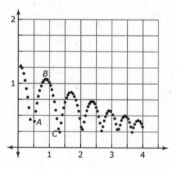

As you can see, the height of each bounce as a function of time creates an arch of a parabola. The data values for 3 points of an arch, labeled A, B, and C on the diagram, are chosen to determine the equation that best models that arch (3 non-collinear points can form a parabola as well as a circle): $A(0.516096, 0.40927)$, $B(0.903168, 1.07254)$, and $C(1.29018, 0.28969)$.

Enter these coordinates into a list and use the quadratic regression tool to get the equation $h = -4.827x^2 + 8.564x - 2.725$. (The gravitational constant used when height is measured in meters is -4.9, half of -9.8. You can see that the data collected by the author for this trial is fairly accurate.)

**Exponential Regression

Processes such as compound interest, population growth, the temperature of a body in a climate-controlled environment such as you might see in a crime show on television, and radioactive decay behave exponentially. The changes that occur over equal time differences are factors of one another rather than differences.

Using the same set of data from the bouncing ball from the example of quadratic regression, the maximum height after each bounce is recorded and examined.

B (.903168, 1.07254)

D (1.67718, .856442)

E (2.36518, .72244)

F (2.96718, .57169)

G (3.44018, .49838)

H (3.82718, .43138)

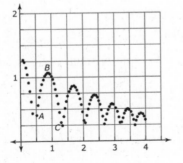

Graphing just these maximum heights:

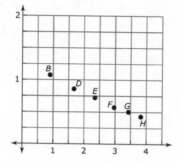

Is this graph linear or exponential? Without the text describing the experiment involved, one could believe that the graph is linear. The results of a exponential regression for these six points is $h = 1.446(.733)^t$. According to this model, the initial height of the ball was 1.446 m when it was released, and the ball rebounds to a height 73.3% of the previous maximum height.

Probability

Probability is the relative frequency of an outcome of a process. When flipping a fair coin—meaning one for which all outcomes have an equal chance to occur—the probability of heads is 1/2. A fair spinner consisting of 4 regions of different colors in equal areas has a probability of 1/4 for any one of the colors to appear.

The probability of the arrow's landing in green on the spinner below is 3/8, because there are 8 equally sized regions, and 3 of them are designated as green.

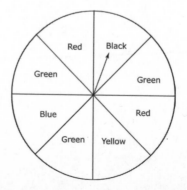

Example: Suppose the spinner on the previous page is spun. What is the probability that the outcome is *not* green?

Three of the eight outcomes are green, so five of the eight are not. The probability that the outcome is not green is 5/8. In general, if the probability of an outcome is p, the probability the outcome will not occur is $1 - p$.

Example: Suppose the spinner is spun. What is the probability that the outcome is green or red?

There are 5 favorable outcomes (3 green + 2 red), so the probability is 5/8.

Example: Suppose the spinner is spun twice. What is the probability that the first outcome is green and the second outcome is red?

The probability for the first outcome is 3/8, and for the second outcome is 1/4. Therefore, the probability of the two events occurring in this order is $(3/8)(1/4) = 3/32$.

Example: Suppose the spinner above is spun twice. What is the probability that the outcome is green and red?

The probability for green is 3/8 and for red is 1/4. A successful outcome could be green first and red second, or red first and green second. Therefore, the probability of the two events occurring is $(3/8)(1/4) + (1/4)(3/8) = 3/16$.

Another classic probability problem consists of marbles in a bag. Suppose a bag contains 5 red and 6 blue marbles. If two marbles are selected, what is the probability that both marbles are the same color (a) if the first marble is replaced before the second marble is picked; (b) the first marble is not replaced before the second marble is picked?

(a) The probability of selecting two red marbles is $(5/11)(5/11) = 25/121$, while the probability of selecting 2 blue marbles is $(6/11)(6/11) = 36/121$. Therefore, the probability of 2 red or 2 blue is $25/121 + 36/121 = 61/121$.

(b) The probability that the first marble is red is 5/11 and the second marble is red is 4/10. Therefore, the probability of *RR* is $(5/11)(4/10) = 20/110 = 2/11$. The other possible successful outcome is blue first,

6/11, and second, 5/10. The probability of *BB* is (6/11)(5/10) = 3/11. Therefore, the probability of *RR* or *BB* is 2/11 + 3/11 = 5/11.

Using the same set of marbles, two marbles are selected without replacement. What is the probability that the second marble drawn is blue if the first marble drawn is red?

If the first marble drawn is red, there remain 4 red and 6 blue marbles in the bag. The probability that the second marble is blue is 6/10. This problem exemplifies *conditional probability*. The probability of an event was *dependent* on a previous condition.

When the marbles are replaced, the probability that the second marble drawn is blue is 6/11 no matter what was drawn first. This is an example of *independent events*.

An important application of independent events is the Binomial, or Bernoulli, distribution. A Bernoulli trial consists of three characteristics:

- there are a repeated number of independent trials

- for each trial, there are two outcomes (designated success and failure)

- the probability for success is constant from trial to trial.

If a Bernoulli experiment has n trials with probability of success on a trial equal to p, the probability of k successes is given by the formula ${}_nC_k$ $(p)^k (1-p)^{n-k}$.

Example: Staying with the bag containing 5 red and 6 blue marbles—5 marbles are drawn from the bag, with replacement. What is the probability that 3 of the marbles drawn are blue?

There are 5 independent trials, each trial has two outcomes (success: blue; failure: red), and the probability of success for each trial is 6/11. The probability of 3 successes, $P(k = 3)$, is

$$P(k = 3) = {}_5C_3\,(6/11)^3(5/11)^2 = 10\left(\frac{216}{1331}\right)\left(\frac{25}{121}\right) = \frac{54000}{161051} = 0.3353$$

Example: Staying with the bag containing 5 red and 6 blue marbles—5 marbles are drawn from the bag, with replacement. What is the probability that, at most, 3 of the marbles drawn are blue?

$$P(k \le 3) = P(k = 0) + P(k = 1) + P(k = 2) + P(k = 3)$$
$$= {}_5C_0 \, (6/11)^0(5/11)^5 + {}_5C_1 \, (6/11)^1(5/11)^4 +$$
$${}_5C_2 \, (6/11)^2(5/11)^3 + {}_5C_3 \, (6/11)^3(5/11)^2$$
$$= 1(1)\left(\frac{3125}{161051}\right) + 5\left(\frac{6}{11}\right)\left(\frac{625}{14641}\right) + 10\left(\frac{36}{121}\right)\left(\frac{125}{1331}\right) +$$
$$10\left(\frac{216}{1331}\right)\left(\frac{25}{121}\right)$$
$$= \frac{139176}{161051}$$
$$= 0.8642$$

The TI-83/84 and the TI-Nspire have a function built in to compute these results. BinomPdf computes the binomial probability for exactly k successes, while BinomCdf computes the probability for *at most* k successes.

Example: What is the probability for at least 4 blues marbles in the last example?

If the outcome of at most 3 blue marbles did not occur, then the outcome must have been at least 4 blue marbles. Therefore, $P(k \ge 4) = 1 - P(k \le 3) = 1 - 0.8642 = 0.1358$.

Example: A committee of 5 students is to be selected from 4 juniors and 6 seniors. What is the probability that there will be more seniors than juniors on the committee?

This is not an example of a Bernoulli experiment, because the probability of success—a person is picked for the committee—is not constant from trial to trial. What is a "successful" outcome for this problem? More seniors than juniors means there could be 3 seniors and 2 juniors, or 4 seniors and 1 junior, or 5 seniors and 0 juniors, on the committee. This is a counting problem using combinations.

$$P(3 \text{ srs}) + P(4 \text{ srs}) + P(5 \text{ srs}) = \frac{\left({}_6C_3\right)\left({}_4C_2\right) + \left({}_6C_4\right)\left({}_4C_1\right) + \left({}_6C_5\right)\left({}_4C_0\right)}{{}_{10}C_5}$$

$$= \frac{(20)(6) + (15)(4) + (6)(1)}{252}$$

$$= \frac{186}{252} = 0.7381$$

Example: A survey of the senior class who indicated an interest in pursuing further education in engineering is displayed in the accompanying Venn diagram.

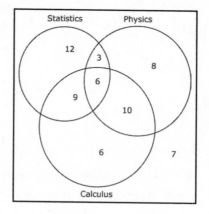

If a member of the senior class is selected at random, what is the probability that student

(a) takes calculus?

(b) takes exactly one of the three courses?

(c) takes exactly two of the three courses?

(d) takes physics but not statistics?

(e) takes physics given that the student takes calculus?

There are 61 seniors who took this survey.

(a) The probability a student takes calculus is 31/61.

(b) The number of students taking exactly one course is 6 + 12 + 8 = 26. Therefore, the probability of taking exactly one of these courses is 26/61.

(c) The number of students taking exactly two of these courses is 9 + 6 + 10 = 25. Therefore, the probability of taking exactly two of these courses is 25/61.

(d) 8 + 10 = 18 students are enrolled in physics but not statistics. Therefore, the probability that a student takes physics but not statistics is 18/61.

(e) There are 31 students in the calculus class. The phrase "given that the student takes calculus" limits the discussion to these students only. Of these 31, 10 + 6 = 16 are taking Physics. Therefore, the probability that a student takes physics given that the student takes calculus is 16/31.

Exercises

1. Approximately 32% of all Americans have blood type A positive. What is the probability that of the next 10 blood donors at a blood drive, 3 will have blood type A positive?

(A) .264   (B) .300   (C) .320   (D) .596   (E) .900

2. Given the data: 23, 25, 29, 35, 35, 39, 42, 43, 47, 52

Which of the following statements is true?

I. The range is 29

II. The IQR is 14

III. The median is equal to the mean

(A) I only   (B) II only   (C) III only
(D) I and II only   (E) I, II, and III

3. Given

x	2	5	7	8	10
y	31	37	42	49	53

The equation for the line of best fit for this data is

(A) $y = 2x + 37$ (B) $y = 3x + 5$ (C) $y = 3.5x + 19$
(D) $y = -4x + 12$ (E) $y = 15x - 1$

**4. The equation of the parabola passing through the points (2,10), (5,2.5), and (8,–14) is

(A) $y = x^2 + 6$ (B) $y = -x^2 + 14$ (C) $y = -x^2 + x + 12$
(D) $y = -.5x^2 + x + 10$ (E) $y = -2x^2 - 3x + 24$

5.   Given the set of data

Score	Frequency
60	4
65	6
70	3
75	5
80	4
85	1

Which of the following could be the box-and-whisker plot for this data?

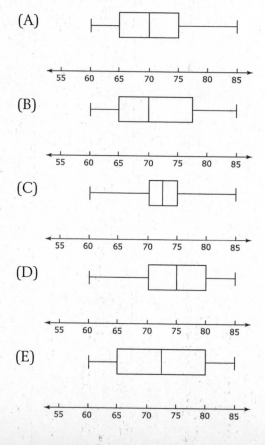

(A)

(B)

(C)

(D)

(E)

Explanations

1. (A) This is an example of a Bernoulli trial with $n = 10$, $p = .32$, and $k = 3$. $P(k = 3) = {}_{10}C_3 (.32)^3(.68)^7 = .264$. This may seem contrary to your intuition in that you would expect an average of 3.2 people in a group of 10, so choice (E) does not work. Choices (B) and (C) are there to trip you up, as these numbers come from the statement of the problem, and choice (D) is a result of reversing the exponents should you incorrectly use the formula.

2. (D) The range is easily computed and, with only 10 data points, Q_1 is the third data point, 29, and Q_3 is the eighth data point, 43. The median is 37. Looking at the differences data–median, the list reads –14, –12, –8, –2, –2 for a total of –38 on the left, and 2, 5, 6, 10, and 15 for a total of 38 on the right. The net sum is 0, so the mean is also 37.

3. (C) The data values are increasing at a fairly moderate pace so choice (D), with its negative slope, and choice (E), with its large positive slope, are not correct. The y-intercept for choice (A) is too large and the y-intercept for choice (B) is too small to fit this data. This leaves choice (C) as the correct answer. You could also enter the data into your calculator and perform a linear regression in a reasonable amount of time.

4. (D) Enter the data points into a list and compute the quadratic regression. All of the equations satisfy the data value (2,10). You can take the time to check another point, but with only three ordered pairs to enter into your calculator, the regression is fairly quick to do.

5. (A) The median of this data is 70, so choices (C), (D), and (E) can be rejected. The first 2 values in the data, 60 and 65, have the 10 values between them, so the first quartile is 65, so a larger share of the rectangle will be between 65 and 70.

THE BIG PICTURE: HOW TO PREPARE YEAR-ROUND

Strategies for Long-Term Preparation

The SAT Subject Test in Mathematics is a cumulative test of all the mathematics that you have learned. As daunting as that may sound, it really is not. You can prepare for this test, and whatever tests you face during your senior year in high school, by taking time daily to prepare yourself.

Pay Attention in Class

As you sit in class and the teacher is giving notes about the topic at hand, do you take notes, or do you simply listen to what is being said? It is difficult to go back into your notes that night or at some point in the future to study if there is not a great deal written in your notebook. (Is your notebook a catch-all for all your classes, or is it just for math class? Keep your notes for each of your subjects together—don't mix math and English and economics, etc. There is a flow in the material from day to day and week to week that you have a better chance of understanding if it is all in one place.) Your notes and your textbook are resources to help you understand the material. Use them.

Anticipate the steps the teacher will perform to solve the problem as she does so on the board. If you think the next step in the problem should be one thing and your teacher does it differently, you have an opportunity to learn. Did you make a mistake (and do you understand the mistake) as to why the teacher's way is correct? If so, make note of it with an asterisk or some notation that you will recognize as a step to be learned. It might be the case that you have an equally valid approach to solving the problem, and this is an excellent opportunity for you to raise the question in class, if time permits, or out of class if needed. You have an excellent opportunity to apply what you know immediately and gain feedback from your teacher.

Use Homework as Practice

Teachers will often have problems for you to work on in class to ensure that you understand the objective of the day's lesson. Do the problems assigned before the teacher provides the answers. If you make a mistake in doing a problem, draw a line through the incorrect material and write the correct solution next to it or below it, wherever you have room. Why not immediately erase the mistake? You want to take the time that night to study your notes. What were you thinking in your attempt to solve the problem? Did you have a concept wrong, or was your error computational? Computational errors require that you be more careful, but conceptual errors are ones that you want to be sure you clarify as soon as possible. Once you decide that you understand the correct process, and can verify your understanding by correctly doing the homework problems, you can erase the error in your notes if you feel the need. However, if you continue to struggle with the concept in the homework, you should take the time to speak with your teacher at the beginning of the next class or outside of class as soon as you can. Don't let days go by, because there is an excellent chance that the concept in question will be the basis of new work. As you well know, things built on poor foundations do not stand for long.

As indicated in the last paragraph, there is more to doing math homework than doing the problems. Take the time to study the notes from the class before doing the assignment. It will refresh your mind as to the object of the lesson and the main thrust of the homework. Do a few of the problems in the homework, but not consecutive problems. Homework problems usually follow a pattern of getting progressively more challenging as you go through them. If possible, check your answers. Most textbooks provide selected answers in the back of the book. Did you get the questions correct the first time you did them? This is different from doing the problem, looking at the answer, and seeing your mistake as you compare your answer with the answer in the text. If you are consistently correcting your answer based on what you read in the back of the book, you have an indication that you do not really have a full grasp of the concept and should seek extra help.

Once you've studied the notes and have done a couple of the homework questions to guarantee your understanding of the material, put yourself to a test. Depending on the complexity of the problems, give yourself 5 minutes to do 3 or 4 problems from the assignment (or, after you've finished your homework, problems that were not assigned). Practicing doing problems in a timed environment will help you when you are placed in the testing situation, when you have only so much time to do so many problems. One of the key pieces of timing yourself is that you learn to quickly assess whether you understand how to start a problem quickly. The SAT Level tests give you 60 minutes to answer 50 questions. You cannot spend minutes thinking about how to start a problem. If you do not recognize the first step within a fairly short period of time, you will be better off skipping the problem and possibly coming back to it once you have finished the questions you have confidence answering.

You should be able to answer questions such as the following in less than a minute:

- Solve $4x^2 - 5x - 7 = 0$ and give your answer in simplest radical form.

- Write a polynomial equation with integral coefficients whose roots are $\frac{-2}{3}, \frac{3}{5}$, and $\frac{1}{4} + \frac{\sqrt{2}}{2}i$.

- Given $\cos(A) = \frac{-5}{8}$ with $90 \le A \le 180$, find $\sin(A)$.

You might take as much as two minutes on a question such as, "Two vectors of 50 N and 80 N act on an object at an angle of 47.3° to each other. Find, to the nearest tenth of a degree, the measure of the angle between the resultant and the larger force." (Keep in mind, you want your *average* time per solution to be no more than 1.2 minutes. Some questions will take you no longer than 30 seconds, so you will have time to answer more involved questions.)

There are some things that you just need to know. Your teacher will tell you that there are certain facts and formulas you need to have memorized. *This is exactly right!* No one expects you to memorize everything you ever studied, but there are key facts you should know, because (a) they are used fairly regularly in the development of many other topics, and (b) your testing time will speed up because you will not need to stop and try to remember the piece of information you need. Here is a list of some of the things you should know. Feel free to add to it.

- Factor formulas

- Difference of squares $\qquad\qquad a^2 - b^2 = (a - b)(a + b)$

- Square trinomials $\qquad\qquad a^2 + 2ab + b^2 = (a + b)^2$

  $\qquad\qquad\qquad\qquad\qquad\quad a^2 - 2ab + b^2 = (a - b)^2$

- Difference of cubes $\qquad\qquad a^3 - b^3 = (a - b)(a^2 + ab + b^2)$

- Sum of cubes $\qquad\qquad\quad a^3 + b^3 = (a + b)(a^2 - ab + b^2)$

- Quadratic Formula $\quad$ If $ax^2 + bx + c = 0$, then $x = \dfrac{-b \pm \sqrt{b^2 - 4ac}}{2a}$,

  the sum of the roots is $\dfrac{-b}{a}$ and the product of the roots is $\dfrac{c}{a}$.

- There is a difference between $(-b)^2$ and $-b^2$. The first will never be negative, and the second will never be positive. This is very important when using a calculator to square negative numbers.

- Equations of a line   Slope-intercept $y = mx + b$

  Point-slope $y - y_1 = m(x - x_1)$

  Standard $Ax + By = C$ (A, B, and C are integers)

- The slope of a line is $\dfrac{rise}{run} = \dfrac{\Delta y}{\Delta x} = \dfrac{y_2 - y_1}{x_2 - x_1}$

- The Pythagorean Theorem states that the sum of the squares of the length of the legs *of a right triangle* is equal to the square of the length of the hypotenuse. It does not say that $a^2 + b^2 = c^2$, as is so commonly stated. Look at the material on the ellipse in the chapter Conics, Parametric Equations, and Polar Coordinates to see why you must be careful.

- The median and altitude to the base of a right triangle are the same lines. This is because all points on the perpendicular bisector are equidistant from the endpoints of the segment.

- The sum of the exterior angles of all convex polygons is 360, and the sum of the interior angles of a convex polygon with n sides is $180(n - 2)$.

- Perimeter and area formulas for triangles, parallelograms, trapezoids, and circles

- The arcs and chords between parallel chords in a circle are congruent.

- Angle relationships with parallel lines

- The diagonals of a rhombus are perpendicular bisectors of each other and they bisect opposite angles.

- The sides of an isosceles right (45-45-90) triangle is 1-1-$\sqrt{2}$ and the ratio of the sides of a 30-60-90 triangle is 1-$\sqrt{3}$-2.

- SOHCAHTOA

- The secant function is the reciprocal of the cosine function and the cosecant is the reciprocal of the sine function.

- Law of Sines and Law of Cosines

- sine, cosine, and tangent of 30, 45, and 60

- Reference angles when using the unit circle

- $\sin^2(\theta) + \cos^2(\theta) = 1$

- The range of the inverse trigonometric functions: $y = \sin^{-1}(x)$ is $-\pi/2 \le y \le \pi/2$, $y = \tan^{-1}(x)$ is $-\pi/2 < y < \pi/2$, $y = \cos^{-1}(x)$ is $0 \le y \le \pi$.

- $\sqrt{-1} = i$ and that $i^{4n+p} = i^p$. Powers of i repeat in a cycle of 4.

- $a + bi = c + di$ only if $a = c$ and $b = d$ and $|a + bi| = \sqrt{a^2 + b^2}$

While studying and doing your homework daily is expected, it is probably unreasonable to think that you can do extra problems. You do have other courses you are taking, and there is life outside of testing. The idea is to get you to practice more efficiently so that you are better prepared. If you homework assignment is set of the first type of question, see if you can answer 4 or 5 in a five-minute period. If the questions on the homework are more involved, such as the vector question, try for 2 or 3 questions in five minutes.

Practice Test Taking

Answering the questions in which you have a high level of confidence first is a good practice when taking a math test. You will score points and be less likely to make a careless mistake by rushing. You can then take the time to answer the rest of the questions on the test. You will most likely find yourself feeling less stress and more confident in your ability to score well as you practice this technique.

Complete Extra Work

It is rare that a teacher will assign all of the problems from a section as homework. Most textbooks arrange their problems to go from straight-forward application of the section's main objective to applications, pos-sibly combining concepts from previous units and/or courses. These are good problems for you to do, as they get you to look at relationships among topics and extend your understanding of the material.

Working through this book over a period of three or four months before you take the SAT Mathematics test will yield better results, as you will be able to set your own pace for how much time you spend studying each of the topics. You may very well find that the informa-tion in this book will provide you with the review and explanations you need. You may also find that you will want to look back a text-book from your geometry class to work on problems. (There is no need to do proofs, as they will not appear on the SAT Mathematics tests.) The exercises and tests in this book and the online tests, which can be downloaded at www.mymaxscore.com, will also provide you with the opportunity to practice.

This book contains one SAT Math Level 1 practice test. Visit mymaxscore.com to download your free second practice test with answers and explanations.

SAT Mathematics Level 1 Practice Test

There are 50 questions on this test. You have 1 hour (60 minutes) to complete it.

1. A shopper found an advertisement for a stereo system that normally sold for $800 and was being offered at a 20% discount. When he arrived at the store he was pleasantly surprised to learn that an additional discount of 15% on the sale price would be taken by the cashier. The store offered him an additional 10% discount for signing up for a store credit card. What was the final pre-tax cost of the stereo?

    (A) $54.40   (B) $400   (C) $489.60   (D) $544
    (E) $797.60

2. If $a(x + b) - b(x - a) = c$, $x =$

    (A) $\dfrac{c}{a+b}$ (B) $\dfrac{a-b}{c}$ (C) $\dfrac{c-ab}{a-b}$ (D) $\dfrac{c-2ab}{a-b}$

    (E) $\dfrac{c+2ab}{a-b}$

3. Given $f(x) = -3x^2 + 4x + 2$, $f(-4) =$

    (A) –62   (B) –28   (C) –26   (D) 34   (E) 66

4. The vertices of $\triangle GHK$ have coordinates $G(-3,4)$, $H(1,-3)$, and $K(2,7)$. The equation of the altitude to $\overline{HK}$ is

  (A) $10x + y = -26$ (B) $10x + y = 7$ (C) $10x + y = 27$
  (D) $x + 10y = 37$ (E) $x + 10y = 72$

5. The measures of the angles of $\triangle QRS$ are $m\angle Q = 2x + 4$, $m\angle R = 4x - 12$, and $m\angle S = 3x + 8$. $QR = y + 9$, $RS = 2y - 7$, and $QS = 3y - 13$. The perimeter of $\triangle QRS$ is

  (A) 11   (B) 20   (C) 44   (D) 55   (E) 68

6. Given the data set: 13, 20, 24, 34, 38, 46, 62, 74, 76, 80

  The difference between the median and the range is

  (A) 13   (B) 25   (C) 42   (D) 46.7   (E) 67

7. If p and q are positive integers with $pq = 36$, then $\frac{p}{q}$ cannot be

  (A) $\frac{1}{4}$ (B) $\frac{4}{9}$ (C) 1   (D) 2   (E) 9

8. Given $g(x) = \dfrac{3x+2}{5x-1}$, $g\left(\dfrac{-3}{4}\right) =$

  (A) $\frac{-1}{9}$ (B) $\frac{1}{19}$ (C) $\frac{1}{11}$ (D) $\frac{7}{16}$ (E) $\frac{1}{2}$

9. Tangents $\overline{TA}$ and $\overline{TB}$ are drawn to circle O from external point T. If $m\angle ATB = 50$, what is the measure of the major arc BA?

  (A) 50   (B) 90   (C) 200   (D) 230   (E)   310

10. The vertices of parallelogram $ABCD$ have coordinates $A(2,5)$, $B(9,11)$, $C(8,12)$ and $D(x,y)$. $x + y =$

  (A) –1   (B) 0   (C) 7   (D) 13   (E)   19

11. $\sqrt[3]{81x^7 y^{10}} =$

   (A) $9x^3 y^5 \sqrt[3]{x}$ (B) $9x^2 y^3 \sqrt[3]{xy}$ (C) $3x^2 y^3 \sqrt[3]{9xy}$

   (D) $3x^2 y^3 \sqrt[3]{3xy}$ (E) $3x^3 y^5 \sqrt[3]{x}$

12. The diagonals of rhombus $QRST$ have lengths 16 and 30. The perimeter of $QRST$ is

   (A) 46   (B) 64   (C) 68   (D) 240   (E) 272

13. A high school musical production sells student tickets for $5 each and adult tickets for $8 each. If the ratio of adult to student tickets purchased is 3:5, what is the average income per ticket sold?

   (A) $5.50   (B) $6.125   (C) $6.25   (D) $6.625
   (E) $7.50

14. Chords $\overline{AC}$ and $\overline{BD}$ of circle O intersect at point E. If the measure of $\overparen{AB} = 46°$ and $m\angle AEB = 57°$, then the measure of $\overparen{CD} =$

   (A) 46°   (B) 68°   (C) 80°   (D) 114°   (E)   123°

15. If $\sqrt{-1} = i$ and $(5 + 7i)(4 - 3i) = a + bi, a - b =$

   (A) –14   (B) –1   (C) 20   (D) 28   (E) 41

16. Allie has two bedrooms whose walls need to be painted. The first bedroom measures 12 feet by 15 feet, while the second room measures 10 feet by 14 feet. Doors and windows occupy 180 square feet in both rooms, combined. The ceilings in each room are 8 feet high. If a gallon of paint covers 400 square feet, and Allie plans to put two coats of paint on each wall, how many gallons of paint will she need to purchase?

   (A) 1   (B) 2   (C) 3   (D) 4   (E) 5

17. The equation of the circle with center $(-3,5)$ and radius 16 is

   (A) $(x - 3)^2 + (y + 5)^2 = 4$ (B) $(x - 3)^2 + (y + 5)^2 = 256$
   (C) $(x + 3)^2 + (y - 5)^2 = 16$ (D) $(x + 3)^2 + (y - 5)^2 = 4$
   (E) $(x + 3)^2 + (y - 5)^2 = 256$

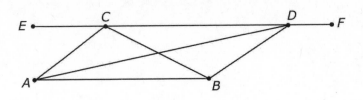

18. $\overline{ECDF} \parallel \overline{AB}$. If $m\angle ACB = 120°$ and $m\angle ADB = 20°$, then the ratio of the area $\triangle ACB$ to the area of $\triangle ADB$ is

(A) 1:1   (B) 4:1   (C) 6:1   (D) 12:1   (E) 36:1

19. A ball is thrown vertically into the air from the edge of a cliff 120 feet above ground. If the height of the ball after t seconds is given by the formula $h(t) = -16t^2 + 180t + 120$, what is the highest point above ground reached by the ball?

(A) 240   (B) 516.25   (C) 584   (D) 626.25   (E) 3930

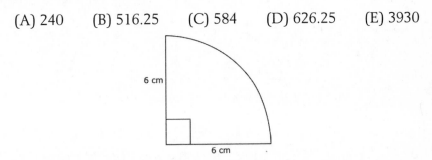

20. When the figure above is spun around its vertical axis, the total surface area of the solid formed will be

(A) 144π (B) 108π (C) 72π (D) 36π (E) $9\pi + 12$

21. Two fair dice are rolled, and the sum of their spots is computed. What is the probability that the sum is a prime number?

(A) $\frac{12}{36}$ (B) $\frac{13}{36}$ (C) $\frac{14}{36}$ (D) $\frac{15}{36}$ (E) $\frac{16}{36}$

22. If $f(x) = 4x^2 - 1$ and $g(x) = 8x + 7$, $g \circ f(2) =$

(A) 15   (B) 23   (C) 127   (D) 345   (E) 2115

23. $\dfrac{\dfrac{2}{3}+\dfrac{1}{x-4}}{1-\dfrac{2}{3x-12}} =$

(A) $\dfrac{2x}{3x-2}$ (B) $\dfrac{2x-8}{3x-2}$ (C) $\dfrac{2x-8}{3x-12}$

(D) $\dfrac{2x-7}{3x-12}$ (E) $\dfrac{2x-5}{3x-14}$

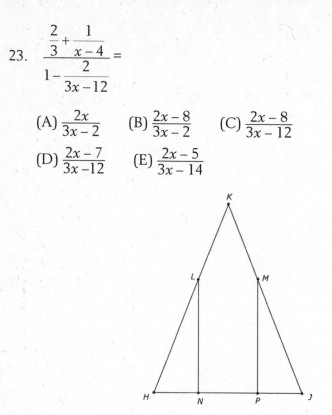

24. In isosceles $\triangle KHJ$, with $HJ = 8$, $\overline{NL} \perp \overline{HJ}$, and $\overline{MP} \perp \overline{HJ}$, if K is 10 cm from base HJ, and $KL = .4\ KH$, the area of $\triangle LNH$ is

(A) 4   (B) 4.8   (C) 6   (D) 7.2   (E) 16

25. The equation of the perpendicular bisector of the segment joining $A\ (-9,2)$ to $B\ (3,-4)$ is

(A) $y - 1 = \dfrac{-1}{2}(x - 3)$ (B) $y + 1 = \dfrac{-1}{2}(x + 3)$

(C) $y + 1 = 2(x + 3)$ (D) $y + 3 = 2(x + 1)$ (E) $y - 1 = 2(x - 3)$

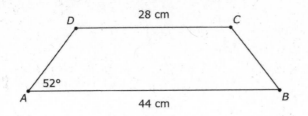

26. The bases of isosceles trapezoid *ABCD* have lengths 28 cm and 44 cm and the $m\angle A = 52°$. Determine, to the nearest square centimeter, the area of *ABCD*.

(A) 177   (B) 225   (C) 227   (D) 369   (E) 737

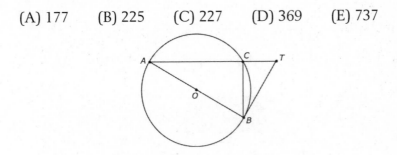

27. Tangent $\overline{TB}$ is drawn to circle O. Diameter $\overline{AB}$ is drawn. If *TB* = 12 and *TC* = 6, find the area of the circle.

(A) 9π   (B) 36π   (C) 108π   (D) 144π   (E) 432π

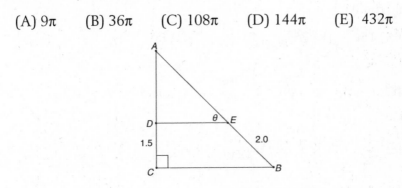

28. In right △*ABC*, $\overline{BC} \parallel \overline{DE}$, *CD* = 1.5, and *BE* = 2.0. tan θ =

(A) $\dfrac{\sqrt{3}}{3}$ (B) $\dfrac{3\sqrt{7}}{7}$ (C) $\sqrt{3}$ (D) $\dfrac{3}{5}$ (E) $\dfrac{5}{3}$

29. Given $k(x) = \dfrac{3x^2 - 4}{2x + 5}$. Solve $k(x) = 5$.

(A) $\dfrac{5 \pm \sqrt{22}}{3}$ (B) $\dfrac{5 \pm 3\sqrt{7}}{3}$ (C) $\dfrac{5 \pm 4\sqrt{7}}{3}$

(D) $\dfrac{5 \pm 2\sqrt{13}}{3}$ (E) No real solutions

30. The 50th term in the sequence $-9, -2, 5, 12, \ldots$ is

(A) 327   (B) 334   (C) 341   (D) 348   (E) 364

31. Given $k(x) = \sqrt{|x - 2| + 1}$. Solve $k(x) = 3$.

(A) {–6}   (B) {0}   (C) {0, 4}   (D) {–6, 10}   (E) {10}

10 20 30 40 50 60 70 80 90 100 110

32. The box-and-whisker plot shows the results of a survey about the number of books read by adults in the past year. The interquartile range for the results is

(A) 15   (B) 25   (C) 45   (D) 50   (E) 85

33. If $\left(\dfrac{1}{125}\right)^{a^2 + 4ab} = \left(\sqrt[3]{625}\right)^{3a^2 - 10ab}$ and if a and b do not equal 0, $\dfrac{a}{b} =$

(A) $\dfrac{4}{21}$ (B) 2   (C) $\dfrac{76}{21}$ (D) 4   (E) $\dfrac{76}{3}$

34. Let $p \,@\, q = \dfrac{p^q}{q - p}$. $(5 \,@\, 3) - (3 \,@\, 5) =$

(A) –184   (B) –59   (C) 0   (D) 59   (E) 184

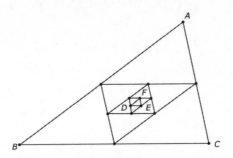

35. A set of triangles is formed by joining the midpoints of larger triangles. If the area of $\triangle ABC$ is 128, then the area of $\triangle DEF$, the smallest triangle formed, is

(A) $\dfrac{1}{8}$ (B) $\dfrac{1}{4}$ (C) $\dfrac{1}{2}$ (D) 1   (E) 4

36. Given $\begin{bmatrix} 5 & 3 \\ -2 & 4 \end{bmatrix}\begin{bmatrix} 2 & a & b \\ 3 & b & a \end{bmatrix} = \begin{bmatrix} 19 & 27 & 29 \\ 8 & 10 & 4 \end{bmatrix}$, $a + b =$

(A) –6   (B) 3   (C) 4   (D) 7   (E) 12

37. $\dfrac{x^2 - x - 2}{x^2 + 9} \le 0$ when

(A) $-1 \le x \le 2$ (B) $x \le -1$ or $x \ge 2$ (C) $-3 < x \le -1$ or $2 \le x < 3$
(D) $x < -3$ or $x > 3$ (E) $-3 \le x \le -1$ or $2 \le x \le 3$

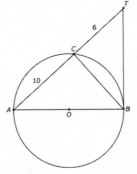

38. Tangent $\overline{TB}$ and secant $\overline{TCA}$ are drawn to circle O. Diameter $\overline{AB}$ is drawn. If $TC = 6$ and $CA = 10$, then $CB =$

(A) $2\sqrt{6}$ (B) $4\sqrt{6}$ (C) $2\sqrt{15}$ (D) 10   (E) $2\sqrt{33}$

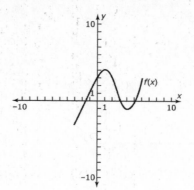

39. The graph of $y = f(x)$ is shown above. Which is the graph of $g(x) = 2f(x - 2) + 1$?

(A)
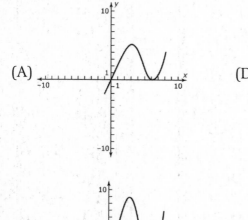

(D)
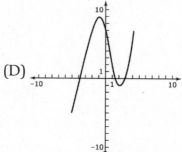

(B)

(E)
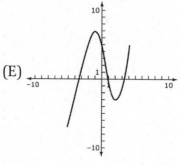

(C)
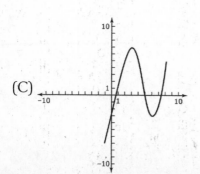

40. An inverted cone (vertex is down) with height 12 inches and base of radius 8 inches is being filled with water. What is the height of the water when the cone is half filled?

   (A) 6   (B) $6\sqrt[3]{4}$ (C) $8\sqrt[3]{6}$ (D) $9\sqrt[3]{4}$ (E) $9\sqrt[3]{6}$

41. The quadratic equation with roots $\dfrac{5+4\sqrt{2}}{3}$ and $\dfrac{5-4\sqrt{2}}{3}$ is

   (A) $9x^2 + 30x - 7 = 0$ (B) $9x^2 - 30x - 7 = 0$

   (C) $9x^2 + 30x + 7 = 0$ (D) $9x^2 + 30x + 7 = 0$

   (E) $9x^2 + 10x - 7 = 0$

42. $\triangle ABC$ has vertices $A(-11,4)$, $B(-3,8)$, and $C(3,-10)$. The coordinates of the center of the circle circumscribed about $\triangle ABC$ is

   (A) $(-2,-3)$ (B) $(-3,-2)$ (C) $(3,2)$
   (D) $(2,3)$ (E) $(-1,-1)$

43. A sphere with diameter 50 cm intersects a plane 14 cm from the center of the sphere. What is the number of square centimeters in the area of the circle formed?

   (A) 49π (B) 196π (C) 429π (D) 576π (E) 2304π

44. A survey of 100 high school seniors asks if they are taking calculus or statistics. The results of the survey show that 60 students are taking statistics, 80 are taking calculus, and 10 are taking neither class. How many of the students are taking statistics but not calculus?

   (A) 0   (B) 10   (C) 20   (D) 40   (E) 50

45. Each side of a regular decagon measures 24 cm. Determine, to the nearest square centimeter, the area of the decagon.

   (A) 576   (B) 1108   (C) 2216   (D) 2494   (E) 4432

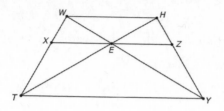

46. In isosceles trapezoid $WTYH$, $\overline{WH} \parallel \overline{XZ} \parallel \overline{TY}$, $m\angle TWH = 120$, and $m\angle HWE = 30$. XZ passes through point E, the intersection of the diagonals. If $WH = 30$, determine the ratio of $XZ{:}TY$.

(A) 1:2   (B) 2:3   (C) 3:4   (D) 4:5   (E) 5:6

47. Isosceles $\triangle QRS$ has dimensions $QR = QS = 60$ and $RS = 30$. The centroid of $\triangle QRS$ is located at point T. What is the distance from T to $\overline{QR}$?

(A) $2\sqrt{15}$ (B) $\frac{5}{2}\sqrt{15}$ (C) $3\sqrt{15}$

(D) $\frac{7}{2}\sqrt{15}$ (E) $5\sqrt{15}$

48. Which of the following statements is true about the graph of the function $f(x) = \dfrac{(2x-3)(x+2)(2x-1)}{4x^2 - 9}$?

I. $f(x) = \dfrac{9}{4}$ has two solutions

II. $f(x) = \dfrac{7}{6}$ has two solutions

III. The range of the function is the set of real numbers.

(A) III only   (B) I and II only   (C) II and III only
(D) I and III only   (E) I, II and III

49. Each side of the base of a square pyramid is reduced by 20%. By what percent must the height be increased so that the volume of the new pyramid is the same as the volume of the original pyramid?

(A) 20   (B) 40   (C) 46.875   (D) 56.25   (E) 71.875

50. Given $g(x) = \dfrac{3x-1}{2x+9}$, $g(g(x)) =$

(A) $\dfrac{9x-4}{6x+7}$ (B) $\dfrac{7x-12}{24x+79}$ (C) $\dfrac{x-10}{21x+80}$

(D) $\dfrac{7x+6}{24x+79}$ (E) $\dfrac{9x^2-6x+1}{4x^2+36x+81}$

Level 1 Practice Test Solutions

1. (C) Because of the advertised discount, the shopper pays 80% of the regular price. The shopper pays 85% of this sale price because of the additional reduction taken by the cashier. Finally, because the shopper signs on for a store credit card, the shopper pays 90% of the reduced price. The result of these successive discounts is that the shopper pays ($800)(.8)(.85)(.9) = $489.60. (FYI: The successive discounts (.8)(.85)(.9) = .6125 of the original price, meaning that the shopper saved 38.75% in total.)

2. (D) $a(x + b) - b(x - a) = c$ becomes $ax + ab - bx + ab = c$. Isolate the x to get $(a - b)x = c - 2ab$. Divide by $a - b$ to get $x = \dfrac{c - 2ab}{a - 2}$.

3. (A) If $f(x) = -3x^2 + 4x + 2$, $f(-4) = -3(-4)^2 + 4(-4) + 2 = -48 - 16 + 2 = -62$.

4. (D) The slope of $\overline{HK}$ is 10, so the slope of the altitude is $\dfrac{-1}{10}$. In standard form, this makes the equation $x + 10y = c$. Substitute the coordinates of G to get $x + 10y = 37$.

5. (D) The sum of the measures of the angles of a triangle is 180, so $2x + 4 + 4x - 12 + 3x + 8 = 180$. Combine and solve: $9x = 180$, or $x = 20$. $m\angle Q = 44$, $m\angle R = 68$, and $m\angle S = 68$. $\triangle QRS$ is isosceles and $QR = QS$. Solve $y + 9 = 3y - 13$ to get $y = 11$. The sum of the sides is $6y - 11$, so the perimeter is $6(11) - 11 = 55$.

6. (B) The range of the data is 67 (that is, $80 - 13$) and the median, 42, is midway between the two middle terms, 38 and 46. The difference between 67 and 42 is 25.

7. (D) The factors of 36 are 1, 2, 3, 4, 6, 9, 12, 18, and 36. $\frac{3}{12} = \frac{1}{4}$, $\frac{6}{6} = 1$, and $\frac{18}{2} = 9$. The ratio of the factors cannot be 2.

8. (B) $g\left(\frac{-3}{4}\right) = \frac{3\left(\frac{-3}{4}\right)+2}{5\left(\frac{-3}{4}\right)-1} = \left[\frac{3\left(\frac{-3}{4}\right)+2}{5\left(\frac{-3}{4}\right)-1}\right]\frac{4}{4} = \frac{-9+8}{-15-4} = \frac{-1}{-19} = \frac{1}{19}$.

9. (D) The angle formed by two tangents is always supplementary to the minor arc contained between the tangents. If the measure of minor arc $AB = 130$, then the measure of the major arc is $360 - 130 = 230$.

10. (C) The slope of $\overline{BC}$ is –1, so the slope of $\overline{AD}$ must be the same. D needs to be 1 to the left and 1 up from A, so the coordinates of D are $(1,6)$ and $x + y = 7$.

11. (D) $\sqrt[3]{81x^7y^{10}} = \sqrt[3]{27x^6y^9} \cdot \sqrt[3]{3xy} = 3x^2y^3\sqrt[3]{3xy}$

12. (C) The diagonals of a rhombus are perpendicular bisectors of each other. The diagonals form four right triangles inside the rhombus, each with legs of length 8 and 15. Use the Pythagorean Theorem to show that the hypotenuse of the triangle (which is a side of the rhombus) has length 17. Therefore, the perimeter is 68.

13. (B) On average, of every 8 tickets sold, 3 will be to adults (raising $24) and 5 will be to students (raising $25). The average is $\frac{\$49}{8} = \$6.125$.

14. (B) The measure of the angle formed by two arcs intersecting in the interior of a circle is the average of the two intercepted arcs. Since the

measure for one of the arcs is 11° below the measure of the angle, the other arc must be 11° more than the measure of the angle.

15. (D) $(5 + 7i)(4 - 3i) = 20 + 28i - 15i - 21i^2 = 20 + 13i - 21(-1) = 20 + 13i + 21 = 41 + 13i.$ $a = 41$ and $b = 13$, so $a - b = 28$.

16. (D) The walls of the room are the same as the lateral sides of a prism. The lateral surface area is equal to the perimeter of the base multiplied by the height. The total perimeter for the two room is 102 feet. Multiplied by the height of the walls, the total surface area of the walls is 816 square feet. Subtracting the 180 square feet of windows and doors leaves Allie with 636 square feet to paint. Two coats of paint must cover the equivalent of 1272 square feet. A gallon of paint covers 400 square feet, so she will need more than 3 gallons of paint and will need to purchase 4 gallons of paint.

17. (E) The equation of a circle is $(x - h)^2 + (y - k)^2 = r^2$. With $h = -3$, $k = 5$, and $r = 16$, the equation of the given circle is $(x + 3)^2 + (y - 5)^2 = 256$.

18. (A) Parallel lines are everywhere equidistant. The distance from C to $\overline{AB}$ is the same as the distance from D to $\overline{AB}$. The two triangles have the same base and the same height, so they have the same area.

19. (D) The ball reaches it maximum height at $t = \dfrac{-180}{2(-16)} = 5.625$ seconds. Substitute into the height equation: $h(5.625) = 626.25$.

20. (B) The figure formed when the figure is rotated about the vertical axis is a hemisphere. The total surface area of the figure is the area of the hemisphere $(2\pi r^2)$ plus the area of the circle that serves as the base (πr^2). With $r = 6$, the total surface area is 108π sq cm.

21. (D) The possible prime sums that can be attained are 2, 3, 5, 7, and 11. There is one way to get a two (1,1). There are two ways to get a three (1,2; 2,1), four ways to get a five (1,4; 2,3; 3,2; 4,1), six ways to get a seven (1,6; 2,5; 3,4; 4,3; 5,2; 6,1), and two ways to get an eleven (5,6; 6,5). There are 36 possible outcomes when rolling two dice, so the probability the sum is a prime number is $\frac{15}{36}$.

22. (C) $f(2) = 4(2)^2 - 1 = 4(4) - 1 = 15$. The composition of functions $g(f(2)) = g(15) = 8(15) + 7 = 127$.

23. (E) Multiply by the common denominator to change the problem into a simple fraction rather than a complex fraction.

$$\left(\frac{\frac{2}{3} + \frac{1}{x-4}}{1 - \frac{2}{3x-12}} \right) \frac{3(x-4)}{3(x-4)} = \frac{2(x-4)+3}{3x-12-2} = \frac{2x-5}{3x-14}$$

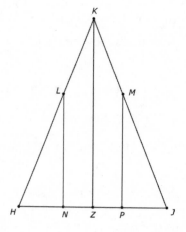

24. (D) $\overline{NL}$ is parallel to the altitude from K to $\overline{HJ}$. Let point Z be the midpoint of line segment HJ. As a consequence, $\triangle NLH \sim \triangle KZH$, $LN = .6KZ$, and $HN = .6HZ$. With $LN = 6$ and $HN = .6(4) = 2.4$, the area of $\triangle NLH$ is $.5(6)(2.4) = 7.2$.

25. (C) The slope of $\overline{AB}$ is $\frac{-4-2}{3-(-9)} = \frac{-6}{12} = \frac{-1}{2}$. The slope of the perpendicular line is 2. The midpoint of $\overline{AB}$ is= $(-3,-1)$, so the equation of the perpendicular bisector is $y + 1 = 2(x + 3)$.

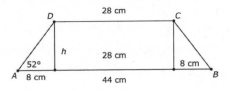

26. (D) Drop the altitudes from points C and D. AB is divided into segments of lengths 8, 28, and 8 cm. Use the tangent ratio to find the height of the trapezoid, $\tan(52) = \frac{h}{8}$. Therefore, the height of the trapezoid is $8\tan(52)$. The area of the trapezoid is $\frac{1}{2}h(b_1 + b_2) = \frac{1}{2}(8\tan(52))(28 + 44) = 368.623$. Rounded to the nearest integer, the area is 369 sq cm. Don't round off the height when computing the area.

27. (C) $\angle ACB$ is a right angle, as it is inscribed in a semicircle. Consequently, $\triangle CBT$ is a right triangle and because leg $\overline{TC}$ is half as long as hypotenuse $\overline{TB}$, $BC = 6\sqrt{3}$ and $m\angle TBC = 30°$. Because $\angle TBC$ is formed by a tangent and a chord, $m\overset{\frown}{BC} = 60°$ and $m\angle A = 30°$. Diameter $AB = 2\,BC$, so the radius of the circle is $6\sqrt{3}$. Therefore, the area of the circle is $(6\sqrt{3})^2\pi$, or 108π.

28. (B) $\tan(\theta) = \frac{AD}{DE}$. Because $\overline{BC} \parallel \overline{DE}$, $\frac{AD}{AE} = \frac{DC}{EB} = \frac{3}{4}$. For simplicity, assume $AD = 3$ and $AE = 4$. Use the Pythagorean Theorem to get $DE = \sqrt{7}$. $\tan(\theta) = \frac{3}{\sqrt{7}} = \frac{3\sqrt{7}}{7}$.

29. (C) Multiply both sides of the equation by the denominator $2x + 5$ to get $3x^2 - 4 = 5(2x + 5)$. Distribute the 5 so the equation becomes $3x^2 - 4 = 10x + 25$. Set one side of the equation equal to 0, $3x^2 - 10x - 29 = 0$.

Use the quadratic formula to solve for x: $x = \dfrac{10 \pm \sqrt{(-10)^2 - 4(3)(-29)}}{2(3)}$

$= \dfrac{10 \pm \sqrt{448}}{6} = \dfrac{10 \pm 8\sqrt{7}}{6} = \dfrac{5 \pm 4\sqrt{7}}{3}$.

30. (B) The difference between successive terms is a constant value of 7, so the sequence is arithmetic. The formula for generating terms in the sequence is $a_n = 7(n - 1) + (-9)$. Therefore, $a_{50} = 7(50 - 1) - 9 = 7(49) - 9 = 334$.

31. (D) Square both sides of the equation $\sqrt{|x-2|+1} = 3$ to get $|x - 2| + 1 = 9$, or $|x - 2| = 8$. Either $x - 2 = 8$ (for which $x = 10$), or $x - 2 = -8$ (for which $x = -6$).

32. (D) The interquartile range (IQR) is the difference between the 3rd quartile (75) and the first quartile (25), the ends of the rectangle in the box-and-whisker plot. The IQR is 50.

33. (A) Rewrite the equation with a common base. $\left(\dfrac{1}{125}\right)^{a^2+4ab} = \left(\sqrt[3]{625}\right)^{3a^2-10ab}$ becomes $\left(5^{-3}\right)^{a^2+4ab} = \left(5^{4/3}\right)^{3a^2-10ab}$. Set the exponents equal to get $-3(a^2+4ab) = \frac{4}{3}(3a^2-10ab)$. Gather like terms $\frac{4}{3}ab = 7a^2$ so that $\dfrac{a}{b} = \dfrac{4}{21}$.

34. (A) $5@3 = \dfrac{5^3}{3-5} = \dfrac{-125}{2}$ and $3@5 = \dfrac{3^5}{5-3} = \dfrac{243}{2}$. $\dfrac{-125}{2} - \dfrac{243}{2}$ $= -184$.

35. (C) The segment joining the midpoints of two sides of a triangle is half as long as the third side. $\overline{DE}$ is the consequence of the 4th set of midpoints, so $\dfrac{DE}{BC} = \left(\dfrac{1}{2}\right)^4 = \dfrac{1}{16}$. The ratio of the areas is the square of the

ratio of corresponding sides, so $\dfrac{area\triangle FDE}{area\triangle ABC} = \left(\dfrac{1}{16}\right)^2 = \dfrac{1}{256}$. The area of

$\triangle FDE = \dfrac{area\triangle ABC}{256} = \dfrac{128}{256} = \dfrac{1}{2}$.

36. (D) $\begin{bmatrix} 5 & 3 \\ -2 & 4 \end{bmatrix}\begin{bmatrix} 2 & a & b \\ 3 & b & a \end{bmatrix} = \begin{bmatrix} 19 & 5a+3b & 5b+3a \\ 8 & -2a+4b & -2b+4a \end{bmatrix} = \begin{bmatrix} 19 & 27 & 29 \\ 8 & 10 & 4 \end{bmatrix}$.
Solve the system of equations from the second column ($5a + 3b = 27$ and
$-2a + 4b = 10$) to get $a = 3$ and $b = 4$. $a + b = 7$.

37. (A) $\dfrac{x^2 - x - 2}{x^2 + 9}$ factors to $\dfrac{(x+1)(x-2)}{x^2 + 9}$. The denominator is always
positive and has no impact on the sign of the answers. $(x-2)(x+1) = 0$
when $x = 2, -1$, and $(x-2)(x+1)$ is negative for all values of x between -1
and 2 (think of the graph of the parabola $y = x^2 - x - 2$: it opens up, so
the section between -1 and 2 must be below the x-axis).

38. (C) $TB^2 = (TC)(TA)$, so $TB^2 = (6)(16)$ and $TB = 2\sqrt{6}$. $\angle ACB$ is
inscribed in a semicircle, so $\angle ACB$ is a right angle. Consequently,
$\angle TCB$ is a right angle and $\triangle TCB$ a right triangle. Using the Pythagorean
Theorem, $TC^2 + CB^2 = TB^2$ yields $36 + CB^2 = 96$. $CB^2 = 60$, so $CB = \sqrt{60} = 2\sqrt{15}$.

39. (B) The function $g(x) = 2\,f(x - 2) + 1$ moves the graph of $f(x)$ right
2, stretches the y-coordinates from the x-axis by a factor of 2, and moves
the graph up 1 unit. Use the points $(0,3)$, $(3,0)$, and $(5,0)$ from $f(x)$ to
follow the motions.

40. (B) The volume of the original cone is $\frac{1}{3}\pi(8)^2(12)$, and the volume
at the time in question is half this amount. The ratio of the radius of the
circle at the water's surface to the height of the water is 2:3. At any given

time, the volume of the water, in terms of the height of the water, is

$\frac{1}{3}\pi(r)^2 h = \frac{1}{3}\pi\left(\frac{2}{3}h\right)^2 h = \frac{4}{27}\pi h^3$. Setting this equal to one-half the original

volume, the equation is $\frac{4}{27}\pi h^3 = 64\pi$. Multiply by $\frac{27}{4\pi}$ to get $h^3 = 864 =$

$9 \cdot 96 = 27 \cdot 32 = 27 \cdot 8 \cdot 4$. Therefore, $h = 6\sqrt[3]{4}$.

41. (B) The product of the roots is $\left(\dfrac{5+4\sqrt{2}}{3}\right)\left(\dfrac{5-4\sqrt{2}}{3}\right) = \dfrac{-7}{9}$. The

sum of the roots is $\dfrac{5+4\sqrt{2}}{3} + \dfrac{5-4\sqrt{2}}{3} = \dfrac{10}{3} = \dfrac{30}{9}$. Therefore, $a = 9$, $b =$

-30, and $c = -7$. The quadratic equation is $9x^2 - 30x - 7 = 0$.

42. (B) The circumcenter of a triangle is the intersection of the perpendicular bisectors of the sides of the triangle. The slope of $\overline{AB}$ is $\frac{1}{2}$, and

its midpoint is $(-7,6)$. The equation of the perpendicular bisector to $\overline{AB}$ is $y = -2x - 8$. The slope of $\overline{AC}$ is -1, and its midpoint is $(-4,-3)$. The equation of the perpendicular bisector of $\overline{AC}$ is $y = x + 1$. The intersection of $y = -2x - 8$ and $y = x + 1$ is $(-3,-2)$.

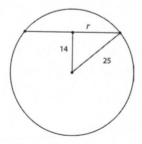

43. (C) The radius of the sphere is 25. The distance from the center of the sphere to the intersecting plane lies along the perpendicular. Use the Pythagorean Theorem to get $r^2 + 14^2 = 25^2$, or $r^2 = 429$. The area of the circle formed by the plane and sphere is πr^2, or 429π.

44. (B) 10 students are taking neither class, so that leaves 90 enrolled in the two courses. The combined number of students listed for the courses is 140, so that means 50 must be in both classes (140 – 90). Of the 60 students in statistics, 50 are also in calculus, so 10 are taking only statistics.

45. (E) Each exterior angle of the decagon measures 36°, so each interior angle measures 144°. Connect a pair of consecutive vertices of the decagon to the center of the decagon to form an isosceles triangle. Each base angle will measure 72°, and the base will have a length of 24. Drop an altitude to the base forming a right triangle with a base of 12. The height of the triangle will be 12tan(72), and the area of the isosceles triangle will be .5(24)(12tan(72)) = 144tan(72). The area of the decagon will be ten times the area of the triangle. The area of the decagon is 10(144)tan(72) = 4431.86 sq cm. Rounded to the nearest integer, this becomes 4432 sq cm.

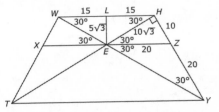

46. (B) Drop the altitude from E to $\overline{WH}$ with the foot of the altitude being L. $LH = 15$. Use the 30-60-90 relationship to determine that $LE = 5\sqrt{3}$ and $EH = 10\sqrt{3}$. $\triangle EHZ$ is also 30-60-90, so $HZ = 10$, and $EZ = 20$. $\triangle EYZ$ is an isosceles triangle making $ZY = 20$. In $\triangle THY$, $\overline{EZ} \parallel \overline{TY}$, so $\frac{HZ}{HY} = \frac{EZ}{TY} = \frac{1}{3}$. Therefore, $\frac{XZ}{TY} = \frac{2}{3}$.

47. (B) The centroid is the intersection of the medians of the triangle. The median from Q to $\overline{RS}$ is also the altitude to $\overline{RS}$. Use the Pythagorean Theorem to show that this altitude has length

$\sqrt{60 - 15^2} = 15\sqrt{15}$. The centroid lies $\frac{2}{3}$ of the way along the median, so T is $5\sqrt{15}$ units from $\overline{RS}$. $\triangle RST$, $\triangle QST$, and $\triangle QRT$ are all equal in area. The area of $\triangle RST$ is $\frac{1}{2}\left(5\sqrt{15}\right)(30) = 75\sqrt{15}$. The area of $\triangle QRT =$

$\frac{1}{2}h(60) = 30h = 75\sqrt{15}$ so $h = \frac{75}{30}\sqrt{15} = \frac{5}{2}\sqrt{15}$.

48. (D) The denominator of the function factors to $(2x + 3)(2x - 3)$, so the function reduces. The graph of $f(x)$ has a hole at the point $\left(\frac{3}{2}, \frac{7}{6}\right)$. $f(2.5) = 2.25$, so statement I is correct, and inspection of the graph of $f(x)$ on your graphing calculator will verify that statement III is also true.

49. (D) The volume of the original pyramid is $\frac{1}{2}s^2h$. The volume of the new pyramid is $\frac{1}{3}(.8s)^2 H$, where H is the new height. Set these expressions equal to get $\frac{1}{3}s^2 h = \frac{1}{3}(.8s)^2 H$. Solve for $H = 1.5625h$. The height needs to be increased by 56.25% to keep the volume the same.

50. (B) $g(g(x)) = \dfrac{3\left(\dfrac{3x-1}{2x+9}\right) - 1}{2\left(\dfrac{3x-1}{2x+9}\right) + 9} = \dfrac{3\left(\dfrac{3x-1}{2x+9}\right) - 1}{2\left(\dfrac{3x-1}{2x+9}\right) + 9} \cdot \dfrac{2x+9}{2x+9} =$

$\dfrac{3(3x-1) - (2x+9)}{2(3x-1) + 9(2x+9)} = \dfrac{9x - 3 - 2x - 9}{6x - 2 + 18x + 81} = \dfrac{7x - 12}{24x + 79}$.

This book contains one SAT Math Level 2 practice test.
Visit mymaxscore.com to download your free second
practice test with answers and explanations.

SAT Mathematics Level 2
Practice Test

**There are 50 questions on this test. You have 1 hour (60 minutes)
to complete it.**

1. Due to poor economic conditions, a company had to lay off 20% of
its workforce. When the economy improved, it was able to restore the
number of employees to its original number. By what percent was the
depleted workforce increased in order to return to the original number
of employees?

    (A) 20   (B) 25   (C) 80   (D) 120   (E) 125

2.   If the binary operation $a \mathbin{\#} b = a^b - \sqrt{b}$, then $(2 \mathbin{\#} 4) - (4 \mathbin{\#} 2) =$

    (A) –32   (B) $\sqrt{2} - 2$ (C) 0   (D) $2 - \sqrt{2}$ (E) 32

3.   Of the 45 countries in Europe, 7 get 100% of their natural gas from
Russia, and 6 get 50% of their natural gas from Russia. If 25% of all the natural gas imported into Europe comes from Russia, what is the average percent
of imported natural gas from Russia for the remaining countries in Europe?

    (A) 3.9%   (B) 20%   (C) 25%   (D) 75%   (E) 78.1%

4. If $f(x) = \dfrac{x^2 - x - 6}{x^2 - 6x - 8}$, solve $f(x) = 3$.

    (A) $\{-5, -1\}$ (B) $\{6, 2.5\}$ (C) $\left\{ \dfrac{17 + \sqrt{73}}{6}, \dfrac{17 - \sqrt{73}}{6} \right\}$

    (D) $\left\{ \dfrac{17 + \sqrt{73}}{6}, \dfrac{17 - \sqrt{73}}{6} \right\}$ (E) $\varnothing$

5. If $\dfrac{a+b}{2} = 4$, with a and b nonnegative integers, which of the following cannot be the value of ab?

    (A) 0   (B) 7   (C) 14   (D) 15   (E) 16

6. In simplest form, $\dfrac{2 - \dfrac{1}{x-3}}{1 - \dfrac{1}{3-x}}$ is equivalent to

    (A) $\dfrac{2x-7}{x-2}$ (B) $\dfrac{7-2x}{x-2}$ (C) $\dfrac{2x-5}{x-2}$

    (D) $\dfrac{2x+7}{x-2}$ (E) 1

7. A 25-foot ladder leans against a building. As the bottom of the ladder at point A slides away from the building, the top of the ladder, B, slides from a height of 24 feet above the ground to a height of 16 feet. How many feet does the bottom of the ladder slide?

    (A) 7   (B) 8   (C) 9   (D) 12.2   (E) 19.2

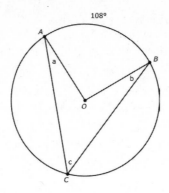

8. The measure of $\overarc{AB}$ in circle O is 108°. $\dfrac{a+b+c}{3} =$

    (A) 18   (B) 27   (C) 36   (D) 45   (E) 54

9. In $\triangle ABC$, $AB = 40$, $m\angle B = 50°$, and $BC = 80$. The area of $\triangle ABC$ to the nearest integer is

    (A) 1120   (B) 1216   (C) 1226   (D) 2240   (E) 2252

10. $QUEST$ is a pentagon. $m\angle Q = 3x - 20$, $m\angle U = 2x + 50$, $m\angle E = x + 30$, $m\angle S = 5x - 90$, and $m\angle T = x + 90$. Which two angles have equal measure?

    (A) E and S (B) Q and U (C) U and T
    (D) T and E (E) U and E

11. If q is a positive integer > 1 so that $q^{3n^2 - n - 4} = 1$, $n =$

    (A) 1   (B) –1   (C) $1, \dfrac{-4}{3}$ (D) $-1, \dfrac{4}{3}$ (E) $\dfrac{1 \pm i\sqrt{47}}{6}$

12. If $\begin{bmatrix} 2 & 1 \\ -3 & 4 \end{bmatrix}\begin{bmatrix} 1 & a & c \\ 3 & b & d \end{bmatrix} = \begin{bmatrix} 5 & -1 & 5 \\ 9 & -4 & -2 \end{bmatrix}$, then $a + b + c + d =$

    (A) –2   (B) –1   (C) 0   (D) 1   (E) 2

13. If $f(x) = 5x + 3$ and $g(x) = x^2 - 1$, then $g \circ f(x) =$

   (A) $5x^2 - 2$ (B) $5x^2 + 2$ (C) $25x^2 - 8$
   (D) $25x^2 + 30x + 8$ (E) $5x^3 + 3x^2 - 5x - 3$

14. An equation of the parabola that passes through the points $(-1,2)$, $(5,2)$, and $(1, -6)$ is

   (A) $y = x^2 - x - 6$ (B) $y = x^2 - 2x - 7$ (C) $y = x^2 + 2x - 9$
   (D) $y = x^2 + x - 8$ (E) $y = x^2 - 4x - 3$

15. In $\triangle QRS$, X is on $\overline{QR}$ and Y is on $\overline{QS}$, so that $\overline{XY} \parallel \overline{RS}$ and $\dfrac{QX}{XR} = \dfrac{1}{4}$. The ratio of the area of $\triangle QXY$ to the area of trapezoid $XYSR$ is

   (A) 1:4   (B) 1:15   (C) 1:16   (D) 1:24   (E) 1:25

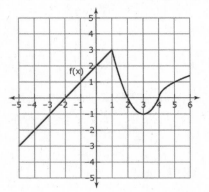

16. Given the graph of $f(x)$ and let $g(x) = f(x - 2) + 1$. For what set of values of will $g(x) = 0$?

   (A) {–2, 2, 4}   (B) {0, 4, 6}   (C) {–4, 2}
   (D) {–1, 5}   (E) Ø

17. Kristen deposits $2500 into an account that pays 4.5% interest compounded annually. If she does not make any further deposits into the account, how many years will she need to wait for the money to grow to $4000?

   (A) 9   (B) 10   (C) 11   (D) 12   (E) 13

18. Which is the equation of the line perpendicular to $4x - 5y = 17$ at the point $(5,2)$?

   (A) $4x - 5y = 10$ (B) $5x + 4y = 33$ (C) $4x + 5y = 30$

   (D) $5x - 4y = 17$ (E) $y = \dfrac{-5}{4}x + \dfrac{15}{2}$

19. In quadrilateral $KLMN$, $KL = LM$, $KN = MN$, and diagonals $\overline{KM}$ and $\overline{NL}$ intersect at P. If $KP = PM$, then which of the following statements is true?

      I. $NP = PL$

      II. $KLMN$ is a rhombus

      III.   The area of $KLMN$ is $\dfrac{1}{2}(KM)(NL)$

   (A) I only   (B) II only   (C) III only

   (D) II and III only   (E) I and III only

20. Each side of the base of a square pyramid is increased in length by 25%, and the height of the pyramid is decreased by $x\%$, so that the volume of the pyramid is unchanged. $x =$

   (A) 20   (B) 25   (C) 36   (D) 50   (E) 64

21. In right triangle QRS, QR is perpendicular to RS, $QR = 12$, and $RS = 12\sqrt{3}$. The area of the circle that circumscribes triangle QRS is

   (A) 108π (B) 144π (C) 288π (D) 576π (E) 1728π

22. Given the two data sets

    Data Set 1:   8, 10, 11, 12, 12, 14, 17, 21, 23, 25

    Data Set 2:   10, 12, 12, 13, 13, 14, 17, 18, 20, 24

Which of the following statements is true?

    I.   The means of the data set are equal

    II.   The median for Data Set 1 < the median for Data Set 2

    III.   The standard deviation for Data Set 1 < the standard deviation for Data Set 2

(A) I only   (B) II only   (C) III only
(D) I and II only   (E) I and III only

23. $(-2 + 2i\sqrt{3})^5 =$

(A) $1024\text{cis}\left(\frac{2\pi}{3}\right)$ (B) $1024\text{cis}\left(\frac{5\pi}{6}\right)$ (C) $1024\text{cis}\left(\frac{4\pi}{3}\right)$

(D) $1024\text{cis}\left(\frac{\pi}{6}\right)$ (E) $1024\text{cis}\left(\frac{\pi}{3}\right)$

24. Six students must be selected from a group of 8 seniors and 5 juniors to serve on a school district–wide committee on rewarding academic performances. What is the probability the committee will contain an equal number of seniors and juniors?

(A) $\frac{7}{429}$ (B) $\frac{140}{429}$ (C) $\frac{6}{13}$ (D) 560   (E) 20,160

25. If $f(x) = \frac{2x-1}{x+2}$, then $f(f(x)) =$

(A) $\frac{4x^2 - 4x + 1}{x^2 + 4x + 4}$ (B) $\frac{3x - 4}{4x + 3}$ (C) $\frac{4x + 4}{3x - 3}$

(D) $\frac{3x}{4x + 3}$ (E) $\frac{3x + 1}{4x + 3}$

26. Solve $|x| + |x - 3| > 5$

(A) $x > 4$ (B) $x < -1$ or $x > 4$ (C) $x < -4$ or $x > 4$

(D) $x > 1$ (E) $x < 1$ or $x > 4$

27. Solve $3 \sec^2(x) + \tan(x) = 5$ for $0 \le x \le 2\pi$

(A) $\left\{\dfrac{\pi}{4}, \dfrac{5\pi}{4}\right\}$ (B) $\left\{\dfrac{3\pi}{4}, \dfrac{7\pi}{4}\right\}$ (C) $\left\{\dfrac{\pi}{4}, \dfrac{5\pi}{4}, 2.554, 5.695\right\}$

(D) $\left\{\dfrac{3\pi}{4}, \dfrac{7\pi}{4}, 0.558, 3.730\right\}$ (E) $\left\{\dfrac{3\pi}{4}, \dfrac{7\pi}{4}, 2.554, 5.695\right\}$

28. If $\log_b\left(a^2\right) = c$, then $\log_b\left(\dfrac{a^4 b^3}{\sqrt[6]{a^5}}\right) =$

(A) $\dfrac{19c}{12} + 3$ (B) $\dfrac{19c}{6} + 3$ (C) $\dfrac{6(2c + 3)}{5c}$

(D) $\dfrac{3(2c + 3)}{5c}$ (E) $\dfrac{1}{3}c^{19/12}$

29. The rectangular form of the parametric equation $x = 3 \sec(t) + 1$ and $y = 2\tan^2(t) - 1$ is

(A) $\dfrac{(x - 1)^2}{9} - \dfrac{(y + 1)^2}{4} = 1$ (B) $\dfrac{(y + 1)^2}{4} - \dfrac{(x - 1)^2}{9} = 1$

(C) $y + 1 = \dfrac{2}{9}(x - 1)^2$ (D) $y + 5 = \dfrac{4}{9}(x - 1)^2$

(E) $y + 3 = \dfrac{2}{9}(x - 1)^2$

30. In parallelogram $ABCD$, W is the midpoint of $\overline{AD}$, and X is the midpoint of $\overline{BC}$. $\overline{CW}$ and $\overline{DX}$ are drawn and intersect at point E. What is the ratio of the area of $\triangle DEW$ to the area of $ABCD$?

(A) 1:2   (B) 1:4   (C) 1:6   (D) 1:8   (E) 1:16

31. $6 - 12 + 24 - 36 + \ldots + 24{,}576 =$

(A) 2731   (B) 8190   (C) 10,923   (D) 16,386
(E) 65,538

32. The graph of $r = 3 + 6\cos(\theta)$ passes through the pole (origin) when $\theta =$

(A) 0   (B) $\frac{\pi}{3}$ (C) $\frac{\pi}{2}$ (D) $\frac{2\pi}{3}$ (E) π

33. If $i = \sqrt{-1}$ and $(a + bi)^2 = -16 + 30i$, given that a and b are integers, $|a + b| =$

(A) 0   (B) 8   (C) 11   (D) 17   (E) 30

34. The equation of the ellipse with foci at $(-3,4)$ and $(7,4)$ passes through the point $(-11,4)$. The equation of the ellipse is

(A) $\dfrac{(x-2)^2}{169} + \dfrac{(y-4)^2}{25} = 1$ (B) $\dfrac{(x-2)^2}{25} + \dfrac{(y-4)^2}{169} = 1$

(C) $\dfrac{(x-2)^2}{169} + \dfrac{(y-4)^2}{144} = 1$ (D) $\dfrac{(x-2)^2}{144} + \dfrac{(y-4)^2}{169}$

(E) $\dfrac{(x-2)^2}{144} + \dfrac{(y-4)^2}{25} = 1$

35. If $f(x) = \tan\left(\dfrac{\pi}{6}(x-3)\right)$, then $f^{-1}(-\sqrt{3}) =$

(A) 1   (B) 2   (C) 7   (D) 8   (E) 13

36. $\triangle ABC$ has coordinates $A(1,0)$, $B(5,3)$, and $C(-3,2)$. $m\angle BAC$, to the nearest tenth of a degree, is

(A) 116.3   (B) 116.4   (C) 116.5   (D) 116.6   (E) 116.9

37. Vector $a = [-4, 5]$, vector $b = [1, -2]$, and $w = 3a - 2b$. The length of $w =$

    (A) 14.7   (B) 15   (C) 23.6   (D) 64.6   (E) 137.4

38. $\sin\left(x + \dfrac{2\pi}{3}\right) =$

    (A) $\dfrac{1}{2}\sin(x) + \dfrac{\sqrt{3}}{2}\cos(x)$ (B) $\dfrac{-1}{2}\sin(x) + \dfrac{\sqrt{3}}{2}\cos(x)$

    (C) $\dfrac{\sqrt{3}}{2}\sin(x) + \dfrac{1}{2}\cos(x)$ (D) $\dfrac{\sqrt{3}}{2}\sin(x) - \dfrac{1}{2}\cos(x)$

    (E) $\dfrac{-1}{2}\sin(x) - \dfrac{\sqrt{3}}{2}\cos(x)$

39. The range of the function $k(x) = \dfrac{|x^2 - 3x - 4|}{x^2 - 1}$ is

    (A) $y \geq 0$ (B) $y \neq -2.5$ (C) $y \leq -2.5$ or $y > 1$
    (D) $y \leq -2.5$ or $y \geq 0$ (E) $y < -2.5$ or $y \geq 0$

40. If p and q are positive integers with $p > q$ and $p^{3q} = 40{,}353{,}607$, then $p + q =$

    (A) 9   (B) 10   (C) 11   (D) 12   (E) 13

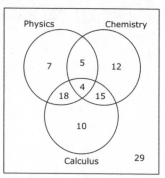

41. The Venn diagram is the result of a survey conducted of 100 college-bound high school seniors at Central High. If one of these students is selected at random, what is the probability that the student is taking chemistry, given that the student is taking physics and calculus?

(A) $\frac{4}{15}$ (B) $\frac{4}{18}$ (C) $\frac{4}{19}$ (D) $\frac{4}{22}$ (E) $\frac{4}{71}$

42. Given $a_1 = 8$, $a_2 = 12$, and for $n \geq 3, a_n = a_{n-2} + \frac{1}{2}a_{n-1} + n + 1$. What is the first value of n for which a_n will not be an integer?

(A) 4   (B) 5   (C) 6   (D) 7   (E) 8

43. Square $ABCD$ has sides with length 20. Each of the smaller figures is formed by connecting midpoints of the next larger figure. What is the area of $EFGH$?

(A) $\frac{25}{64}$ (B) $\frac{25}{16}$ (C) $\frac{25}{4}$ (D) 25   (E) 100

44. Compute $\sin\left(2\tan^{-1}\left(\frac{x+2}{5}\right)\right)$.

(A) $\dfrac{5x+10}{\sqrt{x^2+29}}$ (B) $\dfrac{x+2}{\sqrt{x^2+4x+29}}$ (C) $\dfrac{5x+10}{\sqrt{x^2+4x+29}}$

(D) $\dfrac{10x+20}{\sqrt{x^2+29}}$ (E) $\dfrac{10x+20}{\sqrt{x^2+4x+29}}$

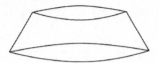

45. A cone with radius 10 cm and height 12 cm is cut by a plane parallel to the base of the cone, so that the volume of the remaining frustum is $\frac{925\pi}{4}$ cubic centimeters. The number of square centimeters in the area of the upper base of the frustum is

(A) 25π (B) 42.1875π (C) 50π (D) 56.25π (E) 75π

46. The function $f(x)$ is a polynomial function with real coefficients. The zeroes of $f(x)$ include $x = -3, 4, \frac{5}{4} + \frac{\sqrt{3}}{4}i$, and $\frac{-2}{3} - \frac{\sqrt{5}}{3}i$. The smallest possible degree of $f(x)$ is

(A) 4   (B) 5   (C) 6   (D) 7   (E) 8

47. In $\triangle QRT$, Q, R, and T are acute angles with $\sin(Q) = \frac{3}{4}$ and $\cos(R) = \frac{5}{6}$. $\sin(T) =$

(A) $\dfrac{15 - \sqrt{77}}{24}$ (B) $\dfrac{15 + \sqrt{77}}{24}$ (C) $\dfrac{5\sqrt{7} + 3\sqrt{11}}{24}$

(D) $\dfrac{5\sqrt{7} - 3\sqrt{11}}{24}$ (E) $\dfrac{3\sqrt{11} - 5\sqrt{7}}{24}$

48. The y-coordinates of the points of intersection of the ellipse $\dfrac{(x-5)^2}{16} + \dfrac{(y-2)^2}{25} = 1$ and the parabola $x = y^2 - 1$ are

(A) ± 1 (B) 1.42, 3.15   (C) –1.86, 1.42
(D) –2.71, –1.86, 1.42, 3.15   (E) –1.86, 1.03, 1.42, 2.46

49. The roots of the equation $x^4 - 20x^3 + 110x^2 - 100x + d = 0$ are in an arithmetic sequence. If the smallest of the roots is –1, determine the value of d.

(A) $\dfrac{-757197}{27}$ (B) –935   (C) –231   (D) $\dfrac{5643}{27}$ (E) 231

50. Which of the statements about the graph of the function $f(x) =$
$-3\sin\left(\frac{11\pi}{6} + \frac{22\pi}{3}\right) + 4$ is true?

     I.   The period of the function is $\frac{12}{11}$.

     II.   The graph is translated left $\frac{22}{3}$.

     III.   The y-intercept is 1.

     (A) I only   (B) II only   (C) III only
     (D) I and II only   (E) II and III only

Level 2 Practice Test Solutions

1. (B) It may help to think of the business as having 100 employees. After the layoffs, the workforce is 80 employees. To bring the workforce back to 100, 20 people must be hired. 20 out of the current level of 80 is a 25% increase.

2. (B) $2 \# 4 = 2^4 - \sqrt{4} = 16 - 2 = 14$. $4 \# 2 = 4^2 - \sqrt{2} = 16 - \sqrt{2}$. $(2 \# 4) - (4 \# 2) = 14 - (16 - \sqrt{2}) = -2 + \sqrt{2}$.

3. (A) 25% of the gas used by all 45 European countries comes from Russia. Let x represent the percent usage by the remaining 32 countries. The solution to the equation $\frac{7(1) + 6(.5) + 32x}{45} = .25$ is $x = 0.3906$. The rest of Europe imports an average of 3.9% of its gas from Russia.

4. (B) $f(x) = 3$ becomes $3 = \frac{x^2 + x - 6}{x^2 - 6x + 8}$, so that $3(x^2 - 6x + 8) = x^2 + x - 6$. Multiply through the left side of the equation to get $3x^2 - 18x + 24 = x^2 + x - 6$ and then $2x^2 - 19x + 30 = 0$. This factors to $(x - 6)(5x - 2) = 0$, so $x = 6, 5/2$.

5. (C) $a + b = 8$ so the values for (a,b) could be $(0,8)$, $(1,7)$, $(2,6)$, $(3,5)$, $(4,4)$, $(5,3)$, $(6,2)$, $(7,1)$, and $(8,0)$. The only product not available from the choices listed is 14.

6. (A) Because $3 - x = -(x - 3)$, $\dfrac{2 - \dfrac{1}{x-3}}{1 - \dfrac{1}{3-x}} = \dfrac{2 - \dfrac{1}{x-3}}{1 + \dfrac{1}{x-3}}$. Multiply the numerator and denominator by the common denominator $x - 3$ to get

$$\left(\dfrac{2 - \dfrac{1}{x-3}}{1 + \dfrac{1}{x-3}} \right) \dfrac{x-3}{x-3} = \dfrac{2(x-3)-1}{x-3+1} = \dfrac{2x-7}{x+2}.$$

7. (D) When the 25-foot ladder originally was at a height of 24 feet, the foot of the ladder was 7 feet from the base of the building. This can be determined using the Pythagorean Theorem: $24^2 + 7^2 = 25^2$. When the top of the ladder falls to a height of 16 feet, the distance from the foot of the ladder to the base of the building must satisfy the equation $16^2 + b^2 = 25^2$, so that $b^2 = 25^2 - 16^2 = 369$, so $b = 19.2$ ft. The ladder slipped 12.2 feet further from the building.

8. (C) Inscribed $\angle C$ has a measure of 54. Draw $\overline{OC}$. $\angle A$ and $\angle ACO$ are congruent, as are $\angle B$ and $\angle BCO$. $m\angle A + m\angle B = m\angle ACO + m\angle BCO = 54$. Therefore, $\dfrac{a+b+c}{3} = \dfrac{54+54}{3} = 36$.

9. (C) The area of the triangle is $\frac{1}{2}(BC)(AB) \sin(B) = \frac{1}{2}(80)(40) \sin(50)$. Do not round $\sin(50)$ to be 0.7 or 0.76, as that is how the incorrect choices (A) and (B) were derived.

10. (C) The sum of the measures of the angles is $12x + 60$. The sum of the interior angles of a pentagon is equal to $3(180) = 540$. (Five sides implies 3 non-overlapping triangles.) Solve for $x = 40$. $m\angle U = m\angle T = 130$.

11. (D) The exponent must be equal to 0. $3n^2 - n - 4 = 0$ becomes $(3n - 4)(n + 1) = 0$, so $n = 4/3$ or -1.

12. (C) $\begin{bmatrix} 2 & 1 \\ -3 & 4 \end{bmatrix} \begin{bmatrix} 1 & a & c \\ 3 & b & d \end{bmatrix} = \begin{bmatrix} 5 & 2a+b & 2c+d \\ 9 & -3a+4b & -3c+4d \end{bmatrix}$. The equality

of the matrices $\begin{bmatrix} 5 & 2a+b & 2c+d \\ 9 & -3a+4b & -3c+4d \end{bmatrix} = \begin{bmatrix} 5 & -1 & 5 \\ 9 & -4 & -2 \end{bmatrix}$ so two systems

of equations are formed.

$2a + b = -1$ $\qquad\qquad\qquad\qquad$ $2c + d = 5$

$-3a + 4b = -4$ $\qquad\qquad\qquad$ $-3c + 4d = -2$

Solve these to learn that $a = 0$, $b = -1$, $c = 2$, and $d = -1$. $a + b + c + d = 0$.

13. (D) If $f(x) = 5x + 3$ and $g(x) = x^2 - 1$, then $g \circ f(x) = (5x + 3)^2 - 1 = 25x^2 + 30x + 9 - 1 = 25x^2 + 30x + 8$.

14. (D) The radius of the inscribed circle is 3, so the area of the circle is 9π. Subtract this from the area of the square to get $25 - 9\pi$.

15. (D) $\triangle QXY \sim \triangle QRS$ so the ratio of the areas of the two triangle will be equal to the square of the ratio of corresponding sides. Since $\dfrac{QX}{XR} = \dfrac{1}{4}$, $\dfrac{QX}{QR} = \dfrac{1}{5}$, so $\dfrac{area \triangle QXY}{area \triangle QRS} = \dfrac{1}{25}$. The area of trapezoid $XYSR$ is the area of $\triangle QRS$ – the area of $\triangle QXY$. Therefore, $\dfrac{area \triangle QXY}{area\, trap XYSR} = \dfrac{1}{24}$.

16. (D) Because the graph is translated right 2 and up 1, you need to find those points for which $f(x) = -1$. These are at $x = -3$ and 3. The graph of $g(x)$ will cross the x-axis 2 points to the right of where $f(x) = -1$, so $x = -1$ and 5.

17. (C) The amount of the money in the account after t years is $2500(1.045)^t$. Set this equal to 4000. Divide by 2500 and then take the

logarithm of both sides of the equation. $\ln\left(\dfrac{4000}{2500}\right) = t\ln(1.0045)$ so

that $t = \dfrac{\ln\left(\dfrac{4000}{2500}\right)}{\ln(1.0045)} = 10.6$ years. Interest is not credited to the account

until the year is over. Kristen needs to wait 11 years.

18. (B) The slope of the line $4x - 5y = 17$ is 4/5. The slope of the per-

pendicular line is $-5/4$. The equation of the line is $y = \dfrac{-5}{4}x + b$. Substitut-

ing 5 for x and 2 for y gives $2 = \dfrac{-5}{4}(5) + b$ so that $b = \dfrac{33}{4}$. $y = \dfrac{-5}{4}x + \dfrac{33}{4}$

becomes $4y = -5x + 33$ or $5x + 4y = 33$. It is faster to know that a line perpendicular to $Ax + By = C$ has the equation $Bx - Ay = D$. You could then have started the problem with $5x + 4y = D$ and determined that $D = 33$.

19. (C) $\triangle KLM$ is an isosceles triangle with legs KL and LM. P is the midpoint of $\overline{KM}$ because $KP = PM$, so $\overline{LP}$ is perpendicular to $\overline{KM}$. LP is part of diagonal $\overline{NL}$, so the diagonals of the quadrilateral are perpendicular. Whenever the diagonals of a quadrilateral are perpendicular, the area is equal to one-half the product of the diagonals (look at the areas of $\triangle KLM$ and $\triangle KNM$ and add them). There is no information to allow you to deduce that $KN = LN$, and therefore you cannot conclude that the quadrilateral is a rhombus, nor is there any information to conclude the diagonals bisect each other to ensure that $NP = PL$.

20. (D) If h is the height of the original pyramid and H is the height of the new pyramid, then the volume equation $\dfrac{1}{3}hs^2 = \dfrac{1}{3}H1.25s^2$, where s represents the length of a side of the base of the original pyramid. Solve

for H to get $H = .64h$. The height of the new pyramid must be 64% of the original pyramid so the height of the original pyramid was reduced by 36%.

21. (B) Triangle QRS must be a 30-60-90 triangle, because the longer leg is $\sqrt{3}$ times longer than the shorter leg. The hypotenuse of the right triangle has length 24. The circumscribed circle about a right triangle must have its center at the midpoint of the hypotenuse, so the radius of the circle is 12 and the area of the circle is 144π.

22. (D) Each data set has 10 elements. The sum of each data set is 153, so the means are equal (I is true). The median for Data Set 1 is 13, while the median for Data Set 2 is 13.5 (II is true). Without computing, you can see that the elements in Data Set 2 are closer to the center than are the elements in Data Set 1 (III is false).

23. (C) Convert $-2 + 2i\sqrt{3}$ to the polar coordinate equivalent

$$4\text{cis}\left(\frac{2\pi}{3}\right). \left(-2 + 2i\sqrt{3}\right)^5 = \left(4\text{cis}\left(\frac{2\pi}{3}\right)\right)^5 = 4^5\text{cis}\left(5\left(\frac{2\pi}{3}\right)\right) = 1024\text{cis}\left(\frac{10\pi}{3}\right)$$

$$= 1024\text{cis}\left(\frac{4\pi}{3}\right).$$

24. (B) No titles are associated with being on this committee, so the order in which the committee is selected is unimportant. The probability that the committee will contain 3 seniors and 3 juniors is

$$\frac{(_8C_3)(_5C_3)}{_{13}C_6} = \frac{140}{429}.$$

25. (B) $f(f(x)) = \dfrac{2\left(\dfrac{2x-1}{x+2}\right) - 1}{\left(\dfrac{2x-1}{x+2}\right) + 2} = \dfrac{\left(2\left(\dfrac{2x-1}{x+2}\right) - 1\right)}{\left(\left(\dfrac{2x-1}{x+2}\right) + 2\right)}\left(\dfrac{x+2}{x+2}\right) =$

$$\frac{2(2x-1) - 1(x+2)}{(2x-1) + 2(x+2)} = \frac{4x - 2 - x - 2}{2x - 1 + 2x + 4} = \frac{3x - 4}{4x + 3}.$$

26. (B) Sketch the graphs of $y = |x| + |x - 3|$ and $y = 5$ to find the points of intersection.

27. (D) Use the identity $\sec^2(x) = 1 + \tan^2(x)$ to change the equation to $3(1 + \tan^2(x)) + \tan(x) = 5$. Simplify this to $3\tan^2(x) + \tan(x) - 5 = 0$. Factor the quadratic: $(3 \tan(x) - 2)(\tan(x) + 1) = 0$ and solve to get $\tan(x) = \frac{2}{3}, -1$. The reference angle for $\tan(x) = \frac{2}{3}$ is 0.588. $\tan(x) = \frac{2}{3}$ when $x = 0.588$ and when $x = \pi + 0.588$, or 3.730. $\tan(x) = -1$ when $x = \frac{3\pi}{4}$ and $x = \frac{7\pi}{4}$.

28. (A) $\log_b(a^2) = c$ becomes $2\log_b(a) = c$ so that $\log_b(a) = \frac{c}{2}$. $\log_b\left(\dfrac{a^4 b^3}{\sqrt[6]{a^5}}\right) = 4\log_b(a) + 3. \log_b(b) - \frac{5}{6}\log_b(a) = 4\left(\frac{c}{2}\right) + 3 - \frac{5}{6}\left(\frac{c}{2}\right) = \frac{19c}{12} + 3.$

29. (E) $x = 3\sec(t) + 1$ becomes $\sec(t) = \dfrac{x-1}{3}$ and $y = 2\tan^2(t) - 1$ becomes $\tan^2(t) = \dfrac{y+1}{2}$. Use the identity $\sec^2(t) = 1 + \tan^2(t)$ to get $\left(\dfrac{x-1}{3}\right)^2 = 1 + \dfrac{y-1}{2}$. This becomes $\left(\dfrac{x-1}{3}\right)^2 = \dfrac{y-3}{2}$ or $y - 3 = \frac{2}{9}(x-1)^2$.

30. (D) Draw $\overline{WX}$. WXCD is a parallelogram because $WD = XC$ and $\overline{WD} \parallel \overline{XC}$. Therefore, E is the midpoint of the diagonals, and the distance from E to $\overline{WD}$ is half the distance from B to $\overline{WD}$. If h is the distance from B to $\overline{WD}$, the area of $\triangle DEW$ is $\frac{1}{2}(WD)\left(\frac{1}{2}h\right) = \frac{1}{4}(WD)h$
$= \frac{1}{4}\left(\frac{1}{2}AD\right)h = \frac{1}{8}(AD)h = \frac{1}{8}$ area ABCD.

31. (D) This is a geometric series with initial term 6 and common ratio
−2. The last term of the series, 24576, must equal $6(-2)^{n-1}$. Dividing by
6, $4096 = (-2)^{n-1}$. $4096 = 2^{12}$ but also $(-2)^{12}$, so $n - 1 = 12$ and $n = 13$.
The sum $S_{13} = \dfrac{6(1-(-2)^{13})}{1-(-2)} = 16386$.

32. (D) $r = 0$ when $3 + 6\cos(\theta) = 0$ or $\cos(\theta) = \dfrac{-1}{2}$. This occurs when
$\theta = \dfrac{2\pi}{3}$.

33. (B) $(a + bi)^2 = a^2 + 2abi + b^2i^2 = a^2 - b^2 + 2abi = -16 + 30i$. Solve the
system of equations $a^2 - b^2 = -16$ and $2ab = 30$. $2ab = 30$ implies that
$b = \dfrac{15}{a}$. Substitute this into $a^2 - \left(\dfrac{15}{a}\right)^2 = -16$ or $a^2 - \dfrac{225}{a^2} = -16$. This
equation is the equivalent of $a^4 + 16a^2 - 225 = 0$ or $(a^2 + 25)(a^2 - 9) = 0$. Therefore, $a = \pm 3$. If $a = 3$, $b = 5$ and if $a = -3$ then $b = -5$. $|a + b| = 8$
in either case.

34. (C) The center of the ellipse is located at the midpoint of the focal
axis, (2,4). Because the focal axis is horizontal, the point (−11,4) is a vertex of the ellipse, as the major axis lies over the focal axis. The distance
from the center to the vertex is a, and the distance from the center to a
focus is c. Using the relationship $b^2 + c^2 = a^2$, $b^2 = 144$, and the equation
of the ellipse is $\dfrac{(x-2)^2}{169} + \dfrac{(y-4)^2}{144} = 1$.

35. (A) Because the range of $y = \tan^{-1}(x)$ is $\dfrac{-\pi}{2} < x < \dfrac{\pi}{2}$, $\tan^{-1}(-\sqrt{3})$.
$\dfrac{\pi}{6}(x-3) = \dfrac{-\pi}{3}$ becomes $x - 3 = -2$ or $x = 1$.

36. (D) $AB = 5$, $AC = \sqrt{20}$, and $BC = \sqrt{65}$. Use the law of Cosines
to solve $(\sqrt{65})^2 = 5^2 + (\sqrt{20})^2 - 2(5)(\sqrt{20})\cos(A)$. $\cos(A) = \dfrac{-\sqrt{5}}{5}$ and
$m\angle BAC = 116.56$, which rounds to 116.6.

37. (C) Linear combination of vectors is basic algebra. $3a = [-12, 15]$, $2b = [2, -4]$, and $w = 3a - 2b = [-12 - 2, 15 - (-4)] = [-14, 19]$. $|w| = \sqrt{(-14)^2 + 19^2} = 23.6$.

38. (B) $\sin\left(x + \frac{2\pi}{3}\right) = \sin(x)\cos\left(\frac{2\pi}{3}\right) + \sin\left(\frac{2\pi}{3}\right)\cos(x) = \frac{-1}{2}\sin(x)$ $+ \frac{\sqrt{3}}{2}\cos(x)$.

39. (E) Factor the quadratics to get $k(x) = \frac{|(x-4)(x+1)|}{(x-1)(x+1)}$. This reduces to $k(x) = \pm\frac{|(x-4)|}{(x-1)}$, with the sign dependent on whether $x < -1$ or $x > -1$. $x = -1$ is not in the domain of the problem, so the point $(-1, -2.5)$ is removed from the graph. (Your graphing calculator will not easily illustrate this, so you need to check the behavior of the function near the removed point.)

40. (B) If $p^{3q} = 40,353,607$, then the result of taking the cube root of each side of the equation is $p^q = 343$. Because $343 = 7^3$, $p = 7$, $q = 3$, and $p + q = 10$.

41. (D) There are 22 students from the survey who are taking both physics and calculus. Of these, 4 are also taking chemistry. Therefore, the probability is $\frac{4}{22}$.

42. (D) $a_3 = 18$, $a_4 = 24$, $a_5 = 32$, $a_6 = 47$, and $a_7 = 63.5$.

43. (D) Joining the midpoints of the sides of a quadrilateral forms parallelograms whose lengths are 1/2 the length of the diagonal of the larger square. The lengths of the sides of the squares, in reduced order, are $AB = 20$, $10\sqrt{2}$, 10, $5\sqrt{2}$, $5 = EF$. The area of $EFGH$ is 25.

44. (E) Let $\theta = \tan^{-1}\left(\dfrac{x+2}{5}\right)$. Then $\tan(\theta) = \dfrac{x+2}{5}$. You are asked to find the value of $\sin(2\theta)$. The hypotenuse of the right triangle with legs 5 and $x + 2$ is $\sqrt{x^2 + 4x + 29}$. $\sin(2\theta) = 2\sin(\theta)\cos(\theta) =$
$$2\left(\dfrac{x+2}{\sqrt{x^2 + 4x + 29}}\right)\left(\dfrac{5}{\sqrt{x^2 + 4x + 29}}\right) = \dfrac{10x + 20}{x^2 + 4x + 29}.$$

45. (D) The volume of the cone is 400π cubic centimeters, and the volume of the frustum is $\dfrac{925\pi}{4}$ cubic centimeters. This makes the volume of the cone that was removed to create the frustum have a volume of $\dfrac{675\pi}{4}$ cubic centimeters. The ratio of the volumes of these similar cones is equal to the cube of the ratio of corresponding linear measurements. Using the radii of the circles, the proportion becomes $\dfrac{\frac{675\pi}{4}}{400\pi} = \left(\dfrac{r}{10}\right)^3$ or $\dfrac{27}{64} = \left(\dfrac{r}{10}\right)^3$. Take the cube root of both sides of the equation to get $\dfrac{3}{4} = \dfrac{r}{10}$ and $r = 7.5$. The area of a circle with $r = 7.5$ cm is 56.25π square centimeters.

46. (C) The Fundamental Theorem of Algebra states that the number of zeroes of a function $f(x)$ with real coefficients must equal the degree of the polynomial. It also states that complex zeroes always come in conjugate pairs. If $\dfrac{5}{4} + \dfrac{\sqrt{3}}{4}i$ and $\dfrac{-2}{3} + \dfrac{\sqrt{5}}{3}i$ are zeroes of the function, $\dfrac{5}{4} - \dfrac{\sqrt{3}}{4}i$ and $\dfrac{-2}{3} - \dfrac{\sqrt{5}}{3}i$ must also be zeroes, giving a total of 6 zeroes to the function.

47. (B) $Q + R + T = 180$, so $T = 180 - (Q + R)$. $\sin(T) = \sin(180 - (Q + R))$. Using the identity for the sine of the difference of two angles, $\sin(180 - (Q + R)) = \sin(180)\cos(Q + R) - \cos(180)\sin(Q + R)$.

$\sin(180) = 0$ and $\cos(180) = -1$, so $\sin(180 - (Q + R)) = 0 - (-1)\sin(Q + R) = \sin(Q + R) = \sin(Q)\cos(R) + \cos(Q)\sin(R)$.

$\sin(Q) = \dfrac{3}{4}$ and $\cos(R) = \dfrac{5}{6}$ give $\cos(Q) = \dfrac{\sqrt{7}}{4}$ and $\sin(R) = \dfrac{\sqrt{11}}{6}$.

$\sin(Q)\cos(R) + \cos(Q)\sin(R) = \left(\dfrac{3}{4}\right)\left(\dfrac{5}{6}\right) + \left(\dfrac{\sqrt{7}}{4}\right)\left(\dfrac{\sqrt{11}}{6}\right) = \dfrac{15 + \sqrt{77}}{24}$.

48. (D) Substitute $y^2 - 1$ for x in the equation of the ellipse to get $\dfrac{(y^2 - 1 - 5)^2}{16} + \dfrac{(y - 2)^2}{25} = 1$ or $\dfrac{(y^2 - 6)^2}{16} + \dfrac{(y - 2)^2}{25} = 1$. Multiply by 400 to get $25(y^2 - 6)^2 + 16(y - 2)^2 = 400$. Expand the binomials: $25(y^4 - 12y^2 + 36) + 16(y^2 - 4y + 4) = 400$. Distribute, combine terms, and set the right-hand side of the equation equal to zero to get $25y^4 - 300y^2 + 900 + 16y^2 - 64y + 64 - 400 = 0$, or $25y^4 - 284y^2 - 64y + 564 = 0$. Use your graphing calculator to graph this polynomial and find the zeroes are -2.71, -1.86, 1.42, and 3.15.

49. (C) There are four roots to this equation because the degree of the polynomial is 4. If the smallest of the roots is -1, the other roots are $-1 + d$, $-1 + 2d$, and $-1 + 3d$ to complete the arithmetic sequence. The sum of the roots is 20. Therefore, $-4 + 6d = 20$ yields $d = 4$. The four roots are -1, 3, 7, and 11. d, the product of the four roots, is -231.

50. (A) The function $f(x) = -3\sin\left(\dfrac{11\pi}{6}\left(x + \dfrac{4}{\pi}\right)\right) + 4$ has a period $2\pi \div \dfrac{11\pi}{6} = 2\pi \times \dfrac{6}{11\pi} = \dfrac{12}{11}$. The graph is translated left $\dfrac{4}{\pi}$. The y-intercept is $f(0) = -3\sin\left(\dfrac{22}{3}\right) + 4 = 1.3975$.

About the Author

Chris Monahan taught high school mathematics in New York State for thirty-three years and also has more than twenty years experience as an adjunct instructor at the college level. He graduated with his BS from Manhattan College in 1976 and an MAT from Colgate University in 1977. He is a past president of the Association of Mathematics Teachers of New York State.

When he and his wife aren't traveling to see their children and grandchild, they live in Wilton, New York. Chris is still active in consulting for the State Education Department, Texas Instruments, and Key Curriculum Press.

Also Available

My Max Score SAT Literature Subject Test
by Steven Fox • 978-1-4022-5613-4

My Max Score SAT U.S. History Subject Test
by Cara Cantarella • 978-1-4022-5604-2

$14.99 U.S./£9.99 UK

Also Available

My Max Score AP Calculus AB/BC
by Carolyn Wheater • 978-1-4022-4313-4

My Max Score AP English Language and Composition
by Jocelyn Sisson • 978-1-4022-4312-7

My Max Score AP English Literature and Composition
by Tony Armstrong • 978-1-4022-4311-0

My Max Score AP U.S. Government & Politics
by Del Franz • 978-1-4022-4314-1

My Max Score AP U.S. History
by Michael Romano • 978-1-4022-4310-3

$14.99 U.S./$17.99 CAN/£9.99 UK

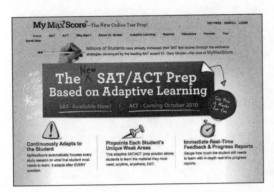

Essentials from
Dr. Gary Gruber

and the creators of My Max Score

"Gruber can ring the bell on any number
of standardized exams."
—*Chicago Tribune*

"Gruber's methods make the questions
seem amazingly simple to solve."
—*Library Journal*

"Gary Gruber is the leading expert on the SAT."
—*Houston Chronicle*

$14.99 U.S./£9.99 UK
978-1-4022-5337-9

$14.99 U.S./£9.99 UK
978-1-4022-5340-9

$14.99 U.S./£9.99 UK
978-1-4022-5343-0

$12.99 U.S./£8.99 UK
978-1-4022-6072-8

Notes

Notes

Notes

Notes

Notes